W9-AYY-856

A NEW EXCALIBUR

Front end-paper: *Mk Vs in front of the smashed Cloth Hall at Ypres.*

'Only the Press and the Germans perceived that a new Excalibur had been forged in England.'

CLOUGH WILLIAMS-ELLIS
The Tank Corps, 1919

LEO COOPER
in association with
SECKER & WARBURG

A NEW EXCALIBUR

The Development of the Tank 1909–1939

A J SMITHERS

By the same author

THE MAN WHO DISOBEYED: Sir Horace Smith-Dorrien and his Enemies
SIR JOHN MONASH
THE KAFFIR WARS 1779-1877
TOBY
DORNFORD YATES: A Biography
COMBINED FORCES
   ETC

© 1986 A J SMITHERS

First published by Leo Cooper
in association with Secker & Warburg Ltd
54 Poland Street, London W1V 3DF

ISBN 0-436-47520-0

Designed by John Mitchell
Printed in Great Britain by
Butler & Tanner Ltd, Frome and London

Title-page: *Gun-carrying Tank with 6″ howitzer*.

Contents

Acknowledgements

ANYBODY WHO ATTEMPTS such a book as this must first visit the Tank Museum at Bovington and seek the benevolence of those in charge of that admirable institution. There I received help far beyond anything I might have expected. The late Lieut-Colonel Kenneth Hill and the present Librarian, Mr Fletcher, did far more than merely answer questions put by an imperfectly educated stranger; they provided information from their important (and under-used) archives that I did not know existed. David Fletcher, author of many books and probably the world's best informed man on the subject, most kindly found the time to direct me to a number of papers containing essential information that could not be found elsewhere. That done, he initiated me into the workings of Tanks of the first generation. I cannot sufficiently thank him.

On published material, I gratefully acknowledge permissions given to me to draw upon books and papers still under copyright. To Colonel A. J. Aylmer and the Estate of the late Major-General Sir Edward Spears for quotations from *Prelude to Victory*. To A. P. Watts Ltd. and the Estate of Lieut-Colonel Sir Albert Stern for those from *Tanks: the Log-book of a Pioneer*. To Newnes Books, a division of the Hamlyn Groups Ltd, for leave to quote from Mr Winston Churchill's *The World Crisis 1911–1918*. To Mr Roderick Suddaby of the Imperial War Museum for telling me of the whereabouts of the Stern Papers and to the trustees of The Liddell Hart Centre for Military Archives at King's College London for making me free of them; my particular gratitude goes to Dr Patricia J. Methven of that Centre for her unfailing help.

Several gentlemen of military antecedents have been good enough to read and comment upon the original typescript, now by no means the same as when it was first submitted. They know of my feelings towards them; I do not mention their names for there is no reason why they should share the blame for such criticisms as are bound to be made.

Last, my thanks to Philippa Arnott who turned a mass of heavily amended paper into the fairest of typescripts, and to Bill Oakes, who spawned the idea of this book.

Acknowledgements to illustrations

Photographs obtained from the Imperial War Museum appear on the following pages: Front end-paper, title-page, 24, 68, 95, 110, 133, 136, 137, 150, 166, 172, 195, 196.
From the Bill Oakes collection: pages 80, 81, 93, 99, 103, 107, 165, 167, 170, 171, 174, 177, 182, 185, rear end-paper.
From various books: pages 19, 20, 25, 28, 37, and from *War Monthly*, page 125 (both subjects).
All the remainder are from the Tank Museum at Bovington.

Introduction

SOMEBODY – I wish I could remember who it was – once said that if Napoleon Bonaparte had only put up a reward of a million francs for the invention of a weapon superior to the flint-lock musket he would have become master of the world. In this there is much truth, but only because Napoleon controlled his War Office. It would have been technically possible to have put a percussion rifle, breech-loading like the Ferguson, into the hands of French soldiers in the early 1800s with incalculable results.

In England we arrange matters differently. It would have been equally possible to have produced a tracked and armoured vehicle driven by an internal combustion engine in the early 1900s. The inventor, however, would not have been rewarded. He would have been lucky to avoid a visit by two doctors accompanied by men in white coats. The story lingers of the Nottingham plumber who submitted designs of just such a machine; they were, naturally, placed in a War Office file with a minute on them saying, 'The man's mad.'

It seems impossible to pick up any book on the subject without encountering the trite observation that nobody invented the tank. John Charteris, Sir Douglas Haig's Director of Military Intelligence was, more often than not, wrong in his conclusions but here he hit the nail on the head. 'The idea of a mobile strong-point, out of which the tank developed, probably occurred to most minds after our first experiences of attacking strongly entrenched positions. I first heard it suggested by an Intelligence Corps officer as early as the Battle of the Aisne. His idea took the form of a group of men carrying a section of bullet-proof shield. Very elementary calculations of weight proved that idea impracticable and the suggestion of using the 'Caterpillar' tractor, which had been experimented with at Aldershot in 1914, immediately arose. I remember discussing the possibility of this with Colonel Swinton in 1914. But it was so obvious a development that it must have occurred simultaneously in many regimental and Staff messes.'

That the Army had fared as well as it had under a Liberal Government was due entirely to one man, Richard Burdon Haldane. Even so, it did not fare well. The Navy, the sure shield, got, however grudgingly, its Dreadnoughts, its turbines and its big guns. The Army, up to 1914, was still Wolseley's army. It was given a superb rifle, better field guns and sensible webbing equipment but that was about all. A man going into battle either walked or was carried by an animal. Should he and his fellows need to dig a hole in the ground they did it in the same way and using the same tools as the builders of the Great Wall of China and the Pyramids of Egypt. And this at a time when mechanical and electrical engineering had reached a degree of skill not far behind that of today. The steam engine was obsolescent but the petrol and Diesel ones were widely used and of high efficiency. British engineers were held in respect everywhere; but nobody asked them to take an interest in military affairs. These were not for civilians, compendiously regarded by the highest military authorities as outsiders and not to be trusted.

Sir Arthur Conan Doyle was possessed of a fertile imagination allied to robust common sense. His articles in the *Strand Magazine*, foretelling exactly what would happen when the Germans unleashed their submarines, were regarded as highly entertaining. When, early in the war, he buttonholed Mr Montagu at the Ministry of Munitions to demand the making of some form of shield he found himself pushing on an open door. 'Sir Arthur, there is no use your arguing here, for there is no one in this building who does not know that you are right. The whole difficulty lies in making the soldiers accept your views.' When all was over Sir Arthur wrote of it again. 'We can never be grateful enough to the men who thought out the Tank, for I have no doubt at all that this product of British brains and British labour won the war, which would otherwise have ended in a peace of mutual exhaustion. Churchill, d'Eyncourt, Tritton, Swinton and Bertie Stern, these were in sober fact, divide the credit as you may, the men who played a very essential part in bringing down the giant'. Even the well-informed Conan Doyle seems to have been unconscious of the existence of a man quite as important as any of these. If Walter Gordon Wilson meant nothing to him it is hardly surprising that most people never heard of him. Yet, but for him there would have been no tank. Not, at any rate, in 1916.

Another well-worn apophthegm is that the effect of tanks in the First War was largely moral. There is something in this, but it calls to mind a remark by Scheibert, the historian of the American Civil War: 'The difference between a Spencer carbine and an Enfield rifle is by no means a mere matter of sentiment.' A great many infantrymen owed their lives to the tank; and to it the Army owed a good part of its greatest victories.

These things did not come about painlessly. As most if not all, of the men involved are long dead it is possible to give a candid account of their doings, successful and otherwise, without hurting the feelings of all who tried their best. That they quarrelled – furiously at times – is hardly surprising, for these were strong-willed men and great affairs were at stake. Who was right and who was wrong no longer matters. There is honour enough for all of them.

When the prophet Joel's palmerworms and locusts had done with the next twenty years the Pioneers were summoned back. By then, however, they were no longer Pioneers but had become in their turn nearer to Mr Kipling's 'eavy-sterned amateur old men. There is a moral in this, somewhere.

PART ONE

from the tents
The armourers, accomplishing the knights,
With busy hammers closing rivets up,
Give dreadful note of preparation.
                                KING HENRY V

CHAPTER 1

Victorian Afterglow

WHEN THE LEGATE, later Emperor, T. Flavius Vespasianus led the IInd Legion Augusta across Hardy's Egdon Heath to its assault upon the great Iron Age fortress of Maiden Castle he did not require his foot soldiers to advance unprotected against expert slingers. On the command being given Augusta carried out a well-practised drill movement. Each shield was raised above the head of its bearer, interlocking with those of his neighbours and the defenders looked helplessly down as the testudo, the great tortoise, advanced upon them. Iron-hard pellets rained down, bounced off and the legionaries arrived at the East Gate practically unscathed. Once there the swords of Rome made a swift and bloody end to the business. To Augusta it was second nature, an exercise that had been carried out times without number by them and their predecessors. Their lesson was not wasted upon posterity. Only a few miles across the heath lies Bovington Camp, home since 1916 to the British armoured forces.

The Roman Army had always been an infantry army; its artillery, in the form of catapults of all shapes and sizes, was efficient for siege work but horses had never been important on the battlefield. Auxiliary cavalry were always useful for scouting and for the pursuit of a broken enemy but had never been the queen of battles. The edged weapon was master and everything else existed only to help the swordsmen get to hand strokes with their adversaries. The next of the really mighty armies to arrive worked on the opposite principle. Mongols were horsemen, excellent horsemen, but they were not cavalry as the West knew it. Their sovereign weapon was not edged but missile, the short bow, and they used it from the saddle with devastating effect. No armour was needed. For a Mongol, as for 'Jacky' Fisher, speed was armour enough, speed coupled with overwhelming numbers. None of their opponents stood a chance. From a professional point of view it would have been of the greatest interest if time and space problems could have been overcome in order to have allowed them to meet in open field the armies of the English longbowmen. It would take some hardihood to pontificate on which side would have come off best. The same may be said of the Swiss phalanx. Though it was the terror of Europe it had the good fortune never to have to take on a missile weapon of such power and precision.

In Western Europe armour had a long and probably undeserved run of success.

The mailed knight upon his barbed horse was irresistible, again until he came face to face with the same simple weapon in very skilled hands. In the Near East, however, he had a less easy time of it. From Manzikert in 1071 to Dorylaeum fifteen years later and finally to the disaster of the Horns of Hattin in 1187 the Frankish-style charge proved ineffective against an enemy who would not stand still to receive it. The Turkish bow was a feeble thing compared to the English but it was good enough to puncture horses, and camel-loads of arrows furnished generous supplies of missiles. The truth was that cavalry ought to have been obsolete hundreds of years before it finally vanished from the field. It continued to exist, as a battering force, only for sentimental reasons and because regular armies had not come into existence. Great numbers of animals were always needed for draught and pack purposes; hunting was the traditional sport of the richer strata of society and it would have been unthinkable that, in the midst of so much horseflesh, a man of high degree should walk into battle.

The old problem remained until our own day. Very possibly it remains still. In essence it is obvious. How do you break a body of armed and determined men if you cannot shoot them down from a distance? Something must hit them with great force, but, before it can do that, it must reach them without being itself destroyed. Many devices were invented over the centuries, most of them never getting further than the drawing board. The majority can be of no more than antiquarian interest, for there are no records of them having achieved anything worth while. Froissart tells of a device called a 'ribaudequin'; it was, so he says 'a high wheelbarrow reinforced with iron and long pointed spikes in front'. In his famous paper of 3 December, 1915, Major The Rt Hon Winston S. Churchill suggested something of the same kind, along with other variants on the offensive. Leonardo da Vinci, inevitably, produced complicated drawings; a great mural at Cowdray, copied before the place was destroyed by fire, depicts a battle-car used at the siege of Boulogne in 1544; as it appears to have been a farm cart pulled by a single horse and carrying one hackbutman plus a bowman it was unlikely to have greatly influenced events. The Germans, ever inventive, produced a number of cognate machines but all suffered from a fatal, if obvious defect. Livy, Silius Italicus and Quintus Curtius told of war-carts or chariots. Later came Nicholas Glockendon of Nurnburg, various Scotchmen of whom the most notable was John Stewart, Duke of Albany, and the inventors of devices pictured by Valturius and Ludwig von Eyb. All foundered on the same snag. Horses can no more push carts than sailors can push rope. It was necessary to be patient and await the discovery of something better than animal-power.

The longbow dropped out before its time, probably because it needed a long training period for the archer, which men became unwilling to take up. Any weakling could be taught to loose off a musket. Thus the cavalries of the world continued in existence, for want of better shock machines and because the aristocracy could not bear to be parted from their horses. They beat each other up relentlessly but their successes against stout infantry were few and far between. Le Marchant's heavy horse wrought famously at Salamanca and von Bock's Germans broke a square at

Garcia Hernandez. The next troops to do this, or something like it, were Osman Digna's Hadendowa, alias 'Fuzzy Wuzzies'. And Fuzzy Wuzzies fought on foot.

With the coming of steam it seemed that a battle car might be at last within the realms of the possible. One such was reportedly built for service in the Crimea, but it never left England and was soon broken up. Anyone who has seen a traction engine will not need further explanation. Steam locomotives are powerful but only on rails have they any turn of speed. And, at the risk of repetition, Jacky Fisher propounded a great truth. Speed is armour; armour without speed merely produces a target.

The ingredients of the tank all came into existence during the eighties of the last century and were produced by several different men working far away from each other. In 1886 Gottlieb Daimler, who had served an apprenticeship with the Manchester firm of Whitworth, came up with the petrol-driven internal combustion engine. It very soon powered a wheeled horseless carriage. Wheels, whether solid-tyred or fitted as they soon would be with Mr Dunlop's inflatable variety, were good enough for metalled roads but of no use off them. Nor did there seem any likelihood of their being needed to go across country. The ploughman and his team still had a long future ahead of them. There were, however, some experiments going on with a view to bringing some degree of mechanical power to the farm additional to the steam traction-engine and reaping machines.

The obvious difficulty was to prevent the machinery from becoming bogged down by sheer weight. The footed wheel, one fitted with pivoted shoes or plates around its circumference so contrived that a flat surface was always presented to the ground, had been known for a long time. The German Army used it in conjunction with its heavy guns. The arrangement was not without its uses but it was hard work for the horses and slowed things up considerably when on any sort of road. With the coming of an engine so much lighter than the steam affair men cast around for something better than the footed wheel; the pressure for results was felt mostly in America whose enormous fields urgently needed something in the way of serviceable tractors.

As long ago as 1770 Richard Lovell Edgeworth had been granted, in London, a Patent for an endless track running over wheels. Once the Patent was granted, Mr Edgeworth seems to have let the matter drop, probably because no financier could be made to take it up. It may well be that the steam engine running on fixed rails seemed a better proposition than a machine that laid its own. Dust gathered on the plans until 1880 when Mr Batter, an American citizen, made a steam-tractor running on endless caterpillar tracks of the same kind. This suited prairie farmers well and soon became established. As time went on other manufacturers appeared and by the beginning of the present century the first name amongst caterpillar-tractor makers was Benjamin Holt. The farmers of Europe were not greatly interested.

The last essential of an armoured fighting vehicle arrived in 1883 when the Patent Office issued its No 3178 for an automatic gun to Hiram Maxim of '57D Hatton Garden, corner of Clerkenwell Road'. Maxim, one of the few American inventors to become a naturalized British subject, was as prolific as Leonardo had been, his discoveries ranging from guns to electric light bulbs. His machine-gun was a masterpiece of ingenuity, working on a different principle from the gas-and-spring affairs that superceded it and are still in service with a number of armies. The recoil forces back the barrel on to the lock which, driven back in its turn, extracts the spent case, feeds in another from a canvas belt, fires it and returns to keep up the process as long as the ammunition lasts. The barrel is encased in a water-jacket and continues operating for a very long time. The drawback is that the gun is heavy, weighing nearly half a hundredweight without its tripod.

As the component parts of the armoured fighting vehicle arrived so did the reason for its existence. Wire had been commonly used in England since the first factory was set up at Mortlake in 1663. Lucien Smith of Ohio is not a name as familiar as Daimler, Holt or Maxim but it deserves to be. In 1867, just after the Civil War, he produced for the farmers of America 'twisted wire studded with points'. Under the name of 'barbed wire' it was patented in this country in 1876 by a Mr Hunt. It became widely used and so unpopular that the Barbed Wire Act 1893 had to be passed in order to limit its use. The first military use of it was in its home country. The Spanish-American war of 1898 taught few lessons apart from some of the 'how not to' kind. It did, however, bring barbed wire into service, though only for the protection of camps. Lord Kitchener used vast quantities of it in South Africa to maintain his lines of blockhouses and in 1905 the Russian General Tretyakov complained that the defence of Port Arthur was made exceedingly difficult by the shortage of a commodity worth its weight in gold. Before 1914 it was an established ordnance store with most armies. When the inventions of Mr Maxim and Mr Smith came to dominate the battlefields it was necessary to take stock of all the means available of overcoming them. At the end of the nineteenth century nothing was further from the military mind. There was then a curious spirit abroad in the British Army.

Everybody will remember the Punch cartoon headed MILITARY EDUCATION:—

General. 'Mr de Bridoon, what is the general use of cavalry in modern warfare?'
Mr de Bridoon. 'Well, I suppose to give tone to what would otherwise be a mere vulgar brawl'.

It was meant as a joke, but it was only half one. Newspaper correspondents fresh from the Sudan who visited the Aldershot Manoeuvres of 1898 were horrified at what they saw. Troops advanced in review order over open country and the very idea of taking cover was regarded as cowardice. The only Maxim guns, until very recently, had been those privately bought by wealthy London Volunteer regiments. The usual orders given to machine-gun officers were to 'get those bloody things out of the way'. The cavalry was still the pride of the service, fresh from its not very difficult success against Arabi at Tel-el-Kebir. Then came South Africa, a war against 'the most formidable mounted warriors since the Mongols' as Mr Churchill called them. Here were lessons in plenty, but few of the senior men seem to have grasped them. Sir John French, at the great house of 94 Lancaster Gate which he shared with his American friend the engineer George Moore, had a visit from Valentine Williams, one of Northcliffe's young men and, later, author of the 'Clubfoot' novels. 'He (French) made a fine portrait of an English gentleman of the old school, in his dinner-coat and white waistcoat, with his silvery hair and healthy pink cheeks, as he sat at the dinner table over the nuts and port, under a large and rather indifferent painting of the "Dash to Kimberley", in the South African War, showing him on horseback, with Haig at his side, sweeping along at the head of the cavalry', Williams wrote in his autobiography *The World of Action*.

In retrospect the Dash to Kimberley was the worst thing that could have happened both to Sir John and to the Army. The *Daily Mail* quoted what it claimed as a letter from one present that the relief of the town was due to the commander's 'masterly decision' to charge through what was believed to be a solid wall of defenders: To do Sir John justice, he would have charged just the same had this been true; in fact the Boers, being sensible men, fired a few rounds from their Mausers and removed themselves from his path. It was claimed that some forty or fifty of them moved too slowly and were either speared or sabred as against losses to the cavalry of less than a dozen. The charge must have been enormous fun for those participating in it, but it was no Gravelotte. Kimberley was certainly relieved, but at a cost. The cavalry had ruined themselves and their horses by overenthusiasm. When Lord Kitchener needed them to support the attack on Cronje's laager a few days later they were not there. The attack went in without them and Kitchener observed to an American correspondent that had he known yesterday what he knew then he would not have tried it at all. Frontal attacks were impossible against the magazine rifle. This lesson Lord K never forgot. Sir John, and to a lesser extent his Chief of Staff Colonel Haig, never quite learned it.

The newspapers went wild over the Dash. It seems sad that television had not arrived for here was the perfect subject. There was, however, another point of view. Doctor Conan Doyle, always an admirer of the regular army, put it this way: 'In the larger operations of the war it is difficult to say that cavalry, as cavalry, have justified their existence. In the opinion of many the tendency of the future will be to convert the whole force into mounted infantry ... a little training in taking cover, leggings instead of boots and a rifle instead of a carbine would give us a formidable force of twenty thousand men who could do all that our cavalry does and more besides.' Which is exactly what happened as the war went on. It was all very well for a civilian to say things like that and even to point to the fact that Lord Airlie had started it all by using his XIIth Lancers dismounted at Magersfontein. A soldier who openly announced the same heresy would have been reckoned not only a professional incompetent but, and worse, a traitor to his class. 'Chevalier', in both the literal and figurative meanings, was still the word of power.

The war ended at last and with it the army's re-education. It had been a horseman's affair for obvious reasons of topography and it had been very expensive; a Commission opened up some interesting scandals over the manner in which the horses had been found. All the same, it was not likely to recur. If the army ever had to fight anybody again it would probably be the Russians and the business would be done by horse, foot and guns as grandfather had done it in the Crimea. Mr Balfour's Conservative government remained in office just long enough to place orders for better weapons of the old kind. The 18-pdr gun, the 4.5 howitzer, the short Lee Enfield rifle and some more Maxims. All were excellent in their way but all were in truth weapons of the late nineteenth century.

The Wolseley Car Company had shown a petrol-driven car with a 16 horse-power Daimler engine at the Crystal Palace show of 1902. It had been designed by Mr Frederick Sims, mounted a Maxim and was in some sort covered with armour plating. In fact it was ahead of its time. The engine was too feeble and the great weakness, as every pioneer motorist knew, lay in the wheels. Pneumatic tyres had been in use for a long time but were still not to be relied upon even on tarred roads. Heavy vehicles still, and for a long time to come, stuck to the solid variety and put up with the jolting and low speed. Nobody was much interested in Mr Sims' car and it was quietly taken to pieces again. In 1908 the Liberal Government gave to the cavalry the only new weapon to be added before 1914. It was a sword; a very fine sword; a shovel would have been far better value.

The reign of Edward the Peacemaker saw much happening in new forms of military hardware. In 1904 a Danish officer, Major-General Madsen, invented a light automatic gun which weighed only five pounds more than a rifle, had a mechanism of the simplest kind and was better by far than anything of the kind for a long time to come. Years later, on 6 June, 1918, an official statement was made in the House of Lords that 'the present Madsen gun is by many considered "the most wonderful machine-gun of its kind ever invented" and that it was admittedly superior in many respects to either the Lewis or the Hotchkiss guns'. The gun was taken into service by the Danish cavalry but the War Office in Pall Mall was not interested. Some years later, when the War Office had moved to its fine new home in Whitehall and handed over Pall Mall to the Royal Automobile Club, it brushed off Colonel Lewis in much the same way. The Madsen gun would have been cheap. By the time of First Ypres the Government would have paid any asking price for such a weapon. By then it was too late. Efforts were made to get hold of some but Germany prevented the sale and collared the guns herself. In a way this disinterest in automatics was a compliment to the soldier. With the SMLE a recruit before leaving his Depot could get off fifteen aimed rounds a minute; real experts could manage thirty. The long-service regular infantryman was the best marksman in any army, as the Germans readily admitted when the clash came. Nobody seemed to understand that hastily raised units could not be expected to come anywhere near this standard.

The attitude of civilian ministers in the new Liberal Government of 1906 was soon made plain to Sir Horace Smith-Dorrien when he held the command at Aldershot; 'One day he (a Minister whose name had been struck out by Lady Smith-Dorrien) honoured me at lunch, and I used the occasion to impress on him, as a member of the Government, that it was most important that we should be armed with the new Vickers-Maxim machine-gun, which was half the weight of the gun we then had, and much more efficient, and I urged that £100,000 would re-equip the six divisions of the Expeditionary Force. Mr —— jeered at me, saying I was afraid of the Germans, that he habitually attended the German Army at training and was quite certain that if they ever went to war "the most monumental examples of crass cowardice the world had ever heard of would be witnessed".' Such, apparently, was Cabinet thinking in 1909. It is hardly wonderful that any soldier of an innovative mind did not waste his time by pressing ideas.

During Smith-Dorrien's tour at Aldershot, in 1910, there was a demonstration by the earliest of the British petrol-engined tractors, a Hornsby chain-track. This was a splendid vehicle that looked as if it owed something to Mr Heath Robinson or Mr Emmett. The exhaust led into an impressive smoke-stack; the chains that drove it were surmounted by wooden blocks about the size and shape of those commonly used for paving roads and the whole was mounted on powerful springs that bounced it about alarmingly. Among those watching was General 'Wullie' Robertson, later to be CIGS under Lord Kitchener. He held the machine 'to have a great future as a tractor for dragging heavy guns and vehicles across broken ground. Universal sympathy was extended to the drivers, who, in consequence of the caterpillar's violent up-and-down motions, experienced all the sensations of sea-sickness, and looked it'. In spite of that there was no denying that the thing worked.

The Committee of Imperial Defence, however, was occupied with more important matters. Between 1907 and 1914 the Channel Tunnel came up for discussion fourteen times. Lord Wolseley's Memorandum of 1882 was resurrected and papers submitted by Field-Marshal Lord Nicholson, Mr Churchill, Colonel Seeley and Sir John French. There is no mention of caterpillar tractors anywhere in the Committee's agenda over these years. As soon as the war started and the demand came for guns heavier than the usual field pieces the question of how they were to be moved along the roads of France demanded answer. Very quickly, for Kitchener was now in charge, the War Office placed orders in America for fifteen of the Holt machines. With 75 hp petrol engines, the best track then on the market, and a weight of 15 tons (the Hornsby weighed 8) they could manage a speed of 15 mph, though this fell to 2 with a gun hooked in. It was still better than a large team of Clydesdale horses and they were soon at work in France. Only a few people saw in them the beginnings of a war-winning fighting machine.

It would be wrong, however, to assume that indifference was limited to the allied camp. The German possessed one great advantage which they, too, neglected. When the Zeppelin first appeared it became plain that engines far more powerful than those used on roads were needful. After much experiment, the firm of Maybach produced one of 450 hp. No other country had anything like this. Fortunately no effort was made to apply the knowledge to land-bound vehicles. The Maybach was far too heavy and clumsy for such uses. Apart from the Rolls-Royce, which was in a class of its own, the best motor-cars were made in France with Germany a good second. England lagged badly behind; the United States produced excellent machines, the Hudson being perhaps the fastest, but these belonged to quite another world.

To blame the Army for living happily in the past would be entirely unfair. Soldiers, like everybody else, could hardly fail to see how swiftly the country was becoming mechanized. As early as 1906 the land speed record had risen to more than 125 miles per hour. At the end of the following year London contained 723 motor taxi-cabs, a figure that had risen within two years to just under 4,000. It was also noticeable that by far the greater number of these were of French manufacture, Unic, Darracq and, above all, the two-cylinder Renault that clung on for a very long time. The year, 1909, saw the first movement of a formed body of troops by road. It was, admittedly, a publicity stunt by the Automobile Association but the fact remained that a composite battalion of the Guards, complete with all impedimenta, was carried from London to Brighton and back in several hundred private cars at a good round speed and without a hitch. The only military lesson learned was that the service cap universally called a Brodrick, though St John Brodrick, Earl of Midleton, denied all responsibility for it, blew off for want of a chin-strap. This omission was made good. It was the AA, months before Lord Kitchener's call, that coined the phrase 'The First Hundred Thousand'. In July, 1914, its membership had reached 89,198 of whom 3,279 had been elected during the previous month or so. It was confidently expected that the magic figure would be reached by the time of the Olympia motor show and a great celebration dinner was planned. Fate, however, got in first. There was no motor show in August, 1914.

It was not the General Staff, however, but the Home Secretary who first realized that the motor car might have an unexpected military use. On a day in the wonderful summer of 1911 Mr Churchill attended a party at No 10 Downing Street where he fell into conversation with Sir Edward Henry, Chief Commissioner of Police. As they talked about the European situation and its gravity, Sir Edward casually remarked that by an odd arrangement the Home Office was responsible, through the Metropolitan Police, for guarding the whole of the Navy's cordite reserves in the magazines at Chattenden and Lodge Hill. This being the first the Home Secretary had heard of it he pressed Sir Edward hard. The guard, it seemed, had for years consisted of a few London bobbies armed with truncheons. To the question of what would happen if a score of armed Germans turned up in motor-cars Mr Churchill received the interesting answer that they would be able to do as they liked. He left the garden party and telephoned the Admiralty. As both First Lord and First Sea Lord were absent he spoke to an Admiral 'who shall be nameless'. He made it quite plain that he was not taking orders from any panicky civilian Minister and flatly refused to send Marines. A second call to Mr Haldane at the War Office had two companies of infantry installed within a few hours. The motor car had introduced something new into military matters.

It was left to that erratic genius Mr H. G. Wells to move things on a little further. Though the son of a professional cricketer, he had some ideas that were certainly not cricket. In 1903, being well into what is now called 'science fiction', a market that he had almost to himself, he sent to the *Strand Magazine* a story of some future war in which armed and armoured machines crawled over the country-side on their tracks and fought battles with each other. It was called *The Land Ironclads*. Later he warmed to his work and told not merely of wars in the air between various branches of the human race but also of battles with invaders from outer space. All were regarded with equal seriousness. The Holt tractor from America, an efficient petrol-driven machine running on tracks, was given a demonstration at Aldershot. Its faults, which were many, were pointed out; its virtues and potential were ignored. The military mind, mercifully, knew no national boundaries. Not only did no other War Office want Mr Holt's tractor; none even wanted buses or lorries.

The scientific Germans, however, did not entirely abandon the idea. In 1913 a Herr Goebel produced a machine of his own design. It was, according to German custom, huge and ponderous; no picture seems to have survived but it was described as resembling what we know as a tank, to have been covered in thick armour and to have bristled with guns. In 1913 he drove it over a high obstacle at Pinne, in Posen; the following year he produced it before a huge crowd at the Berlin stadium. It broke down half way up the first bank and refused to be started again. The crowd became truculent and demanded its money back. Herr Goebel and his machine disappeared from history.

The Belgians took a few of their excellent Minerva cars to the Cockerill works in Antwerp and had them fitted with a mild steel armour. That apart, the armies of the great industrial powers of Europe walked slowly towards each other in the summer of 1914 with masses of man-power and animal-power as great armies had done since man discovered war. A reincarnated Wellington could have taken command of any of them after only the shortest refresher course.

In the rear areas of the BEF some concession was made towards modernity. The War Office as long ago as 1900 had set up a Mechanical Transport Committee. a brave gesture towards the coming century. It found little occupation in Pall Mall but survived the translation to Whitehall in 1907. In 1911, Coronation year, new life was breathed into it with the introduction of two subsidy schemes; these provided a means of mechanizing some parts of the Army on the cheap. Civilian companies were given money on the understanding that they would build vehicles more or less to a specification and would on mobilization hand them over. The scheme did not work out too badly. Each Division had a supply column of motor-lorries, working, theoretically, between railhead and the Divisional Train. Homely names on their sides like Waring & Gillow or J. Lyons rather spoilt the picture of a twentieth-century army but the Army Service Corps drivers plied their new trade well enough. All army ambulances remained horse-drawn; the best of the motor-driven ones were furnished, along with their crews, by those old reliables the British Red Cross Society and the Salvation Army.

On 31 May, 1915, Lord Kitchener submitted a secret report to the Cabinet which set out the entire state of affairs very clearly. On mobilization the Army had owned exactly 80 motor-lorries, 20 cars, 15 motor-cycles and 36 traction-engines. The subsidy scheme brought the lorry total to 807; another 334 had been instantly commandeered. The 20 cars simultaneously jumped by 193 and the motor-cycles by 116. On the day Kitchener signed the report there were on the strength a further 7,037 lorries, 1,694 cars, 2,745 motor-cycles and 1,151 motor-ambulances. The Army Service Corps had grown from 450 officers and 6,300 other ranks to 'a strength today of 4,500 officers and 125,000 other ranks, i.e. 5,000 more than the whole of the Regular Forces in the United Kingdom previous to the outbreak of war'. Petrol, including that for the Royal Flying Corps, was being consumed at the rate of 35,000 gallons a day.

The war was still very young. On Armistice Day 1918 the Army had on charge in all theatres 121,692 motor vehicles along with 735,000 horses and mules.

CHAPTER 2

Farewell to the Sword

SOMEWHERE IN *The World Crisis*, on the subject of the Navy handing over most of its rifles to the Army, Mr Churchill wrote that 'in the last resort Jack will have to trust to his cutlass as of old'. It was, of course, a little Churchillian joke. The writer probably owed his existence, as he well knew, to the fact that before charging with the Lancers at Omdurman he had put his sword back in its case and had bought a serviceable automatic pistol. Like his great ancestor with the flintlock musket and socket bayonet he demanded the best weapon going.

By 1914 skilled engineers had made great battleships with guns throwing shells of a ton weight over a distance of several miles. Submarines had become highly efficient weapons of war. The prospect of Jack's Captain laying his ship alongside an enemy and leading a charge of boarders was remote. In all armies, however, the old ways clung on. The most mathematically-minded gunners, the most skilful aeronauts and all the other technical men existed for one purpose only. Their job was to make it possible for the infantryman to walk up to his enemy and to push a metal spike into his weasand. The bayonet was a comfortable thing to have about one's person and the flash of steel looked splendid on parade. It had its own mystique, with men of outstandingly savage aspect hurling themselves at straw-filled dummies, snarling madly and charged with the duty of instilling into newcomers the 'Spirit of the Bayonet'. A line of steel bearing down must be an unnerving experience, but so long as the defenders are kitted out with a decent rifle – better still a decent light automatic – they are Hallowe'en turnip-masks.

The sword was an incubus even worse. French and German officers, like most continentals, carried theirs around with them everywhere. The sword was not merely a badge of office it was something mystic. Even Mr Asquith, who pretty certainly did not know foible from forte, could not resist making a speech about not sheathing it until various things might happen. When the BEF embarked, every infantry officer was under orders to carry his with him, fresh from the grindstone. Most people found it rather an embarrassment, especially the subalterns; their seniors had horses to ride and to carry their impedimenta. There is no reason to suppose that anybody in any army took hurt from thrust or cut.

Mons and Le Cateau began to explain the obvious. Whatever may have been the principles upon which ancient wars had been fought, the infantry was no longer a wielder of edged weapons. What mattered was fire power; a light machine-gun of the Madsen or Lewis type could make a couple of good men more serviceable than a platoon would be without it. A few hundred of these inexpensive weapons in the early battles would have altered history. There is a further consideration that took time to sink in. Killing an adversary is traditional but wasteful. A corpse demands no more than a hole in the ground, if it is lucky. A wounded man needs to be transported, doctored, nursed, fed, watered, clothed, documented and paid. The bayonet kills: the bullet more often than not, wounds. A far better bargain. So long as the war was being largely carried on by professionals these thoughts would have been dashed aside as unsoldierly. As time went by, and as the amateurs moved in, they became axiomatic. But the 'Spirit of the Bayonet' was too strong for them. In all the battles of 1914, 1915 and 1916 the infantry remained condemned to what Mr Churchill called 'chewing barbed wire'. Old weapons and old ways were no longer enought to give attackers even a quarter of a chance. Something new would have to be found before the pick of the nation either rotted away or died on the wire.

It was not only new machines that were needed; it was new men. Most of the Generals had been born in the 1860s, with the officers of field rank coming along ten years or so later. They had grown up in a world innocent of anything more technical than a steam train and a high proportion had spent their formative years in India or other places where the internal combustion engine was almost unheard of. To be told in their middle age that they must unlearn all that they had acquired over the decades and start again from fresh premises was too much for many good but unimaginative men. Over the years this author has spoken with a good many people who took part in the retreat from Mons. On one point they were unanimous. The middle-piece officers and senior NCOs with South African experience were, generally speaking, useless. They seemed bemused by the whole thing and did not know what to do. It was the Second Lieutenants and the Lance Corporals who brought the Army through its trial. This pointed the next lesson. Youth was hence-forth a quality more to be prized than experience. Already this was showing in the Flying Corps, with its very young Captains and Majors. It would have to leaven the entire Army before the business was over.

Before turning to the subject of mechanical developments it may be useful to consider the military state of mind in the early stages of the war. Inside the Army initiative was not encouraged. For almost every military problem there existed what was called a 'school solution' and such things were Holy Writ. The regimental officer who wanted to get on had well-established things to occupy nearly all of his mind. Company commanders were judged not by any apparent ability to seize initiatives and to exploit them; what mattered were Boot Books and Bath Books, Minor Offence Reports, Pay and Ration Returns, Musketry Returns, Imprest Accounts and half a hundred matters of the like kind. Ensure that all these were in apple-pie order, demonstrate that your Company had a high standard of turn-out, drill and march discipline and you would in due time get your reward, the command of a battalion bearing a famous name. It was the same in the Royal Navy. Nobody wanted Drakes or Rodneys any more. Obey every Regulation, every Standing Order and comply with every known whim of your seniors if you wished to get to the top.

Civilians were another matter. To the Army all civilians were men of a lesser kind, obsessed with the idea of making money by any means, lacking the virtues of discipline and bravery; some of them wore made-up ties, spoke of serviettes and cruets and were never to be trusted since they lacked loyalty. Worst of all were the politicians, a race of inferior men dedicated to the task of keeping the Army starved of everything it needed. Exaggerated, no doubt but there was a grain of truth in it.

When mechanical warfare first began it became, however regrettably, necessary to turn for civilian help. The first operations, it is true, were carried out under the White Ensign, but only just. Commander Charles Samson, RN, was a famous pioneer airman. When the RNAS was given the duty of protecting the homeland against Zeppelin raids it was natural that a base should be set up at Dunkirk. The base had to be defended and, in the absence of any troops for the purpose, Samson, its commander, had to make his own arrangements. With the assistance of his brother Felix, normally a solicitor but for the time being a Marine Lieutenant, he acquired several motor cars; one of them belonged to Felix Samson and was a Mercedes. The best always being good enough for the Navy they acquired several more, all Rolls Royces, and had them armoured after a fashion with boiler-plate fitted on by Les Chantiers de France at Dunkirk itself. The Admiralty found some Maxims to complete the adhockery and during that strange period of the war when the armies had moved beyond Belgium to the Marne and the Aisne the armoured cars made themselves extremely useful. They suffered one grave handicap in that they were completely road-bound but for the moment that did not greatly matter.

It soon became obvious that boiler-plate would not keep out anything much and Samson turned to his Chief, Captain Murray Sueter, for something better. Sueter, Director of the Air Division, formed up to Beardmores, the leading authority on armour, and enquired what they could do. Beardmores told him that they could furnish flat sheets of armour plate but neither they nor anybody else knew how to curve them. It took much trial and error before ways could be found. During this time Samson continued his little raids and General Aston's Marines played the part of a stage army, cruising around empty Belgian roads in charabancs. The end of these exploits came when the Germans finally found out the antidote; all that was necessary was to remove the pavé and dig a trench across the road. Samson ran up some makeshift girder bridges but the armies came back in the autumn and the adventures of the first mechanized units were over.

It was, as Charteris said, the time at which men's thoughts began to turn towards some form of armoured vehicle that could travel across country carrying with it either a small gun or at least a light automatic. Had not almost every officer in the pre-war War Office dashed off to France there might have been somebody in Whitehall who remembered that plans for just such a machine had been filed away in the building for the last couple of years. They had been prepared by a Mr Lancelot de Mole, an Australian engineer whose concern with such things had begun when he interested himself in the problems of transporting heavy loads through his native outback. His first design had been of a multi-wheeled platform with a steering

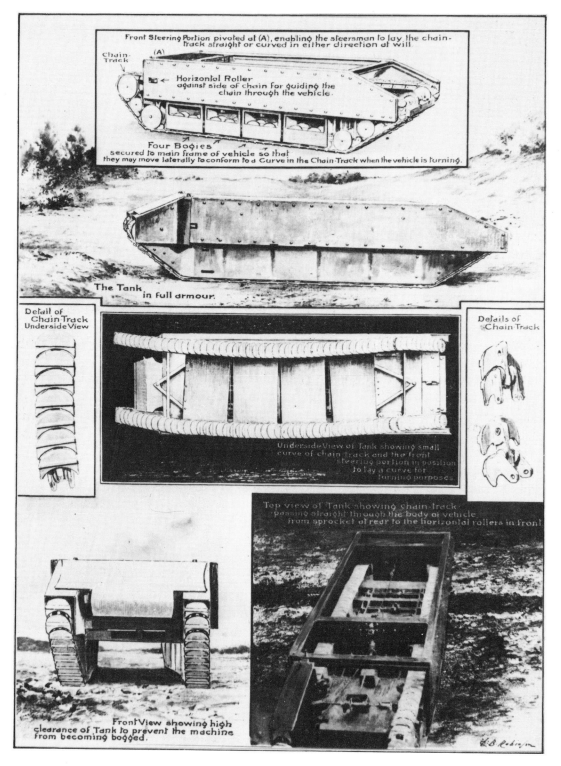

Mr de Mole's tank. A post-war artist's impression.

system of considerable ingenuity; a model of it, picked up in a Brighton junk shop, is in the Tank Museum. Experts say that although the model seems to work well enough it is doubtful whether a full-size version could stand the inevitable strains and stresses. Mr de Mole moved on from it to a design of something easily recognizable as a tank, travelling on tracks and steered by them. This he submitted to the War Office in 1912. The plan was incomplete, for it shows no propulsion unit, but the best opinion is that Mr de Mole was undoubtedly working on the right lines. The War Office filed it. When the war began de Mole joined the AIF and rose to become a Corporal in the 10th Battalion. Some years ago his Colonel, in answer to a letter from the Museum, said that de Mole was an odd sort of chap and had to be given a job in the Orderly Room. Be that as it may, he had sketched out the first armoured fighting vehicle. The Royal Commission on Awards to Inventors spoke highly of his work, but in Australia his unusual name is completely forgotten. The men who produced the first tank never even knew it.

Mr Churchill had a clearer grasp of the future shape of war than had most men. So had his friend Admiral Bacon. Since he had been driven out of the Navy as a result of writing some ill-advised letters critical of his Chiefs, directed to the First Sea Lord but picked up by the Press, Bacon had been general manager of the Coventry Ordnance Works. As his Company produced a third of the turrets for the Navy's guns, Mr Churchill had been at pains to keep it in business. Bacon wanted above all things to get back to the Service and he saw a way of achieving his heart's desire. The war was only days old when he told the First Lord by letter that he had already designed a 15″ howitzer that could be transported by road. Mr Churchill took him up on it and in October, 1914, was shown pictures of the eight big tractors that would do the pulling. When asked to design something that could carry guns and cross trenches the Admiral obliged. An experimental machine was produced on 13 February, 1915; the First Lord ordered thirty of them. In May he proudly demonstrated the prowess of the sample machine to the War Office. It was turned down and the order cancelled. So ended the first attempt at a tank.

If Charteris is right, as he probably is on this occasion, a good many people were simultaneously busy inventing the same thing. Most were too far down in the military strata to do anything about it but one of their number had the entrée everywhere that mattered. Maurice Hankey, Lieutenant-Colonel RMA, had long been Secretary to the Committee of Imperial Defence and no door was closed to him. He, too, possessed what was always called a fertile mind. Amongst his closer friends was Ernest Swinton, a Sapper Colonel of considerable literary ability. From being Hankey's assistant Swinton had been sent to France very early in the war as the official Eye Witness, a substitute for the war correspondents so loathed and despised by Lord Kitchener. His inventive turn of mind appears in his book *The Green Curve* and, at 47, it was still much in evidence. On 20 October, 1914, he visited Hankey at the CID office, spoke about the stalemate caused by machine-guns and wire and speculated about the possible military use of the Holt caterpillar tractor. They agreed that it was something not to be neglected; Swinton was given the unrewarding task of interesting the War Office, whilst Hankey would try his luck amongst the politicians. Swinton, unsurprisingly, was brushed off. Hankey received a hearing from Lord Kitchener but was unable to convince him that tractors could be other than a target for artillery. On Boxing Day Hankey put his thoughts on paper and sent them to, amongst others, the First Lord. Mr Churchill wrote to the Prime Minister, commending the document and saying that it was extraordinary that both the Army in France and the War Office should have allowed three months to pass by without addressing their minds to the problem. He was still thinking in terms of machines driven by steam, to be used by night, and coupled them with a simpler idea for man-pushed shields. As an afterthought he added a note on the use of smoke, the result of a communication from Lord Dundonald with his grandfather's Crimean plan for the use of that ancillary.

As the armies sank into the ground, the war of movement being over for a long time to come, an important character enters this story. Albert Gerald Stern, 'Bertie' to his friends, was 36; about the age of most company and battery commanders. His father, James, was senior partner in the banking house of Stern Brothers which had originated in Frankfurt in 1807. Like the Rothschilds they had three separate establishments; Frankfurt, Paris and Angel Court, London, where they had been since 1834. After Eton and Christ Church, Oxford, Bertie Stern had been sent to study the family trade in Frankfurt and New York and at 25 he had been taken into partnership. While still the age of a subaltern he had been charged with arranging

Foster's 150 h.p. Daimler tractor, as used by Admiral Bacon.

Major-General Sir Ernest Swinton, KBE.

Lieut.-Col. Sir Albert Stern, KBE, CMG.

loans to the Sultan of Morocco – this at the request of the Foreign Office – to the Young Turks in Constantinople and to various big commercial concerns in Canada. Everybody liked Bertie Stern, for he was the most clubbable of men, well known at the Garrick and elsewhere. His first taste of the war came at a meeting at the Bank of England just before the fateful Bank Holiday of 4 August. 'Sir Edward Holden was the commanding figure. "I must pay my wages on Friday," he said, "and we must have Bank Holidays until enough currency has been printed to be able to do so." His advice was followed and all the impending disasters were averted. Here, I first saw (in the war) the advantage of a definite cure administered by a strong man.'

Stern had no mind to spend the war sitting on committees. His two brothers were both in the Yeomanry and would soon be off. A damaged ankle kept him from joining them, but he had an idea of his own. In November, as soon as his feet were cleared, he wrote to the First Lord offering to provide and equip an armoured car, with crew complete, to join Mr Churchill's 'Dunkirk Circus'. He was told that it would be more useful for him to present himself to Captain Sueter, Director of Air, 'and offer the services of the Car and of yourself to the regular Armoured Car section which is being built up and organized under Commander Boothby at Wormwood Scrubbs (sic.)'. Mr Stern walked in. Lieutenant Stern RNVR walked out. Major

Hetherington, the Transport Officer to the Division, 'asked me to join his staff and to work under his Chief Assistant, Lieut Fairer-Smith. I agreed to do so'. The date was the second week in December, 1914.

Armoured cars were, at any rate for the moment, out. A squadron under Lieut-Commander Whittall went to German South-West Africa; 'Bendor', Duke of Westminster, after various misadventures in France, took one to the Western Desert to smarten up the Senussi; Commander Locker Lampson took another one to Russia. 'The enthusiasm of both officers and men of the Armoured Car Division was unbounded. They searched the whole world for war. But war in France had already settled down to trench fighting. In France, Armoured Cars, always an opportunist force, found their opportunities gone.'

Nevertheless several armoured car squadrons remained, their London bases being at the Clement Talbot Works in Barlby Road, Kensington, and at the airship shed belonging to the *Daily Mail* at Wormwood Scrubbs, as it was then usually spelt. For immediate purposes they constituted the entire air defence of London, responsibility for this having been given to Sueter. The cars, most of them in fact being lorries, were an eclectic lot and the weapons even more so. They did, however, muster a number of trained mechanics in their ranks.

Those left behind in the airship shed without any specific duties took counsel amongst themselves about where the Armoured Car Division should go from there. They were young men and between them they mustered a considerable amount of miscellaneous experience. Stern, at 36, was the eldest. The Duke, one year younger, had some military credentials for he had been a Cornet in the Blues and still held a commission in the Cheshire Yeomanry. In South Africa, as ADC to Lord Roberts, he had been chagrined at not receiving a DSO. The initials were then taken as standing for 'Dukes' Sons Only', and Bendor was a Duke already. He earned it a couple of years later with his armoured cars, beating up the Senussi in the Western Desert. Tom Hetherington, at 28, was the youngest member, but what he lacked in years he made up in other ways. Upon leaving Harrow he had declined going to a University but instead passed three years as an apprentice with the famous engineering works of Maudslay. With that behind him he joined the 18th Hussars and represented Great Britain at horse shows in San Sebastian, Brussels, New York and Chicago before deciding that horses were démodé. In 1911 he took up flying and at his own expense won the Aviator's Certificate No 25. He had been a founder member of the Air Battalion RE and in 1912 obtained his Airship Pilot's Certificate. Having been fobbed off with an appointment to the Armoured Cars he at once turned his powerful imagination towards more promising things.

The meeting of minds from which the whole tank idea flowed took place at Murray's Club early in February, 1915; only three of the pioneers, Stern, Hetherington and James Radley, the racing motorist, were present. Most of the talking was done by Hetherington who was thinking in terms of that well-known attraction at Mr Kiralfy's White City, the Big Wheel. Nobody contemplated the years of trench warfare that lay ahead; the thoughts of all three were concentrated on a crossing of the Rhine, presumably to take place quite soon, and for this the plan seemed to have

The one-ton Pedrail machine. As pulled by Mr Churchill.
The same, serving its intended purpose.

something to offer. The Duke of Westminster was captivated by it and agreed to arrange another dinner with Mr Churchill present.

The First Lord accepted and on 17 February sat down with Sueter, Hetherington, Stern and Commander Briggs of the RNAS. Hetherington warmed to his work. As soon as he spoke of a cross-country car Mr Churchill was, says Stern, delighted. He was too well-mannered to cry down his host's immediate plan. The Big Wheel as a weapon of war had, as they admitted, first occurred to Mr Wells but they were working on it. It should be made into a huge tricycle, 100 feet long with 40 foot wheels and weighing 300 tons. There would be three turrets each carrying a pair of 4 inch guns and power would come from a Sunbeam Diesel engine of 800 hp that the Admiralty was developing for its new submarines. The armour would be 3 inches thick over the vital parts. The scheme showed much richness of imagination but was palpably absurd. More VSOP than RNAS. None the less men of imagination were few in 1915 and it seemed a pity to discourage them. To be on the safe side Mr Churchill spoke of it to Admiral Sir John Fisher who turned it down robustly.

The First Lord already had ideas of his own of a more modest kind. Sueter had introduced him to the Pedrail machine made by an eccentric engineer named Bramah Diplock, owner of the Diplock Caterpillar Tractor Company of Fulham. The Pedrail was not much to look at, being merely a builder's skip mounted upon a single track. Its power unit was a horse and it could travel only in a straight line without being hauled round by brute force. The RNAS had borrowed a horse and arranged for a demonstration of the Pedrail on the Horse Guards Parade on 16 February. Mr Churchill stationed himself between the shafts and found himself able to pull a ton weight without difficulty. It was not the only thing on his mind for the Fleet was due to begin bombarding the outer forts of the Dardanelles within a matter of hours.

The First Lord, though carrying a load of responsibility that would have crushed most men, continued to ponder on what he had seen and heard; already he was working towards the idea that there must be some better way of attacking a fortified position than by walking towards it under such cover as the artillery of early 1915 could provide. There were men other than Hetherington and his friends with ingenious minds and knowledge of mechanical engineering. February, 1915, was an eventful month for Mr Churchill. On the 13th he had, on his personal responsibility, ordered thirty of Bacon's machines. On the 16th he had inspected the Pedrail. On the 17th he dined with Hetherington and the others. On the 19th the Navy, of which he was political chief, began to bombard the outer forts of the Dardanelles. On the 20th he ordered the setting-up of what would be called the Landship Committee. One may as well end here the story of Bacon's tractors, though it upsets chronology. After they had been shown to Sir John French and Lord Kitchener on 13 February a report went to the War Office. On 16 May Colonel Capel Holden, the retired officer brought back to be Director of Mechanical Transport – a subject which in nearly 40 years service had never come his way – rejected it because it could not perform impossible feats. Thenceforth nothing mattered but the Landship Committee.

Its brief was to study the entire question of getting men through wire and across

Sir Eustace Tennyson d'Eyncourt, KCB, FRS.

trenches by means of armoured mechanical vehicles. It did not matter whether they would be scaled-down big-wheelers, lashed steam-rollers or forms of the caterpillar tractor. The Committee had the entire responsibility. The War Office would not be invited to have any part in the business, at any rate for the time being. Its Chairman, suitably enough, was to be the Director of Naval Construction, Mr Eustace Tennyson d'Eyncourt. It would not have been reasonable to expect d'Eyncourt to devote all his time to landships; his speciality was the big, fast submarine. In 1913 he had designed one driven by steam and displacing 1700 tons, bigger than many destroyers and unmatched for size until recent times. It had never got beyond the model stage. In January, 1915, he followed it up with plans for another, using three Diesel engines with 36 cylinders between them. At the time of joining the Landships Committee he was at work on the most spectacular plan of them all, the huge steam-driven 'K' boats. Six of them were to sink and one was to disappear without trace. Nobody could accuse d'Eyncourt of lack of imagination. Only Mr Wells or Jules Verne had more. His Committee's Secretary, appointed a few days later, was Lieut Albert Stern, RNVR. From the beginning he admired d'Eyncourt greatly, later writing that he alone was the tank's true father.

On the following day the First Lord wrote an Appreciation of the war situation. It was a thorough *tour d'horizon* and had strong views about the Western Front.

24

'Little Willie'. The ancestor of them all.

'The Anglo-French lines in the west are very strong and cannot be turned ... We ought to welcome a German assault on the largest possible scale. The chances of repulsing it would be strongly in our favour.' Sir John French took a different view. On 10 March fourteen British battalions attacked at Neuve Chapelle, with the object of pushing the cavalry through to Lille. The wire and the machine-guns claimed 13,000 men. On 22 April, around Ypres, came the German counter-attack. It was not Neuve Chapelle in reverse. IG Farben, chemists to the world, had worked out a plan for dealing with the twin killers of infantry. Clouds of greenish-yellow chlorine gas swirled around the British wire and engulfed the men behind the Vickers guns. Only the steadiness of the Canadians, most of them going into their first battle, prevented the secret weapon from winning a mighty success. Once the secret was out, however, the tool turned in the makers' hands. Gas of all kinds would be a valuable ancillary; but it would not breach a trench-line.

The Landship Committee got seriously down to the work with which it had been entrusted. Perhaps between all their experts they could come up with something better. The War Office remained quite indifferent. If Mr Churchill wanted to waste the Navy's money it was nobody's affair but his.

CHAPTER 3

The Landship Committee

OTHERS, APART FROM THE LANDSHIP COMMITTEE, were interesting themselves in turning warfare from a physical to a mechanical business. Some of the brightest military minds had in the beginning been relegated to the duties of chauffeuring the great because they had made the mistake, if such it was, of quitting the Service before time. By this means many of them managed to get back into harness again.

Toby Rawlinson, General Sir Henry's younger brother, had a task of his own. When ordered by the General to provide trench-mortars with which to make some reply to the Germans he scoured French military museums, rescued a number of pieces dating from the Crimea or earlier, recruited Belgian refugee labour to make shells for them and finally brought several batteries of 'Toby Mortars' – their official name – into action at Aubers Ridge on 9 May. There remained Christopher d'Arcy

The Hornsby chain-tracked tractor of 1909.

Major-General Sir G. M. Harper,
KCB, DSO.

Bloomfield Saltern Baker-Carr, late Rifle Brigade but now a civilian in a uniform bought off the peg from Burberrys and lacking all insignia and badges. Though several years retired he was still only 36 and lusted after a fighting command. Baker-Carr knew more than most about modern weapons. He had seen at Omdurman what a belt-fed machine-gun could do to unarmoured masses. He had been an instructor at the Small Arms School, Hythe, where the Regular Army had been trained to its 1914 excellence. In South Africa he had got into 'terrible trouble' because when bidden to make a barbed-wire entanglement he had quite deliberately made it more difficult to surmount by being irregularly spaced and loosely stretched. His next senior officer, in addition to abusing him roundly, made him take it down and reassemble it properly; tightly drawn and dressed by the left. Baker-Carr had a fine contempt for the military mind, based wholly upon experience.

The trouble with the military mind was that many of those who best exemplified it were in every other respect admirable men. Such a one was George Montague Harper, late of the Royal Engineers, later Lieutenant-General Sir George, but in the Spring of 1915, plain Colonel, GS. Though only 50 his hair had become prematurely white, contrasting strongly with his black moustache. There was something symbolic about this for in his world everything was of either one or the other of these colours. He had been known as 'Uncle' ever since his days as an Instructor at the Staff College under Henry Wilson, upon whose translation to the War Office in 1911 as Director of Military Operations 'Uncle' had followed as his acolyte. Everything covered by a Staff College school solution was white; everything else black. It was impossible not to like him. No unpleasant man has ever been called 'Uncle' in the Army. It is a patent of merit.

Major-General Thomson Capper, GOC 7 Division and the rock upon which the Germans had broken at First Ypres, was the complete fighting leader and he had no interest in anything but beating the Germans in the field. It so happened that when Lord Roberts died at St Omer, a few days after the Ypres battle had petered out, Baker-Carr went to his funeral. There he met Capper who invited him to watch a parade by one of his Brigades and afterwards to luncheon. The parade showed how Capper's Division had fought. A small field easily held all that was left of four strong battalions; one of them mustered a solitary officer and about fifty men; the total came to less than 300 all ranks. The War Establishment of an infantry brigade was just over 4,000. During the meal Capper spoke of re-building. 'You were an Instructor at Hythe, Baker-Carr. Why don't you come and do a real job of work?' Baker-Carr jumped at the chance. 'Come to my Division and train my machine-gunners for me. There isn't a single one left.'

GHQ consent being needed, Baker-Carr visited Colonel Lambton, Sir John French's Military Secretary. They agreed that Baker-Carr should train machine-gunners, not merely those of Capper's Division but of the whole British Army in France. There were few enough of them. He was bidden to see 'Uncle' Harper and fix up details. Baker-Carr walked into 'Uncle's' office 'and touched my cap. "Colonel Lambton told me to see you about training some machine-gunners for the Divisions, Sir," I began. "Yes," said "Uncle", "he telephoned me about it. Why don't you get on with it?" "I want some sort of authority before I can start, sir." "All right," replied "Uncle," "you've got it. Now get on with it." "But ...," I began again. "Look here, Baker," said "Uncle", "are you running this show or am I? Go away and do what you like, but don't bother me. I'm busy."' Thus began the Machine Gun School; from it descended the Machine Gun Corps and from that the Tank Corps.

The *faites et gestes* of Baker-Carr and his Machine Gun School fall outside this narrative but they are not irrelevant. One of the most frequent visitors was the 'Eyewitness', Colonel Swinton. Another was General Sir Charles Monro who had been Commandant at Hythe when Baker-Carr had been an Instructor; to him more than to any other man the Army owed its 1914 skill at arms. Towards the end of 1915 the General announced that he would like to see a range practice. You will remember, if indeed you needed to be told, that a trained soldier could get off more than thirty aimed shots during the 'mad minute'. The prize on this occasion was won by a sergeant in a Guards battalion; he managed to fire precisely twelve rounds. To such depths had skill with the rifle fallen in a single year.

Baker-Carr had much to say to Swinton about this and many other things. The two men between them mustered an enormous amount of campaigning experience and the talk naturally enough turned to machine-guns, their use and how to circumvent them. Swinton told of the fate of Hankey's Boxing Day paper at the hands of the War Office department to which he had sent it. The note pinned to it on its return read 'If the writer of this paper would descend from the realms of fancy to the regions of hard fact a great deal of valuable time and labour would be saved'. It seems a reasonable assumption that Swinton had not included the name of the author.

Swinton and Baker-Carr talked caterpillars and armour for many hours. Both railed against the closed minds of the hierarchy in Whitehall and at St Omer where GHQ still resided. The case for serious experiment seemed unanswerable but nothing appeared to be happening. Nothing either man could do would make any difference.

All seemed hopeless until the month of July, 1915, arrived. Mr Asquith invited Swinton to become Secretary to the War Committee and in that capacity he learned of the existence of the struggling Landship Committee. Stern was summoned before him. Their initial conversation has gone down in history. 'Lieutenant Stern, this is the most extraordinary thing that I have ever seen. The Director of Naval Construction appears to be making land battleships for the Army who have never asked for them, and are doing nothing to help. You have nothing but naval ratings doing all your work. What on earth are you? Are you a mechanic or a chauffeur?' 'A banker', Stern replied. 'This', said he, 'makes it still more mysterious.'

The two men got on from the start. At last Stern had the opportunity of telling somebody with authority exactly what his Committee had been up to and he took it. Henceforth the progenitors of the tank were joined together in something like lawful wedlock.

Much work had been done during the last few months. Mr Churchill, before the Dardanelles had swallowed him up, had ordered one dozen Pedrail machines and half a dozen 16-foot Bigwheel Landships. The Pedrail, designed by Colonel Crompton, the grand old man of civil, mechanical and electrical engineering, was a larger version of the Diplock machine.

Rookes Evelyn Bell Crompton deserves more than a passing mention. Apart from being the senior mechanical engineer in active practice, he was the connecting-file between the armies of Wellington and of Haig. In 1855, at the age of 10, he had accompanied his mother's cousin Captain William Houston Stewart, RN, to the Crimea where the Commander-in-Chief was Lord Raglan who had served throughout the Peninsula as the Duke's Military Secretary. Stewart was Captain of HMS Dragon and in order to find a berth for his young kinsman he had had him regularly enrolled as a Naval Cadet. On the strength of a visit to the trenches to see his elder brother Crompton qualified and he was duly awarded the Crimean medal with the Sebastopol clasp. Thus decorated, he went on to Harrow. During school holidays he built himself a full-sized steam-driven road locomotive. Very possibly this owed something to his war experience, for the Crimea had more in common with the early stages of the Kaiser's War than is generally realized. After the charges of the Heavy and Light Brigades were over serious men had produced machines that might have hastened mechanization of the Army had the war not come to an abrupt conclusion. Steam engines running on rails were beginning to bring order into the chaos that existed between port and army, and steam tractors with footed wheels were of greater sophistication than anything yet seen. Had the war continued for another year the Crimean tank might have put in an appearance. It was well within the capacity of Brunel's generation.

After leaving Harrow Crompton had been commissioned into the Rifle Brigade and served with them in India from 1864 to 1868. There he had been given a grant of £500 for furnishing the Viceroy, Lord Minto, with a serviceable steam road-train with which to replace his elephants. In 1875 he had sent in his papers and turned his talents towards electricity. The Mansion House, the new Law Courts and the Ring Theatre in Vienna all had their electric lighting systems designed and installed by the Crompton Company. So also did a good part of London. Lord Roberts had summoned him to South Africa where he raised and commanded a corps of electrical engineers whose efficiency at maintaining communications became a byword. That war over he left the Army again, with the entirely genuine rank of Lieut-Colonel, to become engineering member of the Roads Board whose business was to produce highways fit for motor traffic. The man who had seen the Crimea lived to see Hitler's tanks preparing to carve up a later BEF. He died in 1940.

The design of the Pedrail was his; construction of the Big Wheeler, as it was called, was entrusted to Mr Tritton of Foster & Co, Engineers and Boilermakers, of Wellington Foundry, Lincoln.

The Pedrail machine, called by Crompton the 'Articulateur', would, had it been possible to take enough time over it, have been the first articulated vehicle. It was intended not as a tank but as a carrier for fifty men, 'standing in two ranks at each side', and it was to be protected by armour about $\frac{1}{4}''$ thick. Originally it was designed for a length of 40 feet by a beam of 13 and it soon became obvious that it could never go round a corner. Crompton therefore cut it in half, the two parts being connected by 'a special form of joint'. Motive power was to come from a pair of Rolls Royce engines. Probably fortunately, it soon became apparent that the Pedrail form of caterpillar was nowhere near up to the demands made upon it and Articulateur was scrapped before it had got very far. Parts of it were sold off to the Trench Warfare Department for conversion into a flamethrower.

Tritton dealt with all these things in a long letter to Crompton dated 5 June, 1915. 'It would take men of very strong nerves to fight such a machine while being attacked by an enemy' was not an over-statement. He had, however, another suggestion. 'An electrically driven wagon or fort could be made, driven by a dynamo attached to an independent tractor, connected by a cable unwound from a drum in the wagon and carrying a length of up to a mile. The well-known advantages of a series-wound motor enable enormous torque to be applied by the road wheels, thereby enabling the engine to come out of shell holes in which a petrol drive tractor would be held fast'. This was undoubtedly true; equally true was the fact that severance of the cable would halt the whole thing. It was not followed up. It appears strange now that practical and highly trained men should have set so much store by electric engines. Unfortunately they did not vanish for good with Tritton's proposed machine.

In May Mr Churchill left the Admiralty; he was the firmest and possibly the only friend to the Landships. Fortunately his successor, Arthur Balfour, asked him to stay on unofficially in order to watch over the activities of his Committee.

Members of the Committee were kept up to the collar. Lieut Wilson, for example, spent 12 April at Derby where Rolls Royce were working on chassis plans for the Big Wheeler. Next day he was at Lincoln with Tritton. Fosters needed armour plate from Beardmores and permission to buy six 105 hp Daimler engines from the makers. Wilson saw to this. Hetherington and Stern had been to Paris a few days earlier to interview a M. Derocle who claimed to know all about armour. Syme, the expert on this subject, arranged for a test to be carried out at Woolwich on 21 April. M. Derocle was there with 'a patent material and certain other substances'. Two pieces of plate and '1½ inches of Derocle jelly' were made into a sandwich and set up. A Mk VI bullet from a Lee-Metford – obsolete these many years – achieved 'complete penetration and a bad tear in the back plate'. The Derocle jelly went the same way as the Pedrail, the Articulateur, the Lemon Wheel and the Elephant's Feet, early travellers down a road to be littered with disappointments. Syme turned his mind to more conventional forms of armour. The Landships Committee by early June had little to show for its hard work.

Important things were, nevertheless, beginning to happen. Everybody agreed that caterpillar tracks would be the only means of carrying heavy weights over bad ground. The difficulty was that the only two systems known, the Holt and the Killen-Strait, were too short for the purposes of the Committee. Sueter says that Commander Briggs happened to go into 'one of those foreign book-shops off Leicester Square' and came out with a copy of the *Scientific American* for 18 February, 1911, which contained details of a much longer machine designed for moving heavy loads of an agricultural kind over bad surfaces. This had to be investigated. Mr Field, one of Crompton's men, was hastily commissioned as Lieutenant RNVR and packed off to Chicago with orders to examine and report upon the Bullock Creeping Grip. His report was enthusiastic and two Giant machines using the system were ordered.

Crompton, meanwhile, wanted more information about the nature of the obstacles that any machine of this kind might have to cross. With Stern and Hetherington for company he set off for France. Once the party got to GHQ at St Omer, however, they received a dusty reception. Nobody knew anything about them and a Staff Officer was inexcuseably rude to the old Colonel. They came home no better informed about the size and quality of German trenches than before.

The old gentleman was undeterred. As soon as he learned that a Creeping Grip machine was known to be at work in the marshes at Greenhithe he arranged for an inspection. The Greenhithe Machine, as it came to be called, was really a half-track, with a pair of iron wheels in the front by which it was steered. Apart from a canopy over the driver's head there was no sort of protection from weather or anything else. Unlike the Hornsby this machine had no suspension, a circumstance which at least reduced the likelihood of sea-sickness. Crompton made Hetherington drive it through the marsh and was pleased by its performance. It was not yet sufficiently convincing for him as he wanted to try two machines in tandem and this appeared to be the only one in the country. Final judgment would have to await the arrival of Field's purchase.

The Landship Committee was not a heavy burden on the taxpayer. The Office of Works invited it to occupy a room in Whitehall. It later admitted the room to be small, stuffy and at the top of many flights of stairs. Stern, accustomed to far better things, took one look at it and made some enquiries on his own. Lord Kitchener, in the words of his May statement on the war, had decided that 'the only course open was impressment of every available motor vehicle which was in running order' and he had collared some 8,000 lorries, about a quarter of the total commercial vehicles in the Kingdom at August, 1914. The Commercial Motor Users Association was glad to offer a weekly tenancy of Room 59 in its office at 83 Pall Mall for £2 a week. Stern took it and moved in at once. The Office of Works was furious and one of its understrappers wrote a minute complaining that a temporary officer, 'a certain Lieutenant Stern', had had the temerity to send in a bill for the rent. The matter smoothed itself down in time. The poky little room at the top of all those stairs was

Opposite: *The Chicago-built Bullock Creeping Grip tractor.*

A pair of Creeping Grips coupled up. Col. Crompton on right.

The Greenhithe machine.

given to an Admiral. For a time Stern paid the rent himself. He would hardly have noticed £2 a week. It was, however, his introduction to Governmental ways of doing things and these ways he soon came to hate and despise. They were not business-like and, to a merchant banker, business was everything.

On 8 June the Committee, including Mr Bussell of the Admiralty and Cmdr Boothby, OC Armoured Car Section, met in Mr Churchill's room at the Official Residence in Whitehall. The big wheel was given its quietus; what mattered was that two Giant tractors from America with the Creeping Grip were at sea on board s.s. *Lapland*. They should arrive in a fortnight at worst. Approval was given to the purchase of one Killen-Strait tractor which looked promising. On the 21st Crompton reported that the Bullocks had arrived and were at the factory of McEwan Pratt & Co, Burton on Trent. Since there was no place for trying them out Wilson leased a field at Sinai Park from Mr Loverock for a year; the two-guineas rent came out of his own pocket.

The Giants represented most of the Committee's assets, for the only others were the Killen-Strait tractor at the Clement Talbot works in Barlby Road and two of the builders'-skip-on-a-track machines. Wilson took over the Giant testing on his

Major W. G. Wilson, CMG.

field with some help from Colonel Crompton, whose small, neat figure appears in a number of photographs bent over the mechanism. The Giants were coupled back to back and set to work, one pulling whilst the other idled; then back again in reverse order. Wilson learnt little from this, nor had he expected to. His interests were in the track and the transmission, neither of which had been designed for his purposes. The track came up to Crompton's expectations, for Sinai Park was better holding ground than Greenhithe Marshes. The transmission was quite another matter. It served for an agricultural tractor but was clearly not going to be man enough for a heavy-bodied vehicle with the much bigger Daimler engine.

Walter Gordon Wilson, born in 1874, was the same age as Mr Churchill. He had remained only a very short time in the Navy and at 20 had moved to King's College, Cambridge, where he gained a First in mechanical engineering. Through Lord Braye he had become acquainted with Percy Pilcher, then a lecturer in naval architecture and a pioneer of flying. The two men formed a little company to build what might have been the first internal combustion engine to power a flying machine; when Pilcher was killed by a gliding accident in 1899 Wilson seemed to lose interest in flight and turned to road transport. In 1904 he designed and built a car which he called the Wilson-Pilcher. It still stands, under a glass case, in the Tank Museum.

After that he moved to Armstrong-Whitworth where he designed their first car and between 1908 and 1914 he was with J & E Hall at Dartford, designing the Halford lorry. Though under no compulsion but that of conscience he threw up well-paid work on the outbreak of war to come back to the Navy, where he naturally gravitated to the Armoured Cars. His *specialité* was the gear-box; probably no living man knew as much as Wilson about this interesting subject. He is said to have been a prickly man who did not suffer fools or those who did not understand mechanical engineering. 'Genius' is a word of which one should fight shy; yet it is hard to think of another for Walter Gordon Wilson. Some of his later designs are still in use with tanks of the present day.

According to his evidence given to the Royal Commission on Awards to Invesntors in 1919 Wilson first met Stern on 15 July, 1915. Stern complained to him that the Committee seemed to be getting nowhere and asked whether Wilson would prefer to work with Colonel Crompton or with Mr Tritton. Wilson replied that if Tritton and he were put on the job 'we would soon produce a machine that could do something'.

Wilson was a dedicated engineer, by no means the clubbable kind of man like Bertie Stern. He and Tritton spoke the same language and, as their correspondence shows, they liked each other. Together they did great things, for every British tank used during the Kaiser's War was built to their designs. D'Eyncourt supplied ideas; Stern was, in the jargon of the day, 'the man of push and go'. There was need of all of them.

It has to be realized that Fosters was a commercial concern and, war or no war, was in business for profit. When Tritton had taken over conduct of its affairs in 1905 the Company, founded in 1856, was in low water. Only just before the war came had he pulled it round to the point when it was beginning to show a decent return. Whatever happened the shareholders expected their half-yearly dividends and the workmen expected to be paid on Fridays. No firm particularly wanted work on experimental machines; the constant changes in design were irksome, the finding of raw materials difficult since they were at the end of the queue and the money available for such things was not plentiful. It says much for Fosters' patriotism that they took on the job at all. Tritton in due time was to receive his knighthood but no great profits were made. The Company, indeed, made the Government a free gift of its royalties from the use of the Foster-Daimler engine, for which it held the patents; Tritton put this at about £115,000. In 1915 he was just 40 and with his bald-head, pince-nez and expression of general benevolence could never have been regarded as a hard-faced man who looked as if he had done well out of the war.

By mid-summer 1915 matters were not going well. On 29 June the Admiralty had invited the War Office to interest itself in landships; the invitation was accepted but with some economy of enthusiasm. To the Army this was still a silly, time-wasting business, but if it had to be kept going the War Office ought to be informed about what was going on. Stern, in a moment of unusual gloom, admitted that he and the others came near to abandoning the whole project as hopeless since every technical expert on traction had assured him that the problems were beyond solution.

In order to keep the flickering flame alive he staged a demonstration at Wembley Stadium on 30 June, the day after the War Office had come in. There was not a lot to show. The main attraction was an exhibition of wire-cutting by one of the Committee's few assets, the American made Killen-Strait tractor. It was an unmilitary looking machine, completely open and propelled by two small sets of caterpillars aft and an even smaller one forward. The driver sat high up, steering with a wheel. When fitted out with Navy wire-cutters the Killen-Strait showed itself able to tear its way through a barbed wire entanglement of a not very formidable kind. Amongst those present were Mr Churchill, Mr Lloyd George, now Minister of Munitions, and a Mr Wilfrid Stokes who had invented a trench-mortar of simple but effective design. Stern had been greatly taken by it and did not affect surprise when Stokes told him of the impossibility he had experienced in getting the War Office to show interest in his gun. Stern took him straight to Mr Lloyd George who watched the inventor put three shells into the air before the first one had hit the ground. To his question about how long manufacture of the mortar would take Stokes gave a proper East Anglian answer. 'It depends whether you or I try to make them'. The Minister, suitably impressed, ordered a thousand of them at once. Even though the Killen-Strait achieved little else it earned its keep by being the indirect means of getting the Army a weapon second only to the machine-gun in value.

Though the Killen-Strait performance was nothing to excite anybody over much it did furnish evidence that the Landship Committee had possibilities, however remote at the time. The Admiralty, presumably at the instance of Mr Churchill, agreed that Squadron 20 RNAS should be relieved of all other duties and placed at the Committee's disposal. This was a wise decision for it gave the pioneers all the man-power needed to continue with its work. The association was to last throughout the war, despite occasional attempts at breaking it; by November, 1918, Squadron 20, then of infantry battalion strength, worked on both sides of the Channel at the testing and delivery of every tank used by the BEF.

Better things than the Killen-Strait were coming along. Once it had shown off its paces it was furnished with rude armour and promptly set aside. It ended its days towing aircraft around the RNAS base at Barrow-in-Furness. Squadron 20 was moved to Burton-on-Trent under command of Hetherington there to await the next experiment.

The Giant tractors had yielded up all their technical data to Wilson and he was ready to use his knowledge on something more practical. Tritton had been working on his own and had built a trench-crossing machine of some ingenuity; it would have done well over drainage ditches but it was not a weapon of war. In fact it was one of the Bacon tractors with 8-foot wheels pushing an integrally built sledge mounted on two pairs of small wheels. Colonel Crompton, whose vast and expensive designs were becoming an embarrassment, left on termination of his 6 months contract early in August.

At the end of July the Committee asked Tritton and Wilson to make a machine which would incorporate the Bullock track, the Daimler 105 hp engine as used on Bacon's tractors and an armoured body. The planned weight was about 18 tons and

The Killen-Strait tractor shows its paces.

the machine must be able to cross a trench four feet wide. Like the Giants it would be steered by wheels but this time they should work from behind.

The designers established themselves in the White Hart at Lincoln. This was a sensible move, for difficulties were many and comfortable quarters needed. Some of the less technical were removed by Swinton who persuaded the Prime Minister to call an inter-departmental conference on 28 August. D'Eyncourt wrote to Stern on the following day that 'the conference has distinctly cleared the air and put the whole thing on a sounder footing. I'm glad you had a good talk with Swinton; you seem to have arranged it very well, and I hope now we shall be able to go on steadily without more tiresome interruptions.' Again he emphasized the need for utmost secrecy. This Stern effected by telling all enquirers that things were going very badly indeed and they were probably all about to lose their jobs.

For the time being all those concerned with producing a prototype caterpillar trench-crosser worked very happily together and there was a family atmosphere about the White Hart. This was just as well, for plenty of irritants remained. On 27 July Tritton wired Stern in London that the drawings supplied to him by Crompton and one of Fosters' own men, Mr Rigby, were mere sketches and that until proper ones arrived work was at a standstill. Stern was at his best prodding laggards and the detailed drawings soon arrived. On 9 August he attended a meeting chaired by

Dr Addison of the Munitions Invention Committee on the subject of money for landships. It was agreed that £80,000 should be made available, out of which some £10,000 had been spent. It was the matter of money that had finally finished Colonel Crompton. The estimate for his Rolls-engined landship had come from the Metropolitan Carriage and Wagon Company and it amounted to £68,676. Such amounts were far beyond thinking about.

Wilson and Tritton and Fosters' workmen produced without too much difficulty a large metal box driven by the Daimler engine and mounted on Bullock tracks. These last caused all the trouble, for the ones sent by the American factory were badly made and of inferior metal. As soon as the machine moved around the factory floor they either snapped or fell off. The Giant machines were still under test at Burton under the care of Hetherington and Squadron 20. Reports came to Fosters' works that the machine was proving a good wire-crusher but when it came to crossing trenches something in the way of a differential lock was needed. One track on land and the other hanging over a drop made the whole machine useless. Wilson left Tritton working on tracks at Lincoln and hurried north. Already the two men had come to the conclusion that the armoured box would not do and were moving towards something better. The nature of this was not committed to paper but by late August d'Eyncourt was writing to Stern that he should go at once to Lincoln and hurry Tritton along with whatever he was doing. In fact both Tritton and Wilson were working at speed almost beyond belief. Wilson was constantly travelling between Lincoln, Burton and Coventry in intervals between working at drawing board and on factory floor. There was plenty to occupy him. Designs for a transmission system for the second machine took much time; work on more serviceable tracks took even more. D'Eyncourt, in desperation, suggested that they try Balata belting. Little Willie, as the armoured box came to be called, waddled round the

The Killen-Strait tractor faces barbed wire.

A view of Sir Willliam Tritton's trench-crossing machine.

factory on 6 September under his own power.

On 22 September Stern received the famous telegram, handed in at Lincoln: 'Balata died on test bench yesterday morning. New arrival by Tritton out of Pressed Plate. Light in weight but very strong. All doing well thank you. PROUD PARENTS'. In a letter written after the war Wilson complained that Stern gave undue prominence to this cable. By that time, however, they had fallen out and he goes on to grumble about 'the absurd scramble for credit that developed later'. For the moment everybody was happy in the White Hart.

On 19 September Tritton and Wilson decided to leave Little Willie to be completed by Fosters' people and to concentrate on his successor. This was a far longer business than the building of the first machine. Sketch followed sketch, two like-minded men beavering away with nothing to guide them in the direction of a machine that would change the face of war and the composition of armies. It was Wilson who first drew out the shape of a slightly deformed rhomboid but both men spotted at once the possibility that they had found what they were seeking. The track would run on rollers round the entire circumference; this would prevent top-heaviness. The nose would be cocked-up and would thus get some sort of grip upon the face of any bank it might have to climb. The engine would go amidships, driving toothed wheels called sprockets at the rear and the sprockets would push the track

Sir William Tritton with his trench-crossing machine.

'Little Willie'.

over the rollers and an idler wheel in the bows, laying it down as if it were a carpet.

It is commonly said, even by Stern, that the underside was deliberately made as the arc of a 16 foot wheel. Wilson says flatly that this is nonsense. First mention of it comes in Williams-Ellis' *The Tank Corps* published in 1919. Wilson was very cross, for professional engineers would see the absurdity of the proposition and would blame him. As the book was quasi-official, he wrote a protest 'but without result'. Wilson's contribution was the transmission system, of which more later. Even working at their pace it took the two men from August, 1915, until January, 1916, to produce the first sample of their work.

Little Willie – presumably named for the Crown Prince – was given his road trials on 15 September. Tritton and Wilson now found him rather a bore but they had to be there. Swinton (then Secretary of the CID) told the Royal Commission on Awards to Inventors after the war how it had all gone. 'I was asked my opinion and I said that Willie would not do. He did not comply with the specification sent from France and could not climb a 5 foot vertical height. Little Willie was a steel box.' Swinton was quite right and nobody disputed it. Little Willie was what the cavalry calls 'cast'. He spent the next few years ingloriously lying around and after the war was shifted to the Tank Museum at Bovington. There you may see him, as good as new.

In 1919 Stern's book *Tanks: The Log Book of A Pioneer* was published. In the

The Mark I. The Tank of the Somme.

A Mark I Tank with original tail attachment.

The Mark IX Tank, the first armoured personnel carrier. Late 1918.

following year Wilson presented a copy to his friend and colleague Major Buddicum of the Tank Corps who had been a member of the design team during the early days. Attached to it were a number of notes from which the sequence of events during the late summer and autumn of 1915 can be extracted. It was during August that Wilson suggested to Tritton 'a quasi-rhomboidal shape with tracks running outside'. On 24 August Tritton submitted a sketch to d'Eyncourt who approved and told him to get on with it. Two days later, at Tritton's request, Stern came to Lincoln with a specification drawn up by Swinton. Immediately after this visit work began on the machine that was to become known as 'Mother'. At the end of September a 'mock-up' had been completed and this was taken by lorry to Wembley for Stern to show to a party of senior officers. All save General von Donop approved of what they saw; the MGO's objection was to the wooden gun which had been put in without his consent.

On 30 September Stern, with authority from the Landship Committee, instructed Tritton to go ahead and make the machine whose model had been shown.

One difficulty remained. Nobody knew where to mount the gun. If in front it would dig into the ground whenever the nose went down. The roof was plainly out of the question. D'Eyncourt came up with the answer. The Navy constantly had to mount guns along the sides of ships capable of being swivelled about over many degrees. It was done by 'sponsons', steel boxes protruding from the side and bolted on to it. Stern made a sketch and sent it to Tritton who developed an exact drawing of what was needed. Admiral Singer agreed to let the Committee have some surplus 6-pdrs which ought to fit nicely into it. The guns were 8 feet long and 6 feet from the centre. Two sponsons plus two guns added three tons to the weight of the Wilson. The Daimler engine, designed only for a big tractor, had another burden added; but sponsons were clearly the answer and sponsons were made.

There were only enough track plates to make up one side of the new machine by the end of November but more were being fabricated. The hull was ready on the 23rd, the engine and gear-box a day or two later. Stern was, metaphorically, hopping from one foot to the other in his anxiety to have something substantial to show off. No doubt his pestering was a nuisance and quite needless. The job would be done when the men were finished and not before. On 3 December, 1915, they announced themselves ready for the first trial.

CHAPTER 4

'Mother'

LET US LEAVE THE LANDSHIPS for a moment and return to Baker-Carr in France. For a long time he had been trying to force a great truth into unreceptive minds. The Vickers gun, a better and lighter Maxim, was not the same thing as a Lewis gun. The Vickers, weighing just under half a hundredweight and mounted upon a tripod of about the same, was a true machine-gun. It could, and should, be used to fire by means of instruments from a position where it could neither see nor be seen by its target. The long beaten zone – at a range of 1,000 yards it swept an ellipse 150 yards long by 15 across at its widest point – could interlock with the beaten zones of many other guns and smother large areas with bullets by day or night. The Lewis, though an excellent weapon, was a mere automatic rifle. Vickers guns should be grouped together and worked by specialists, leaving the Lewis as a bonus for infantry. In October, 1915, Baker-Carr got his way. The Machine Gun Corps came into being, as distinct from other Corps as were Gunners or Sappers. One hears and reads much of the excellent German machine-gunners. Few people now remember that the Machine Gun Corps had them beaten all ends up. By the end of the war 170,000 men had passed through its ranks and its dead numbered more than 13,000. The Tank Corps, at the peak of its strength, never reached 20,000 all ranks.

It had taken the personal order of Lord Kitchener to get for Baker-Carr the first 40,000 men he needed for the new arm of the service. The Adjutant-General, Sir Henry Sclater, had refused point-blank, with the words 'Can't be done'. Nor was this mere stubbornness. A secret paper for the Cabinet printed in October over the initial K began with the words 'The voluntary system, as at present administered, fails to produce the numbers of recruits required to maintain the Armies in the field. The returns show that the total yield is much less than the 35,000 a week required.' Two days previously, on 6 October, Lord Kitchener had had to turn down a proposal from Mr Lloyd George at the Ministry of Munitions for the supply of a thousand heavy guns over and above those already ordered by the War Office. The Army simply could not find the men. Already it had to scrape up from somewhere nearly 2,000 officers and 43,000 other ranks to man the guns already ordered but not delivered. It was no time to demand men for a new and possibly futile venture. Lord Kitchener had suggested sending to Russia guns that the Army would one day need.

If he was to be induced to invest in armoured vehicles he would need a lot of persuasion, quite apart from the factor of which Baker-Carr spoke. 'The average Englishman's deep-rooted dislike and mistrust of machinery in general'.

Some Englishmen, professional and enthusiastic amateur alike, were trying to overcome it. Syme had produced armour plate, with the help of the Beardmore company, that would more often than not keep out the ordinary German 'S' bullet. On 24 June, six days before the Wormwood Scrubbs demonstration, General Scott-Moncrieff (now Chairman of the Landship Committee) had come up with ideas for arming the vehicles with a two-pounder pom-pom either side of the bows, two machine-guns further back and loopholes wherever possible for musketry. The pom-pom, though made by Vickers, was not a British service weapon. A number of them had been captured during the Boer War and were used, whenever spare parts could be found, as anti-aircraft guns. A few had gone to France during the early days of desperate expedients and had been found useful for clearing villages. All the same, these were weapons off the scrap-heap, for the Army had nothing better to offer. A 2·95 mountain gun - Kipling's screw-gun - was lent to Stern but it was obviously unusable. An experimental mortar, firing a 50 lb bomb, was tried out at the Clement-Talbot works in Barlby Road, Kensington, where the armoured cars still had their HQ. Again it was plainly not what was wanted.

Syme was deputed to try his luck with the Navy which had a number of small guns dating from the '80s and were designed as secondary armament for shooting at torpedo boats. Here he had better fortune. The 2 and 3 pounders were, for various reasons, unsuitable but the 6-pdr seemed to be just what was wanted. The Navy agreed to provide as many as it could. This gun, with its barrel shortened, became the standard tank weapon throughout the war.

The exhibition at Wormwood Scrubbs on 30 June had been no more than an expedient to keep up interest in mechanized warfare, the only real turn being the demonstration of wire-cutting by the Killen-Strait tractor but Mr Lloyd George (now Minister of Munitions), Mr Churchill and the entire Committee came to watch it. For Stern it was an opportunity, probably of his own creation, to keep in personal touch with Lloyd George whom he had, of course, known passably well in financial circles. The future of Mr Churchill seemed doubtful but LG had to be kept well disposed. Stern, as later correspondence shows, was also at pains to cultivate the great man's secretary-cum-mistress, Frances Stevenson, who was at this time worrying both the Minister and herself with an unfounded belief that she was pregnant. Such an ally was not to be despised.

On 29 September, 1915, Squadron 20 brought a full-sized model of Little Willie's successor to Wembley for examination by invited officers from the War Office and GHQ. Sir John French sent his aide Major Guest, a stockbroker by trade and Sir John's main link with the outside world. Guest's report cannot have been enthusiastic; when Sir Douglas Haig took over three months later there was nobody at GHQ who could tell him anything about what was happening over the development of a fighting vehicle.

For Tritton the show was a triumph, and a deserved one. As recently as 27 July he had had to send an agitated telegram to Stern saying that the drawings given him were mere sketches and until proper ones were in his hands no work could even be started. Within a couple of months Fosters had turned out the model of a recognizable tank. Nearly all the spectators, of whom only Mr Moir of the Inventions Board was a civilian, were suitably impressed. Only General von Donop thought little of it. He complained that the whole business was highly irregular and, worse, that artillery pieces were being used without his approval.

This was the kind of thing Stern had come to expect and he took no notice. On the following day he gave Tritton instructions to build 'Mother' in accordance with the Committee's plans. As might have been expected another complication immediately arose.

Men engaged in munitions production had been issued with badges, the possession of which demonstrated that they were not hanging back. The work at Fosters, being of a highly secret nature, was not reckoned by the War Badge Department to qualify. Many of Fosters' best men, sick of being accused of 'dodging the column', began to leave. Correspondence achieved nothing. Stern marched down to the office in Abingdon Street, threatened to bring Squadron 20 to take the place by force, and marched out with a sackful of badges. A couple of years later Albert Thomas, the French Minister of Munitions, complained officially of Stern's 'bullying methods' and he may have had a point. Bullying is sometimes necessary with Government departments. On this occasion Tritton wrote that he 'was very grateful to you for the trouble you have taken in the matter and I feel I must congratulate you on the promptness with which you have overcome the entanglement of red tape'. Work on 'Mother' was resumed. On 3 December her trials took place at Lincoln and 'were very successful indeed'. D'Eyncourt, wishing to find out what happened when a 6-pdr was fired from a sponson, arranged to have the machine taken to a lonely field outside Lincoln, within a mile of the Cathedral, for practical tests. Hetherington and Stern motored up with some rounds of solid armour-piercing shot. Early in the morning 'Mother' was driven into position, Hetherington took his place at the gun and pressed the trigger. Nothing happened. While he and Stern were examining the breech the gun suddenly went off of its own accord and the shot headed towards the Cathedral. Two hours of consternation and digging followed until it was found buried in the earth.

Then came trials of the lighter weapons. Enfield Lock produced specimens of Vickers, Lewis, Hotchkiss and Madsen guns. Where this last came from is a mystery; it would have been the ideal weapon. There seems no obvious reason why the existing gun should not have been copied but people were punctilious about patent rights in 1915. The Hotchkiss was chosen as second best. The bulky cylinder surrounding the cooling flanges of the Lewis made this excellent weapon hardly practicable for use in a sponson's loop-hole. Nor was its drum of cartridges as handy as the clip employed by the Hotchkiss.

By Christmas 'Mother' was in all respects ready for service. A full meeting of the Committee of Imperial Defence was held on Christmas Eve with Scott-Moncrieff in the chair; Swinton was present in his new capacity of Assistant Secretary with

Stern and d'Eyncourt representing the Admiralty. The first item on the agenda was a paper prepared by Swinton entitled 'The Present And Future Situation Regarding The Provision Of Caterpillar Machine-Gun Destroyers Or "Land Cruisers"'. There was no longer any mention of mere armoured personnel carriers; these machines were to seek out and destroy in regular naval tradition. Much of the paper dealt with matters of only transient interest, such as manning the RNAS Squadrons, the only Service personnel so far engaged, the organization of Committees and the important question of who should pay for what. So far every penny had come out of the Navy Vote and the Navy did not much care for it. On one point Swinton made a firm recommendation. 'To whatever Department the production of the Caterpillars is finally allotted, it is suggested that it be entrusted to one business man of proved capacity, preferably one who has been connected with the experimental construction up to date.' It is not hard to guess the name he had in mind. Stern notoriously hated all Committees.

This was a little too much for the War Office to swallow. Sir Charles Callwell, brought from retirement to be Director of Military Operations at the War Office, has left on record that body's distrust, based on experience, of The Man of Business and The British Working Man. To appoint a Tank Supply Dictator would be going too far, but a fair compromise was reached on 12 February, 1916. There would be a Tank Supply Committee, as an off-shoot of the Ministry of Munitions with Stern as President and Wilson, Swinton, Syme and Mr Bussell of the Admiralty Contracts Branch as Members, along with two soldiers from branches of the War Office. D'Eyncourt, not being able to give anything like all his time to Landships, was appointed a Consultant. The Committee was empowered to place orders on its own authority and would be given a Bank Account starting with 'the estimated cost of fifty machines'. When they were made they would be handed over to the War Office whose business it would be to find and train crews. The officers of the RNAS engaged in tank affairs would 'cease to belong to that Service' and arrangements would be made 'for their appointment as military officers with rank suitable to the importance of their duties'. The War Office reckoned that the equivalent of an infantry company commander was quite high enough. Stern and Wilson became Majors; though Stern did achieve one step to Lieut-Colonel, Wilson was never promoted above his new rank. Holden, even when he became British Representative in America, remained no more than a Captain. Admiral Singer undertook to supply a hundred 6-pdr guns by June, 1916, but 'it was not possible at the moment to say how many of them would have non-recoil mountings'.

The word 'Tank', coined by Swinton, seems to have crept into the records of the Committee almost by accident. Clearly some jargon word was needed and, though no mention is in the record, everybody agrees that it was debated. 'Water Carrier' was suggested but turned down; the initials by which it would certainly be called were misleading beyond necessity. The first machine was called by various names at the beginning. In letters it can be found as 'Big Willie', 'Wilson', 'Centipede' and 'HMS Caterpillar', before there was general agreement on 'Mother'. Even this was confusing, for it had already been adopted by Gunners for the first 9·2 howitzer. 'Mother', however, stuck; 'Willie' was not lost, for in everyday speech tank men usually referred to their ships as either 'Willies' or 'buses'. And, as everybody knows, 'My Boy Willie' is still the quickstep of the Royal Tank Regiment.

Everything now turned on the success or otherwise of the demonstrations. Wembley, being too open to the public, would not do. Stern and d'Eyncourt sought out Mr McCowan, Lord Salisbury's agent, and obtained from him the use of a part of Hatfield Park. A company of Hertfordshire Volunteers, under RE supervision, dug trenches and put up wire. Squadron 20 oiled, greased, polished and painted 'Mother' in proper Bristol-fashion. Her first performance in front of an audience bound to be highly critical was fixed for 29 January, 1916.

The audience was almost entirely a Service one, the only exceptions being people immediately concerned with Landships. One officer who might have wished to be there was not. Lieut-Col W. S. Churchill, OC 6th Royal Scots Fusiliers, was with his battalion at Plug Street. The 9th Division, of which his unit formed a part, had had a very rough passage at Loos. The Divisional General, Thesiger, had been killed and his place had been taken by W. T. Furse who was to succeed von Donop as MGO at the end of the year. Colonel Churchill was at that moment a worried officer. On 3 December, 1915, before taking command, he had written his famous paper 'Variants of the Offensive'. A copy had gone to the Committee of Imperial Defence and a proof had been returned to him. While the Colonel was addressing himself to revising the paper his HQ came under heavy shell fire and he 'did not suggest that my departure was hurried, but neither was it unduly delayed.' When he returned to his room an hour and a half later the paper was gone. Terrible thoughts of spies, about whom there had been many warnings, sprang to the mind. Even then this frightfully important paper might be in an aeroplane bound for the Fatherland. Colonel Churchill had a very bad time until three days later he found the missing sheets in an inside pocket of a jacket that he hardly ever used.

A copy of the paper had gone to GHQ, BEF. On 25 December Sir Douglas Haig had written in the margin 'Is anything known about these caterpillars referred to in para. 4, p. 3?'. The answer being negative a 35-year-old Lieut-Colonel of Sappers named Hugh Elles was sent home to find out. Elles must have gone quietly about his business for his name does not figure in the lists of those present at the two Hatfield tests.

The conditions in which 'Mother' was to operate were based on those of the battle of Loos, which was a pity. During the days of preparation for 'Mother's' debut great numbers of German guns of immense power were being turned upon the brave defenders of Verdun. Loos was already ancient history and new dimensions of warfare were being introduced. In France, Sir Douglas Haig needed no telling that before long it would be the imperative duty of the British Army to find some way of taking pressure off the French before they collapsed.

There was in 'Mother' about every fault that a tank could have. The 90 plates on each track were fabricated from brittle steel: the 105 hp Daimler engine was not powerful enough: the exhaust lacked a silencer, trailed over the top, belched out smoke and became red hot: lubrication was simply by means of oil swilling around

'Mother' at Hatfield.

in a trough: the petrol tanks were inside, up in the bows and fed the carburettor by gravity, with the result that when nose-down supply was cut off: the machine was steered as an oarsman steers a skiff, pulling on one side but not the other, with the assistance of a pair of large iron wheels trailing behind and worked hydraulically. All that said, she was a genuine armoured fighting vehicle and the only one in the world. Immense credit is due to Fosters. The whole business had had to be carried out in the utmost secrecy and here again Fosters had shown good East Anglian sense. When asked what they wanted in the way of guards and such Tritton had replied that the only way of drawing attention to the strange activities of harmless agricultural instrument makers would be to surround the place with sentries. Work had simply gone on as usual.

It took eight men to drive and fight the Mk 1 Tank. This rather large number was due to the transmission system. Up in front was the driver, sitting alongside the subaltern in command. He had two levers, one for each track, and a clutch connected to a two-speed gear box; the drive then continued through a differential which was fitted with a secondary two-speed gear-box on the outer end of each shaft. These were the care of two gearsmen who worked them with hand-levers. It then continued by chains to the driving sprockets – the toothed wheels at the stern which engaged with the underside of the track and drove it forward – the front wheel being a mere idler. Only about five feet of track was in contact with the ground, with the result that the tank always had a slight rocking motion. As the point of balance was in the middle an experienced driver could see-saw the machine over the edge of a jump and lower it fairly gently over steep drops. If the gravity feed failed it was necessary

51

to pour petrol into the carburettor out of a can; not a pleasant exercise against a hot exhaust inside a fume-filled metal box. The gunners and their mates knelt inside the sponsons, adding cordite fumes to the stench of petrol and contributing substantially to the already hellish din of the engine. To swing the machine it was necessary to lock the differential and signal to one gearsman by hand to put his side into neutral. The officer then applied the brake on the same side and the tank turned pretty well on its axis.

None of this, apart from the smoke, could be understood by observers. The Programme for the first test was printed and this is how it read.

'TANK' TRIAL

Description of 'Tank'

This machine has been designed, under the direction of Mr E. H. T. d'Eyncourt, by Mr W. A. Tritton (of Messrs. Foster, of Lincoln) and Lieutenant W. G. Wilson, R.N.A.S., and has been constructed by Messrs. Foster, of Lincoln. The conditions laid down as to the obstacle to be surmounted were that the machine should be able to climb a parapet 4 feet 6 inches high and cross a gap 5 feet wide.

	Over-all Dimensions	
	Feet	Inches
Length	31	3
Width with sponsons .	18	8
„ without sponsons	8	3
Height	8	0

'Mother's' rear view.

A Mk I Tank at work.

Protection

The conning tower is protected generally by 10 millim. thickness of nickel-steel plate, with 12 millim. thickness in front of the drivers. The sides and back ends have 8 millim. thickness of nickel-steel plate. The top is covered by 6 millim. thickness of high tensile steel, and the belly is covered with the same.

	Weight	
	Tons	Cwt
Hull	21	0
Sponsons and guns . .	3	10
Ammunition, 300 rounds for guns and 20,000 rounds for rifles[1] . .	2	0
Crew (8 men) . . .	0	10
Tail (for balance) . .	1	8
Total weight with armament, crew, petrol, and ammunition . . .	28	8

[1] Removable for transport purposes.

Horse-power of engines .	105 h.p.
Number of gears . .	4 forward,
	2 reverse.

Approximate speed of travel on each gear .

$\begin{cases} \frac{3}{4} \text{ mile,} \\ 1\frac{1}{4} \text{ miles,} \\ 2\frac{1}{4} \text{ miles, and} \\ 4 \text{ miles per} \\ \quad \text{hour.} \end{cases}$

Armament

Two 6-pr. guns, and
Three automatic rifles (1 Hotchkiss and 2 Madsen).

Rate of Fire

6-pr.: 15–20 rounds per minute.
Madsen gun: 300 rounds per minute.
Hotchkiss gun: 250 rounds per minute.

NOTES AS TO STEEL PLATE OBTAINED FROM EXPERIMENTS MADE

Nickel-Steel Plate

12 millim. thickness is proof against a concentrated fire of reversed Mauser Bullets at 10 yards range, normal impact.

10 millim. thickness is proof against single shots of reversed Mauser bullets at 10 yards range, normal impact.

8 millim. thickness is proof against Mauser bullets at 10 yards range, normal impact.

High Tensile Steel Plate

6 millim. thickness will give protection against bombs up to 1 lb. weight detonated not closer than 6 inches from the plate.

(N.B.—It is proposed to cause the detonation of bombs away from the top of the tank by an outer skin of expanded metal, which is not on the sample machine shown.)

PROGRAMME OF TRIALS
Reference to Sketch, Plan, and Sections
The trial will be divided into three parts, I, II, and III

———

Part I.—*Official Test*

1. The machine will start and cross (*a*) the obstacle specified, *i.e.* a parapet 4 feet 6 inches high and a gap 5 feet wide. This forms the test laid down.

Part II.—*Test approximating to Active Service*

2. It will then proceed over the level at full speed for about 100 yards, and take its place in a prepared dug-out shelter (*b*), from which it will traverse a course of obstacles approximating to those likely to be met with on service.

3. Climbing over the British defences (*c*) (reduced for its passage), it will—

4. Pass through the wire entanglements in front;

5. Cross two small shell craters, each 12 feet in diameter and 6 feet deep;

6. Traverse the soft, water-logged ground round the stream (*d*), climb the slope from the stream, pass through the German entanglement;

7. Climb the German defences (*e*);

8. Turn round on the flat and pass down the marshy bed of the stream via (*d*), and climb the double breastwork at (*f*).

Part III.—*Extra Test if required*

9. The 'tank' will then, if desired, cross the larger trench (*h*), and proceed for half a mile across the park to a piece of rotten ground seamed with old trenches, going down a steep incline on the way.

January 27th, 1916.

The trial course, though it did not bear close resemblance to any 1916 battle-field, was an honest effort to show what a tank could do. One thing was missing. Cold January weather does not provide mud. Nobody could have been expected to appreciate that the bigger guns now coming into use on both sides could do things other than kill men and smash their works. They had an unprecedented ability to turn great tracts of good agricultural land into bottomless lakes of brown porridge.

This, however, was for the future. 'Mother' having behaved very well on 29 January, d'Eyncourt wrote next day a personal letter to the man who, above all others, could decide her fate. His message to Lord Kitchener was unequivocal in its terms. 'The machine has had a satisfactory preliminary trial at Hatfield and proved its capacity, and I trust your Lordship may be able to come there and see a further trial on Wednesday afternoon next, February 2nd, when you will have an opportunity of judging its qualities yourself.'

Kitchener, though still the nation's most revered soldier, had never suffered from Baker-Carr's Military Mind. He accepted with alacrity; so did Mr Balfour, Mr Lloyd George, General Robertson and a long list of grandees both naval and military of whom Maurice Hankey was one. The earlier demonstration had been important but this one was crucial. Tritton, Wilson, d'Eyncourt, Swinton and Stern would have been more than human had they not endured much trepidation.

In spite of all the prospects of a successful performance d'Eyncourt cannot have been a happy man. On the same day, 29 January, 1916, the first of his great steam-driven fleet submarines, K 13, had sunk on her trials with the loss of 31 good men.

The petrol was turned on, four men swung the huge starting handle and the Daimler engine burst into life. Dense clouds of smoke belched from the exhaust but the machine, bearing the name HMLS *Centipede*, trundled round the course. Mr Lloyd George was captivated; 'I can recall the feeling of delighted amazement with which I saw for the first time the ungainly monster plough through thick entanglements, wallow through deep mud and heave its huge bulk over parapets and across trenches,' he wrote nearly twenty years later. 'At last, I thought, we have the answer to the German machine-guns and wire. Mr Balfour's delight was as great as my own and it was only with difficulty that some of us persuaded him to disembark from

HM Landship whilst she crossed the last test, a trench several feet wide.' AJB, having extruded his lanky frame through the little door below one of the sponsons was heard to remark plaintively that there must be some more artistic way of leaving a tank. There was none. To enter, it was necessary to stoop under the sponson, insert the head and trunk and finally pull up the feet; to leave one lowered the feet until they touched ground and then folded the body downwards until the head was clear. On Lord Salisbury's golf course it cost a number of bruises; in action, with the machine on fire, it took great good fortune to emerge at all. The last resort was a small manhole in the roof, provided with holes for revolver fire at intruders; it would have admitted only a very undersized man in great desperation. Once the engine had warmed up the inside temperature commonly touched 125°.

It was satisfactory to have made allies of the Minister of Munitions and the First Lord of the Admiralty, but one man remained with power of life or death in his hands.

It is odd how much nonsense has been written about Lord Kitchener's attitude to the first tank, and this would have pleased him. His whole military life had been spent among people of devious minds and his own had been shaped in the Near East. He trusted none of his Cabinet colleagues any more than he had once trusted the Mudir of Dongola and with good reason. 'Leaky' was the adjective he applied to them more than once. When, during his Egyptian days, he had been faced with any dogmatic statement about anything the natural consequence would have been for him to ask himself not 'Is that true?' but 'Why did he say that?' So he managed his own affairs. Lord Kitchener ostentatiously left the demonstration before it was over, announcing that the tank would soon be knocked out by artillery and that the war would not be won by such things. Even Sir Basil Liddell Hart, in his obituary of Swinton in the *Dictionary of National Biography*, says simply that 'Kitchener dubbed it a pretty mechanical toy "which would be quickly knocked out by the enemy's artillery"' and leaves it at that. No doubt Lord K did say something of the kind. The deception plan plainly worked well. It deceived most historians.

Of all people, it was Mr Lloyd George who brought the truth to light. In his *War Memoirs*, written during the years 1933 and 1934, he tells of the demonstration and of Kitchener's departure. Then, to his eternal credit, he quotes from 'a letter I have quite recently received from General Sir Robert Whigham, who in 1916 was a Member of the Army Council and accompanied Lord Kitchener to the Hatfield trial.' He writes: 'Lord Kitchener was so much impressed that he remarked to Sir William Robertson that it was far too valuable a weapon for so much publicity. He then left the trial ground before the trials were concluded, with the deliberate intention of creating the impression that he did not think there was to be anything gained from them. Sir William Robertson followed him straight away, taking me with him, to my great disappointment as I was just going to have a ride in the tank! During the drive back to London, Sir William explained to me the reason of Lord Kitchener's and his own early departure, and impressed on me the necessity of maintaining absolute secrecy about the tank, explaining that Lord Kitchener was rather disturbed at so many people being present at the trials as he feared they would get talked about and the Germans would get to hear of them. It is a matter of history that after these trials fifty tanks were ordered and that Lord Kitchener went to his death before they were ready for the field. I do know, however, that he had great expectations of them, for he used to send for me pretty frequently while he was S of S and I was DCIGS, and he referred to them more than once in the course of conversation. His one fear was that the Germans would get to hear of them before they were ready.'

His good deed for the day done, Mr Lloyd George returned to form. 'If this is the correct interpretation of Lord Kitchener's view, I can only express regret that he did not see fit to inform me of it at the time, in view of the fact that I was responsible as Minister of Munitions for the manufacture of these weapons.' Lord Kitchener, one may suspect, ranked Mr Lloyd George somewhere below the Mudir of Dongola as a trustworthy confidant.

Stern says that before Robertson left the ground he told him that 'orders should be immediately given for the construction of these machines', though he makes no mention of numbers. General Butler, Haig's Deputy CGS, asked how soon he could have some and what alterations could be made. Stern, regardless of the gulf between General officers and Lieutenants RNVR, told him flatly that if GHQ wanted any in 1916 no alterations could be made, except to the loop-holes in the armour.

D'Eyncourt sent an ebullient letter to his former First Sea Lord, still commanding his battalion of Jocks at Plug Street and, between duties, sketching his HQ at Lawrence Farm. 'Dear Colonel Churchill, It is with great pleasure that I am now able to report to you the success of the first landship (Tanks we call them). The War Office have ordered one hundred to the pattern which underwent most successful trials recently ... The official tests of trenches, etc., were nothing to it, and finally we showed them how it would cross a 9 feet gap after climbing a 4 feet 6 inches high perpendicular parapet. Wire entanglements it goes through like a rhinoceros through a field of corn. It can be conveyed by rail (the sponsons and guns take off, making it lighter) and be ready for action very quickly. The King came and saw it and was greatly struck by its performance, as was everybody else. It is capable of great development, but to get a sufficient number in time I strongly urged ordering immediately a good many to the pattern which we know all about. As you are aware it has taken much time and trouble to get the thing perfect and a practical machine simple to make; we tried various types and did much experimental work. I am sorry it has taken so long but pioneer work always takes time, and no avoidable delay has taken place though I begged them to order ten for training purposes two months ago. After losing the great advantage of your influence I had some difficulty in steering the scheme past the rocks of opposition and the more insidious shoals of apathy which are frequented by red herrings, which cross the main line of progress at frequent intervals. The great thing now is to keep the whole matter secret and produce the machines all together as a complete surprise. I have already put the manufacture in hand, under the aegis of the Minister of Munitions, who is very keen; the Admiralty is also allowing me to continue to carry on with the same Committee, but Stern is now Chairman. I enclose photo. In appearance it looks rather like a great antediluvian monster, especially when it comes out of boggy

Excalibur, with swordsmiths. Foster's men at Lincoln.

ground, which it traverses easily. The wheels behind form a rudder and also ease the shock over banks etc. but are not absolutely necessary, as it can steer and turn in its own length with the independent tracks.' D'Eyncourt ended with his 'congratulations on your original project' and good wishes.

Admiral Singer, Director of Naval Operations, was sufficiently taken by the demonstration to propose a machine three times the length and with '3 feet protection over fore part'. Though this may have been premature, the Army Council on 10 February sent to Their Lordships formal congratulations to everybody concerned, including the much-humbugged Squadron 20. 'The thanks of the War Office are thoroughly well deserved,' replied Mr Balfour.

From being a friendless and despised orphan of doubtful legitimacy the Tank had, at a bound, become the friend of man. It would have to do remarkably well to live up to what everybody now expected. Contracts went out to the Metropolitan Carriage Wagon and Finance Co, Armstrong Whitworth, to Kitson Clarke of Leeds, Marshalls of Gainsborough and the North British Locomotive Company of Glasgow. The engineers, once it had been explained to them, undertook to build Tanks with every possible speed. Hankey, not a convert but an original believer, wrote to Swinton on 7 February, 'I shall get as many Tanks as they will let me have. Hundreds, I agree, are necessary.' His diary entry for the day of the Trial did not carry modesty to excess: 'A great triumph for Swinton and me as we have had to climb a mountain of apathy and passive resistance to reach this stage.' It is possible that D'Eyncourt,

Stern, Tritton, Wilson and even Colonel Crompton might have taken another view.

The specifications, it will be remembered, spoke of Madsen guns. These excellent weapons, in appearance much like the Bren, would have been by far the most suitable. They formed part of the agenda for a CID meeting on 21 June. Hankey explained that 900 had been ordered from Copenhagen and half the price of £230,000 had been paid. There was, however, a difficulty. The Roumanians, lured at last into the Allied camp, wanted them too, and were proposing to order a further 1500. Mr Lloyd George told the meeting that the Danes would not part with them except to neutrals. If the Roumanians took them they would have to go through Russia, 'and the Russians would probably taken them en route'. The Prime Minister observed that 'the Roumanians could be told that they could have them if they would arrange for getting them. He thought it doubtful that they would ever arrive in Roumania but we should be making a show of virtue.' Nobody mentioned that the War Office, in a letter dated 5 February, three days after the trials, had told the Committee that 'they do not require any Madsen guns for equipment'. This is hard to explain away. The guns, badly needed, were bought and half paid for. Even though the United States was in its semi-permanent condition of a Presidential election it ought to have been possible to find a well-disposed neutral to make the necessary arrangements. Instead of that, merely to 'make a show of virtue', this invaluable weapon was thrown away. What happened to them is unclear. There are many photographs of German cavalry equipped with the Madsen; certainly, by one means or another, that is where they ended up.

After guns came men. In France there were fifty-two regiments of cavalry, eleven of them Indian, with an average strength of 600 each. Timid suggestions were made to Sir Douglas Haig that some economies might be made in this department. His answer was uncompromising. 'I am very strongly of opinion that no reduction should be made in the Cavalry and it is essential, looking to the future, that the Cavalry should be thoroughly trained, as Cavalry, throughout the ensuing winter.' Before that letter was written the Battle of the Somme had been fought.

CHAPTER 5

Now thrive the Armourers

FINDING MEN FOR THE ARMY is the business of the Adjutant-General's Department, and Sir Henry Sclater did not welcome the additional demand. During 1915 he had had to produce men for a variety of new units, from Mobile Bath Sections and Blanket Delousing Companies to the Machine Gun Corps and the Welsh Guards. Swinton was the obvious person to take on the day-to-day running of the Tank people and, in order to tidy up loose ends, he was appointed to command a body to be known as the Heavy Section (sometimes Heavy Branch) of the six-month-old Machine Gun Corps. It was tactfully - reasonably tactfully - made clear to him that at his time of life he could not expect to lead it into battle, but he must first of all assemble it and then give it whatever training might occur to him as appropriate.

There was an existing body of men that could serve as a nucleus. Early in the war there had come into being a unit called the Motor Machine Gun Corps. It had been modish among young men with cars or motor-cycles of their own, or at any rate with experience of other peoples' cars or motor-cycles, and it had acquired recruits who would not have been over-enthusiastic about joining the older established regiments. In particular it had attracted into its ranks quite a number of what were then called Colonials, some from Colonies whose allegiance had been renounced quite a long time ago. There was Captain Kermit Roosevelt, son of ex-President Theodore, and several Canadians who claimed to come from Provinces with names like New York and Texas. They were a very welcome accretion of strength, especially at a time when recruiting had so fallen off that conscription was coming in. In addition to them there were men of vaguely seafaring antecedents, lately of Squadron 20 RNAS. The Squadron, when threatened with collective transfer to the Army, had declined to oblige, but a good many men who had seen the beginnings of the Tank were determined to share its fortunes. Stern and Wilson, as already mentioned, were transferred in the same way, each with the rank of Major, MGC. Hetherington, already an Army officer in spite of his rank of Flight Commander RNAS, was similarly promoted. None of them, of course, was expected to become a Regimental officer. Stern, after a skirmish between the War Office and the Ministry of Munitions, each of which claimed to own him, was seconded to the Ministry as Chairman of the Tank Supply Committee, with Wilson and Syme both members. Sueter did not remain for long but returned to his first love, the flying service.

As had always happened, and as would happen again a generation later, a call was made for volunteers to serve in something new and exotic. The word was passed round, rather as it had been at the time of the South Sea Bubble, for 'a Company for carrying on an undertaking of Great Advantage but no one to know what it is'. All that was known was that the volunteers sought should have some mechanical or engineering experience and there was talk of an experimental armoured car unit. It sounded rather attractive, certainly a lot more attractive than infantry life, and men of the right calibre came in. The mystery deepened for two of them. A temporary camp, to which they were bidden to report themselves, had been set up at Bisley. On arrival they were told that the Motor Machine Gun Corps had left two days earlier for Siberia. It was nothing to do with Locker Lampson's squadron; Siberia was the code-name of a new camp a few miles away. Russia had been pressed into service as part of the deception plan, the men making the tanks being told that they were water-carriers for the Czar and words in Cyrillic script adorned their sides. Whoever thought the idea up did not know his East Anglians. They have never been that easily fooled; but they kept their thoughts to themselves in the East Anglian way and asked no questions.

The first specialist instruction given was in the Vickers and Hotchkiss machine-guns. When a reasonable competence in these had been attained the plot was thickened by sending everybody to Whale Island where Naval Petty Officers taught them the mysteries of the six-pounder gun. That done, and filled with rumours about the strange machines to whose service they were assigned, they were encadred into a battalion and sent by train to Elveden, near Thetford in Norfolk. Once there the new tank men found themselves wrapped in a security not seen again until the eve of 'D' Day. Five square miles of Norfolk had been cut off from the world. Every farm and cottage had been evacuated, the road running through it closed and nobody was allowed in without a pass. Sentries were posted everywhere, reinforced by patrols of cavalry, and aircraft were forbidden to fly over the area on pain of being shot down. Once in, it was only possible to leave upon production of a special pass which was almost unobtainable. A local belief, not discouraged, was that a great shaft was being dug from which tunnels were to be driven right under Germany.

The men knew, of course, that some sort of machine was awaited and rumours ran around. It could climb trees, cross rivers and jump like a kangaroo. The camp opened in June, 1916. Weeks passed before the first arrivals, for there had been labour troubles and shortages of everything. So scanty were the supplies of 6-pdr shells that 25,000 had had to be bought from Japan. Then, at dead of night, they heard the sound of engines and rushed out to look. Some 'Willies' had arrived and serious training could begin.

Seldom have men been so dedicated to a new thing. The tanks broke down regularly, but this was regarded merely as an agreeable chance to try out their knowledge of the mechanisms. There were nothing like enough to go round and men queued for their turns to drive and shoot. Swinton's famous Memorandum of

February, 1916, was their vade-mecum. *Notes On The Employment Of Tanks* was very firm on one point. 'Surprise cannot be repeated. It follows ... that these machines *should not be used in driblets* (for instance as they may be produced) but that the fact of their existence should be kept as secret as possible until the whole are ready to be launched, together with the infantry assault, in one great combined operation'. This is exactly what did not happen. Swinton's *Notes* mark the beginning of the great divide, between the men who produced the tanks and those who were to command them in battle: it lasted throughout the rest of the war.

It has to be said that the few weeks of training at Thetford were elementary; it could hardly have been otherwise. The first business of a tank crew is, rather obviously, to keep the machine moving. To keep it moving in the right direction is almost as important. The course at Thetford was nearer to reality than Lord Salisbury's golf course had been but it gave little idea of what lay in store. Map reading and compass work were hardly touched on and signalling not mentioned at all. Nor was any consideration given to Staff work. Operation Orders for a Division are long and complicated. The commanders of its component parts needed to be practised in extracting such portions of the Order as concerned them and making their own dispositions for carrying them out. None of the crews had had the smallest experience of any serviceable kind. Few had ever been out of England, hardly any had ever seen battle; most had never seen anything more frightening than a Regimental Guest Night or wounds more hideous than a cut finger. The sheer noise, the smoke, the stench and the fog of war were only dimly understood from Bairnsfather cartoons and the like. The fact that, as *Weekly Tank Notes* put it, 'except for a few small breaks, a man could have walked by trench, had he wished to, from Nieuport almost into Switzerland' seemed picturesque but little else. Nobody should be criticized for this. There is high authority for saying that when the blind lead the blind they shall both fall into the same ditch. This happened.

The Somme had been planned as a gunner's show piece. At long last the British Army had what seemed a sufficient artillery and it set to work to blast the Germans off the face of the earth, wire, machine guns and all. The Germans, well knowing this, dug. Cyril Falls, who walked in the ruins of Thiepval after it had finally been taken, told of 'underground refuges, some two stories deep, fitted with bunks, tables and chairs and lit by electricity: stocks of canned meat, sardines, cigars and thousands of bottles of beer'.

The artillery, despite enormous effort, failed. Much of the ammunition bought in America was defective and, even more important, the sensitive 106 fuse was not yet in service. 'Dud' shells lay everywhere and infantry casualties mounted to figures that staggered belief. From the dreadful 1 July the battle raged on throughout the summer. The pressure had been taken off Verdun, it is true, but other advantages gained, if there were any, had been bought at an impossible price. By the end of the first month it seemed that anything must be tried which had the smallest chance of

Opposite: *A gun-carrying Tank of 1916.*

stopping the slaughter while keeping up the momentum of the attack.

Stern now found himself in a position of great difficulty. As the batteries were moving up for the opening bombardment he had been working with General du Cane on one of Wilson's new designs, this time for a tank capable of carrying a 60-pdr medium gun. The main object of this was to find work for factories which had completed the first order and saw no signs of any others coming in. On 19 June experiments had been carried out at Shoeburyness and, as Wilson says elsewhere, they had proved the idea to be entirely sound. Mr Lloyd George was convinced and ordered that fifty be built. All tanks, incidentally, were to be camouflaged with the dazzle painting used on ships and the task was given to a Sapper officer, Lieut-Colonel Solomon J. Solomon, the only man entitled to the suffixes RE and RA, for he was an Academician. It was also at this time that Stern met Sir Arthur Conan Doyle who had been conducting a vigorous Press campaign for body armour. Stern was bidden by the Minister, Mr Montagu, to let him into the great secret. He was enthusiastic about it, but doubted the validity of Stern's idea for using large numbers in a surprise attack. After Cambrai he ate his words handsomely. On 10 July General Burnett Stuart wrote from GHQ asking that twenty existing machines should be sent to France in order to make it possible to decide whether it was worth persevering with them. Stern passed the letter to Swinton who replied that it was essential to keep going. 'The absolute continuity of supply is, as a matter of fact, already broken but so far the skilled men have not been dispersed.'

At about the time that the demand for tanks to be sent to France came the friendship between Stern and Wilson broke up. The Committee was behaving very tiresomely, demanding that every piffling detail be put before it for a decision, even though the technical knowledge of some members was scanty. The day came when Stern had had enough. At a meeting in July he demanded that this be stopped as it was not merely irritating but a brake on production. His proposition, that the status of the Committee be reduced to an advisory one was, he says, 'carried unanimously'. Wilson, who was there, put it differently. 'Such pandemonium reigned owing to the Chairman's (General Scott-Moncrieff's) attitude to Col Swinton that any resolution might have been recorded.' The one that found its way on to the record eliminated the Supply Committee and appointed Stern Director of the Tank Supply Department with Norman Holden, an officer still recovering from his Gallipoli wounds, as his assistant. With all powers and duties vested in him, Stern picked a quarrel with Wilson. Exactly how they got across each other is not clear, but Stern was the entrepreneur who demanded quick results, whereas the other man was the professional who refused to be hurried or to accept anything slapdash. Early in July, 1916, he had sent Stern a report complaining of bad workmanship in a number of places: 'I do not approve of the work being done at Lincoln and must repudiate any responsibility for it,' he said. Stern wrote back, not unreasonably, pointing out that the responsibility was Wilson's and he could not avoid it, adding that 'these machines are not for peace wear but are rush orders for warfare'. On 17 July he wrote again that 'I have made many complaints about the quality of the work.... Lives will be risked in these machines and it is no argument in excuse for bad or careless work to say that it is alright for trial machines'. The quarrel between the two men erupted on 14 August. In a routine report on a piece of equipment Wilson ended by saying that he would like a decision of the Committee. Stern sent for him and gave a direct order that the words be altered to 'your decision'. Since he had by then been appointed Director of the Tank Supply Department and the Committee was only an advisory body he was probably strictly correct, though pettiness of this kind was not his usual style. Wilson, much angered, demanded the order in writing, something that every officer is entitled to do when faced with what he considers an improper command. Stern sent for Lieut Anderson as a witness and, says Wilson, 'I was told to leave the room'.

The unattractive scene demonstrates as nothing else could the strain under which men were working. Wilson cannot have enjoyed speaking ill of his friend Tritton. Stern at another time would not have treated so senior a man as if he had been a clerk caught with his hand in the till. The tanks were needed in France and both men were working themselves into the ground to see that they arrived there. Both were apprehensive about what would happen to them. It is hardly remarkable that something snapped. Unfortunately it was more than a fire of straw. The happy days of the White Hart were never to come again and other quarrels were to follow. It is too easy to call such displays of temper childish, for most people today simply do not understand the feelings of those active during the summer of 1916. The present writer's father, the least imaginative of men, once told him of how, waiting to go over the bags with his platoon and half-deafened by the guns, 'I seriously thought for a few seconds, "This must be the end of the world"'. Minds were stretched to a point beyond what would be considered possible in peacetime, for what was seen as the decisive battle upon which the fate of the Allies hung was being fought. Our history was these mens' immediate future and it is not seemly to blame any of them for behaving out of character.

When the order to send tanks to France arrived at the end of July Stern came near to losing his temper. The machines were nowhere near ready, stocks of spare parts hardly existed and crews had only had an elementary training. Furthermore the whole tank concept was based upon the use of masses of machines at a time when all the preparations for a great armoured attack had been completed. Enquiries at the Repair Shop Unit in Thetford told him of most of the deficiencies. The machinery and skill for taking off tracks simply did not then exist. Two months' work for the infant Corps lay ahead if the order was to be obeyed. Stern descended upon everybody in authority, from the Prime Minister to the CIGS, Sir William Robertson. They persuaded him to agree that every available machine should be made ready within ten days. No suggestion seems to have been made that they should be pitched straight into the battle.

To make this promise good demanded more than Thetford could offer. Stern went instead to Birmingham, to the Metropolitan Carriage Company which was the biggest single manufacturer of tanks. There he asked for volunteers to come to Thetford and do what was necessary. Forty good men turned out, led by Mr Wirrick of the Company. The Army refused to house or feed a bunch of civilians. At Stern's urgent request the Chief Constable found billets and the Great Eastern Railway provided a restaurant car. There are so many dismal stories about wartime strikes that it is a pleasure to quote Stern's words about the men of Birmingham: 'This is only one of the instances of the magnificent patriotism and unselfishness of the industrial workers, who were ready to labour night and day for the Tanks, from the making of the first experimental machine until the Armistice was signed in November, 1918'.

Sir William Robertson mentions it nowhere in his published writings but he had allowed the idea to get about that he wanted to use the tanks at the earliest possible moment, no matter what their state of battle-worthiness might be. Stern, who missed very little, spoke with d'Eyncourt (now Chief Adviser to the Tank Supply Department) and together they descended upon 'Wullie' at the War Office. The CIGS was not a happy man. When Kitchener had been Secretary of State it had been the duty of his old enemy Lord Curzon to oppose everything he said or did. Most of Kitchener's Memoranda for the Cabinet, whether on the state of the war, the evacuation of Gallipoli, conscription or anything else, have attached to them long and windy papers initialled 'C of K' flatly contradicting almost everything. Now the enemy was the Minister, for 'Wullie' Robertson and David Lloyd George, in the words of the song, 'thought nowt of each other at all'. Lloyd George was of Swinton's mind about not revealing the secret until plenty of tanks were ready. Stern and d'Eyncourt took the same view. Together they urged that 'the tanks should not be used until they were ready in great numbers. We urged him to wait until the Spring of 1917, when large numbers would be ready'. 'Wullie's' reply is not on record. It was probably his customary grunt. He did, however, agree to the placing of an order for 150 new tanks.

On 3 August Stern put it into writing, addressed to his masters at the Ministry of Munitions: 'I beg to refer to our conversation regarding the order for 150 Tanks. My Department was originally given an order to produced 150 Tanks with necessary spares, and I was under the impression that these would not be used until the order had been completed, therefore the spares would not, in the ordinary way, be available until the 150 machines were completed. From the conversations I have had with Mr Lloyd George and General Sir William Robertson, and information received from Colonel Swinton, I believe it is intended to send small numbers of these machines out at the earliest possible date, and I beg to inform you that the machines cannot be equipped to my satisfaction before the 1st of September. I have therefore made arrangements that the 100 machines shall be completed in every detail, together with the necessary spares, by the 1st of September. This is from the designer's and manufacturer's point of view, which I represent. I may add that in my opinion the sending out of partially equipped machines, as now suggested, is courting disaster.' The French, who were themselves into the early stages of the tank business, also begged for delay until all was ready. Stern was not being entirely candid. The first fifty tanks were being finished off by the men at Thetford as he wrote.

These were strong arguments. Equally strong were those of the men in France. The end of the battle was nowhere in sight; winter was not all that far off; if winter

Interior view, looking aft from driver's seat. Screw-threaded object is the engine governor.

came before any substantial success had been won – as it probably would – the morale of even this Army, the finest ever assembled, must inevitably fall off. 'The slightest holding back of any of our resources might, at the critical moment, make the difference between defeat and victory,' they were told. Stern and the others could not stand out against these urgings. Tremendous events which might shape the history of the world for years to come trembled in the balance. Perhaps it was their duty to let the tanks, with all their imperfections, at least have a try. In any event once they were in France it would be up to GHQ.

On 15 August, 1916, thirteen tanks of C and D Companies, their sponsons

Information technology, 1916. Releasing a pigeon.

unbolted and carried on specially made trollies, travelled by train from Thetford to Avonmouth from whence they sailed to Havre. It was a back-breaking business, for each sponson with its gun weighed some 35 cwt and the only machinery available to move them was a girder with block and tackle. Between Thetford and the temporary base at Yvrench near Abbeville they had to be loaded and unloaded five times. By the end of the month fifty Mk I tanks were assembled in France along with their unpractised crews to await whatever might be in store for them. Wilson, to his intense anger, was not allowed to go with them. When he wrote to Stern asking for more information he received a reply that would have justified knocking the writer down. Everything to do with tanks 'is entirely under my control and whatever I think necessary will be done ... I will arrange for all useful information to be passed on to you. You should not give orders.' Tritton, being a mere civilian, was told to stay at home. According to Wilson Major Sommers, who commanded the first Company to go, and Major Knothe with the workshop staff, were delayed in England

- he does not say why - and arrived in France only on 12 September, three days before the battle. Again it is Wilson who asserts that if it had not been for these two officers 'the tank would have died on the Somme'. Ten days after the battle had come to an end permission was granted for Wilson to go and find out what had happened to the tanks that were so largely his creation.

In spite of all these things a demonstration was mounted on 26 August for the edification of Sir Douglas Haig and Sir Henry Rawlinson, commanding Fourth Army. Five dazzle-painted tanks accompanied by a battalion of infantry put on a brave show. Sir Douglas wrote of it that 'The tanks crossed ditches and parapets, representing the several lines of a defensive position with the greatest ease and one entered a wood which was made to represent a "strong-point" and easily "walked over" fair-sized trees of six inches diameter! Altogether the demonstration was quite encouraging, but we require to clear our ideas as to the tactical handling of these machines.' In the published part of his diaries Haig tells of the various conferences he attended during the next couple of weeks and of the plans made there for renewal of the attack. No mention anywhere is made of the tanks or of how he planned to use them.

On 10 September, 1916, the first fifty moved up to the forward area, by train to the Loop, near Bray, a couple of miles from the river and thence across country. Aerial photographs of enemy positions, common coinage to the rest of the army but new and barely comprehensible to the tank men, were produced and pored over. Anti-bombing nets were slung over the tops, spares, pigeons in baskets, signal lamps and two days' rations stowed away, while the crews were issued with leather anti-bruise helmets. Each 'male' tank - the slightly larger one equipped with 6-pdrs - carried 324 gun rounds and 6,300 of SAA. The 'female' - designed for trench clearing - had no less than 31,000 rounds for the machine-guns crammed away in the poky inside. Nobody, even now, had more than the roughest idea of what they would be expected to do. The guns on both sides continued to roar, the shell craters grew more and bigger. Four miles of devastated land, far worse than anything that could have been imagined, had to be traversed before they could begin to come to grips with their enemy.

Charteris, who had every reason to know, says that the secret had not been as well kept as people thought. A demonstration attended by a number of MPs, as well as other people, had been followed by letters to neutral countries which had certainly given the Germans cause to realize that something was up. They would pretty certainly have known all there was to know well before the Spring of 1917 and anti-tank weapons could be made far more quickly than tanks. It was possible that even now they were expected.

Under these less than perfect conditions the Heavy Branch, Machine Gun Corps, made ready for its first battle.

CHAPTER 6

Innocence Lost

O N A DAY LONG AGO, somewhere in the Middle East, bearded men had once pushed a wheeled tower towards a walled city. Very probably the wheels fell off, the tower fell over and rude Assyrian laughter rang out. For all that, walled cities were never again entirely safe. Five hundred and seventy years before the Somme battles French bombardiers are supposed to have brought their fire-crakes to the field of Crecy. They made so little impression upon observers that nobody bothered to record the fact. It would be interesting to see whether the tank could do better. Mr Churchill, who had seen the searchlights sweep the desert at Omdurman, had always called for a mass onfall by night guided by the same means. What actually happened was a piecemeal 'chipping in wherever we could', as Sir Hugh Elles was to call it. Nobody was in command; the Divisions lacked even the tank equivalent of a CRA or CRE.

Baker-Carr, as senior Machine Gun Corps officer about the place, was asked to keep some sort of eye on them. He found the Company and Section commanders 'harassed almost beyond endurance by their domestic problems of packing equipment, ammunition, food, water, blankets and a hundred other things into a space already overcrowded with machinery and human beings, called upon to answer at a moment's notice a hundred conundrums that were suddenly hurled at them'. Orders, already incomprehensible, were constantly changed. Up to midnight on the 14th several commanders were still unclear about what they were expected to do or even at what hour to start. In one instance a group of tanks had no petrol at all, nor did they know where to get any. Baker-Carr provided it just in time. The only comfortable words he had to say were that 'for once the weather was not unfavourable'.

Forty-nine tanks set out for the assembly area. Of these seventeen broke down on the way, mostly with clutch trouble. The proportion sounds high but it was unreasonable to expect anything even as good. The Daimler sleeve-valve engine – still in use today – had never been designed to push nearly thirty tons of metal and humanity along steel tracks. Many of them had not had time to be properly run in and some had been hastily made up from such spare parts as could be found. The petrol supplied was of the lowest quality imaginable. The Heavy Branch deserve great credit for getting any of its 'Willies' across the start line at all. The crews of those that managed it had passed a sleepless night following upon an unrestful day.

After spending hours trying to digest complicated operation orders, only one copy being provided for each section of three machines, the commanders had at 5 am received a message cancelling all of them. Fresh ones, equally incomprehensible, were given verbally. As soon as it was dusk each tank had been driven to a point a little behind its jumping-off place and the crews had tried to snatch some rest. They got very little, for it takes long practice to sleep through a bombardment. At 5.30 am on 15 September the starting handles were swung, each by four men, the engines spluttered and, after a moment, most of them roared into life belching out great clouds of black smoke. About thirty tanks, iron capsules cutting off their occupants from the world and each with its clumsy pair of wheels trailing behind, lurched towards the German lines, following the tapes laid down by the Reconnaissance Officers. Charteris swears that one was led into battle by a man carrying a red flag as in the earliest days of motoring.

All night long the medium and heavy batteries had been banging away, stirring up yet again the sea of whitish mud that lay ahead. Maps were useless, for everything looked like the surface of the moon. At 6.20, Zero hour, the field guns joined in, putting down the creeping barrage behind whose curtain tanks and infantry were to move forward.

The attack was on a two Corps front. On the right was Lord Cavan's XIVth, made up of the Guards, 6th and 56th (London) Divisions. To their left was the XVth Corps of General Horne, consisting of 14th, 41st and New Zealand Divisions. In accordance with custom, the right-hand formation will be followed first. The 6th was a Regular Division that had come to France just before the Battle of the Aisne. Its task, along with the other two formations, was to attack the line Lesboeufs to Morval. General Marden, the GOC, left his record of the part the tanks took in his battle: 'As far as the Division was concerned (it) was a failure, for of the three allotted to 6th Division two broke down before starting, and the third, moving off in accordance with orders long before the infantry, had its periscope shot off, its peep-holes blinded, was riddled by armour-piercing bullets and had to come back without achieving anything. A perfect stream of fire was directed at it and the driver badly wounded.' The 56th, London Territorials, also had three tanks. The instructions given to their commanders were to move off at a time (apparently to be decided by themselves) which would put them on the first objective five minutes before the infantry arrived. That done, they were to move on, halt and turn themselves into strong-points. 'Departure from this programme to assist any infantry held up by the enemy was left to the discretion of the Tank Commander.' For the third and fourth objectives the tanks would go on ahead without the creeping barrage, the infantry following behind them. Signals were arranged. Red flag meant 'Out of action'; Green for 'On objective'.

The main objective of 56th Division was Bouleaux Wood; this had to be cleared before defensive flanks could be formed. One brigade was to hold the line through Leuze Wood and to capture the notorious Loop Trench to the south-east which ran into the sunken road to Combles. One tank, called the Right Tank, was to advance on the right of the wood, drive the enemy beyond the sunken road and halt. The

Centre and Left Tanks were to work along the left of Bouleaux Wood and 'proceed to a railway cutting, which promised to be a point of some difficulty'. The right Tank 'gave valuable assistance, but was set on fire by a field gun'. The Centre Tank broke down on its way to the assembly position. The Left Tank is not mentioned again, but was included in the general conclusion that 'the Tanks were by no means a success'. Nobody blamed the gallant crews. Evidence of the impossible task set them comes from one of the Brigade Majors in 56th Division, Philip Neame, already VC and in due time to become Lieut-General Sir Philip. 'One of the tanks was not bullet-proof; it came crawling back past our HQ with a very frightened officer inside whose first sight of fighting this had been. The steel walls were riddled with bullet holes. I imagine that by mistake inferior boiler-plate instead of armour-plate must have been put in.'

The Guards Division were given nine tanks, later increased to ten. In accordance with immemorial practice, long and careful Orders were drawn up. Guards Division Orders No 75 devoted all of Appendix IV to the subject. Gaps 100 yards wide were to be left in the barrage to accommodate them, but the attacking troops were warned that in no circumstances were they to wait as, on such heavily cratered ground, the tanks were not thought likely to manage even fifteen yards a minute. At 6.20 am the creeping barrage opened up. It was an historic moment, for more reasons than one. For the first time ever three Coldstream battalions marched off in line, 'as steadily as if they were walking down the Mall'. They took hideous punishment. Behind them, late but pursuing, the first armoured fighting vehicles lurched and rumbled, smoke belching from each exhaust. The crews had been up since 3 am when their commander had had to report to Major-General Feilding that only seven of his machines, parked on the southern outskirts of Trones Wood, could be persuaded to start. He cannot have enjoyed the interview. The report on the day of battle was not encouraging. 'It was an infantry battle throughout, for the tanks in this their first cooperation in the field with the troops of the Guards Division proved of little or no assistance to the infantry. They were late in crossing the parapet and so were unable to move forward in advance of the leading battalions. The tank to which had been entrusted the important task of dislodging the Germans from their position at the south-eastern corner of Delville Wood does not appear to have come into action. The remaining tanks wandered about in various directions and are reported to have done a certain amount of useful fighting on their own account either in the area of the Guards Division or in that of 6th Division, but they certainly failed on this occasion to carry out their main task and were of no help to the infantry in the subduing of machine-gun fire … the moment they started they lost all sense of direction and wandered about aimlessly.' There is not a kind word about the crews in the Guards Divisional History. But the Guards are seldom lavish with praise.

Now to General Horne's area, with the left-hand XVth Corps. Apart from four tanks given to the 47th (London) Division of IIIrd Corps to help in the attack on High Wood, all of which came to grief early on broken tree stumps and in shell holes, this was the only remaining tank area. The 14th (Light) was one of the senior

New Army Divisions, 41st its newest and last. So low had manpower stocks fallen that its immediate predecessor, 40th, had been made up of infantry of low medical category in the hope that an unusually good artillery might even things up. It had not worked. The category men had had to be discharged and new recruits found. No Kitchener divisions were raised after the 41st. All those with later numbers, save for 63rd (Naval), were either first- or second-line Territorials. The 41st, mostly made up of south country regiments, had only been raised the previous September and had arrived in France in May, 1916. Like so many formations from which nobody expected much, it turned out to be an uncommonly good one.

Again at 6.20 the barrage opened. The 14th, on the right, faced a maze of trenches before it could reach its objective, the now non-existent village of Guedecourt. In the centre the 41st looked out at what remained of Flers; the task of the New Zealanders was to secure the spur north-west of the same village. Eighteen tanks had been given to the Corps to try and make the job of the infantry a little less impossible than it seemed. An hour before the main attack was due to start General Horne had decided to give the tanks a chance to see what they could achieve by surprise. Three of them had been sent off on their own to set about the tenacious German unit that was clinging so grimly on to the south-east corner of Delville Wood. Only one arrived, but Lieutenant Mortimore's 'male', No 1 of D Company, got there, straddled Hop Alley and opened up with both 6-pdrs and machine-guns. The stupefied Germans poured out with hands in the air. On the way back Mortimore's tank took two direct hits from a field gun and was put out of action, two of the crew being killed, but they had shown what a tank could do, given a little luck.

Away to the left Gough's Reserve Army had been allocated seven machines which he had passed to 2nd Canadian Division. They had come out of the darkness at 4.30, their engines roaring, and drove into a counter-barrage. It did no particular harm, but as the Canadians moved on Courcelette four hours later they had to manage without them. One had broken down, two were bogged in the German support area while the others pitched and rolled slowly behind the infantry incapable of so much as a foot pace. They did, however, put the wind up many Germans and induced them to surrender for fear of what they might be able to do. ('Not war but bloody butchery,' one of them complained.) A solitary tank, its mate dead, attached itself to 15 (Scottish) Division and clanked down the Martinpuich road clearing trenches as it went.

It was on the front of the 41st that the tanks made themselves felt. Four of them, D6, 9, 16 and 17, rumbled through the 11th Royal West Kent and 15th Hampshires at about 8 o'clock. Number 16, Lieutenant Hastie's tank, barged its way into Flers, slewed on its tracks to face down the main road and opened fire with all it had. The others joined in, smashing down wire entanglements, lurching over ruined buildings and shooting up everything. The two infantry battalions, who had been up all night carrying stores, cheered their hearts out and followed along behind as if Flers had been Lord Salisbury's golf course. A bright young man in the RFC, watching it all from above, wrote and dropped his famous message which reached Swinton as he was about to disembark at Boulogne. It was a message of which the

Heavy Branch was to become heartily sick, but it sounded splendid at the time: 'A tank is walking up the High Street at Flers with the British Army cheering behind.' It was a small incident in a battle of gigantic size, but it was not insignificant.

It was eleven days after the battle, on 26 September, that the first DSO came to the Heavy Branch. 21st Division, one of those New Army formations so wantonly thrown into the mincer at Loos, was attacking towards Guedecourt and one of its Brigades - Leicestershire men - had once again come up against uncut wire in front of the strongly defended Gird Trench. Lieutenant Storey and D14 were whistled up to see what they could do. D14 was a female, designed for the job of clearing trenches with her machine-guns. She waddled off at 6.30 am, followed by a party of bombers. The German defenders opened up with machine guns, and potato-masher grenades burst around and in front. It did nothing for them. D14 swept the wire aside, swung right and clanked down the 1500-yard length of the trench, firing bursts as she went, assisted by an aircraft of the RFC which did much the same thing. The Germans fought well, but their case was hopeless. Up and down went D14 until white handkerchiefs appeared. 362 men surrendered to the Leicesters as Storey headed for Guedecourt, meditating further havoc. Before he could wreak much more D14 ran short of petrol and had to come home; all but two of the occupants were wounded but at that price they had done something that would otherwise have demanded a full brigade of infantry and hundreds of dead and wounded. DSOs to Colonels and above are usually no more than glorified service stripes; very rarely do they come the way of subalterns.

A few miles away, across the Albert-Bapaume road, eight other tanks were achieving something just as valuable. Thiepval, where the great archway commemorating the Missing stands, had been a name of dread since the day when 36th (Ulster) Division had been decimated in its first battle. The fortress, still untaken but absolutely necessary if the long battle was to achieve any sort of results, was in the sector of Sir Hubert Gough's Reserve Army and, after the disaster of Gommecourt, Gough's stock stood low. This time, as a rather desperate expedient, he decided to do without any preliminary bombardment and to give the tanks some chance of showing how they could manage on their own. The result was entirely successful. The role of the tanks was admittedly ancillary to that of the infantry but eight of them set off up the shell-blasted slope, through the mounds of what had been buildings and across the shattered orchards. Most of them got to their destination and, as Williams-Ellis quoted from an officer then present, 'our men were over the German parapets and into the dug-outs before the machine-guns could be got up to repel them'. Once again the point had been made. Tanks could save casualties amongst our own men as nothing else could; besides this the business of killing Germans was far less important.

The performance of the tanks, however, had been patchy. Four were given to 18 Division, the main assaulting formation, commanded by Major-General Ivor Maxse who would become a tank enthusiast in time. One, Creme de Menthe, certainly earned its rations. The 12th Middlesex, 'cleared line after line of trenches until they reached the château, where one company was checked by deadly machine-gun fire. Just at this critical moment the leading tank came up, having crossed over from Thiepval Wood; its arrival was most opportune as it dealt with the enemy machine-guns and the leading companies of the Middlesex passed determinedly round both flanks of the château. Two Tanks had been assigned to the Brigade and were intended to lead the infantry into Thiepval and then on to the Schwaben Redoubt. Unfortunately, having done excellent service, this tank subsided into the mud and remained there, whilst its fellows arrived a little later and suffered the same fate. That was the end of Creme de Menthe and Cordon Bleu as active combatants on this great day,' says the Divisional History. The other tanks are nowhere mentioned.

Williams-Ellis made out a score card. Forty-nine tanks were employed. Thirty-two reached their starting points. Nine pushed ahead of the infantry and caused considerable loss to the enemy. Nine others did not catch up the infantry but did good work in 'clearing up'. Five became ditched. Nine broke down from mechanical trouble. The casualties amongst tank personnel were insignificant, though one officer of great promise was lost.

Though the operations had not been an unqualified success, there was justification for the pioneers, when faced with the question of what use tanks were, to give Michael Faraday's reply: 'What use is a baby?'

With October the rain came back. Six miles of mud lay behind the front line, between the men in the trenches and supplies of every sort. There would be no more battles for a while. The main business was to keep the army in being.

The War Committee, under the Prime Minister, held a meeting on 18 September with the object of deciding what should be publicly announced about the Caterpillar Machine-gun Destroyers. Mr Montagu, ex-Financial Secretary to the Treasury and now Minister of Munitions, disliked the original draft submitted by the CID because 'it did not give sufficient credit to the Ministry or to Major Stern. Nor did it do justice to Mr d'Eyncourt and Mr Tritton, who were responsible for the design'. Stern, he asserted 'was responsible for the production,' but nobody thought to mention Wilson. He would not have minded, for he was a self-effacing man. Mr Lloyd George 'thought that the training of the "Tank" Corps (it did not yet exist under that name) had not been entirely satisfactory and for that Colonel Swinton might be held to some extent responsible.' The others were having none of that. 'Very great credit was due to Colonel Swinton,' said Mr Asquith. Mr Montagu 'thought that the reason why the training was not satisfactory was that the "Tanks" were used before the training of the Corps had been properly completed.' The upshot of it was that no official statement was made but Mr Lloyd George would say something rather vague in the Commons. Which he in due course did.

CHAPTER *7*

Complications

NOW CAME THE INQUEST. Stern, in his capacity of coroner, set out for France on the morning of 15 September. Already he was in a vile temper, the result of another brush with authority. Just as he had been about to leave, a civil servant had arrived bearing a message. The Tank Supply Department, being now of no importance, was to give up its office and move all its rubbish to a small flat in a back street opposite the Metropole Hotel in Northumberland Avenue. Today was Friday; everything must be out by Sunday. Stern, whose state of mind as he waited for news of the debut of his tanks can be imagined without a lot of difficulty, exploded. Addressing the Assistant Secretary as if he had been a customer of ill-repute asking for a bigger overdraft, he spoke. His Department was concerned with matters of the highest national importance; not only did it refuse to move, it required a very large building of its own. To avoid any possibility of misunderstanding, an officer of Squadron 20 was ordered to maintain an armed guard over the office during the Director's absence. Should any attempt be made to enter the place the Assistant Secretary was to be put under close arrest, taken to the Squadron HQ at Wembley and tied to a stake for twenty-four hours. A full account of the proceedings would then be sent to every editor in Fleet Street.

That done, Stern left Charing Cross and arrived in France the next day. There he met Colonel Elles and was told of the events of the 15th. Elles appeared well pleased, but not everybody else shared his feelings. Sir Henry Rawlinson had written a long letter to Lord Derby at the War Office; he gave a thorough exegesis of what had happened on the fronts of the various Corps engaged without mentioning tanks at all. At the end of the letter, as a kind of coda, he spoke of them: 'The tanks in certain circumstances, such as at Flers and Martinpuich, rendered very valuable service, but they failed to have that effect on the fighting which many of their strongest advocates expected. They laboured under great difficulties. The officers and men who were driving them had not been under fire before; they had had great difficulty in maintaining their direction, owing to their limited vision; and their very low speed over ground torn by shells was a very serious handicap.... Until they have more engine power, can maintain a speed of four miles an hour over really bad ground, and until the personnel has had more experience, they will not be of much value to an infantry assault.' He then turned to the more important subject of artillery.

That sound judge of the new warfare Christopher Baker-Carr had had more time than the Army Commander to think the matter through. 'Two facts emerge from the long tale of mishaps and misadventures which had taken place. The first, and one which was completely ignored by the British High Command, was the moral effect on the Germans.... Not only did captured officers and men admit that they felt absolutely helpless when attacked by tanks, but the German official Press lost no time in proclaiming to the world the inhumanity of the British in employing "these cruel and barbarous weapons". Our friends, the enemy, always "squealed" when frightened, but the reason for this particular paroxysm of righteous indignation appears to have been overlooked by GHQ. The second fact which strikes the observer is that if one or two of the new machines were capable of achieving a great success, there should be no reason why, given good organization and favourable conditions, the large majority should not achieve equally good results.' Baker-Carr was ordered to put in a detailed report. He dealt fairly and faithfully with the business, tank by tank, and ended with the assertion that, given more reliable and less complicated machines, the tank, 'under favourable conditions and given suitable organization, would prove to be of inestimable assistance to breaking the deadlock on the Western Front'. As usual he was reviled for his pains.

Not, however, by Sir Douglas Haig. On Sunday 17 September Swinton and Stern presented themselves at Montreuil to pay a call on General Butler. As they waited outside his office the Chief himself appeared and called them to him. 'We have had the greatest victory since the Battle of the Marne. We have taken more prisoners and more territory with comparatively few casualties. This is due to the Tanks. Wherever the Tanks advanced we took our objectives, and where they did not advance we failed to take our objectives. Colonel Swinton, you shall be head of the Tank Corps: Major Stern, you shall be head of the construction of Tanks. Go back and make as many Tanks as you can. We thank you.' When d'Eyncourt arrived a few days later and a further audience was granted this had been watered down a little: 'Go home and build as many Tanks as you can, subject to not interfering with the output of aircraft and of railway trucks and locomotives, of which we are in great need.'

The bull market for Tanks at GHQ was by no means universal at the next stratum down. Amongst the Corps Commanders, Pulteney, a very experienced General who had been in every battle since the beginning, had personally over-ruled the commander of 47th Division over the tank part in the attack on High Wood. Major-General Barter had accepted the tank subaltern's statement that the tree stumps of the wood itself made an obstacle that his machines could not cross; another route must be found. The Corps artillery said equally firmly that this would ruin their carefully worked-out barrage programme. General Pulteney preferred known to unknown quantities, and who can blame him? The result, of course, was that all the tanks became firmly stuck long before they could do anything useful. General Horne left XIV Corps shortly afterwards, to succeed Sir Charles Monro in command of First Army. His successor, 'Sandy' du Cane, knew little about Tanks. Lord Cavan, at XV Corps, had not seen enough to make a convert of him. And of the

Divisional Generals only Lawford of the 41st could be reckoned a friend.

From inside the tanks themselves had come a number of lessons. Not only had Charteris had a point in saying that the Germans might have armour-piercing bullets but the invulnerability to small-arms fire had been exaggerated. Fragments of lead from squashed nickel-jacketed rounds ('splash' in the vernacular) that had hit the armour mysteriously found their way inside through the tiniest of orifices. In addition to that, bursts of fire from machine-guns had a way of detaching minute fragments of steel from the inner faces of the armour plate, fragments that ricochetted around inside and were capable of blinding a man. The exhausts were a great source of weakness, running up from inside and along the top. The low-grade petrol on issue made smoke, the pipes became red-hot and the noise was abominable. Some crews made make-shift silencers out of biscuit tins; others covered the pipes with layers of the one commodity that was available in quantity, mud. The 8-foot-long 6-pdrs had a way of digging themselves into the ground, should the tank go nose down; they needed to be truncated. The open-trough lubrication system was wretched, but there was no obvious way of bettering it. The improved Creeping Grip slid happily round in mud giving no forward movement; an easy amelioration was the provision of 'spuds' on the tracks, protruding metal bars that served as do studs on a football boot. Above all some means must be provided of helping a crew to unditch. It was absurd to have so powerful a weapon kept out of battle when by sweat and ingenuity it might be got on the move again. Some sort of stout bar fastened to the tracks athwartships on top of the tank might work. It would be carried down by the tracks under the belly where it might serve to give enough lift to get the tank out of its hole. It might equally well wrench the tracks off; experiment was needed. The trailing wheels were, everybody agreed, quite needless and a nuisance.

Though Stern had fiercely opposed the use of his tanks before they were ready, he was reasonably well satisfied with the results. He visited the Railway Loop near Bray where the survivors of the battle had gathered along with the newer arrivals and had a word with his brother in the Yeomanry who, like the rest of the cavalry, was glumly leading his horse home again. Next morning, with Swinton and General Butler, he set out for Paris by road to visit Colonel Estienne to find out what the French were doing in the matter of armoured fighting machines. The first of them had just arrived at Marly and Stern was invited to come and look at it.

Estienne was, as near as no matter, the French equivalent of Colonel Swinton, with M le Breton for his Wilson. His ideas were in advance of his time, for Estienne was not thinking in terms of mechanical pill-boxes but of mechanized cavalry. He wanted lots of little tanks, little tanks that could be brought to the edge of the battlefield in the backs of lorries. Already he had tried something like 'Little Willie' with the original St Chamond, but it had shown all of 'Little Willie's' failings. He therefore turned to M Louis Renault, the best man by far for his purpose. At the time of his meeting with Stern, however, French development lagged rather a long way behind. For immediate purposes there was no tank superior to the Tritton-Wilsons.

Swinton and Stern were very busy during the last days of September. On the 19th they returned to London and next morning there was a meeting at the War Office. Mr Lloyd George was there, along with Dr Addison for the Ministry of Munitions and Generals Butler and Whigham. It must have been painful for Mr Lloyd George to find himself and Sir Douglas Haig in such perfect accord, for Butler demanded, on behalf of his Chief, that 1,000 tanks be put in hand at once. This was agreed, although it demanded 30,000 tons of steel, 1,000 6-pdr guns and 6,000 machine-guns. Orders were placed, but orders did not mean that the tanks would appear.

On the 23rd Stern set off again for Paris, this time with a large party of experts. D'Eyncourt, Wilson and Tritton were there, along with representatives of the manufacturers and Mr Searle of the Daimler Company. On the same day Stern had been promoted Lieut-Colonel, possibly to put him on an equal footing with the Frenchman. They visited the Schneider factory at St Ouen where a sizeable tank was being built and discussed the St Chamond with the designers. The only common language, for most of them, was German. It goes to show what a hold Germany had in what we would now call 'advanced technology'. America still lagged far behind in many things.

Wilson examined everything with an engineer's care, interesting himself particularly in gear-boxes and transmissions. He did not reckon much of what he was shown. Already he was working in a pencil-stub and back-of-envelope way on an entirely new system of his own.

The party was back in London on 28 September. The Assistant Secretary had acknowledged defeat and the Tank Supply Committee had been given new offices at 14, 17 and 18 Cockspur Street. Before long even these proved too small. The thought in front of the minds of the English contingent was, inevitably, engines. If they had hoped to get something more powerful from the French they had been disappointed. Stern's men ransacked the American factories but found nothing. On 16 October, no new design for the projected 1,000 having been settled, orders were placed, just to keep the factories going, for 100 more Mk 1s.

Though Mr Lloyd George was present at at least three meetings attended by Stern there is no record amongst the latter's papers of any controversy about whether or not the tanks should have been used at all. Both Mr Lloyd George and Mr Churchill in their own writings are bitter about what they considered the throwing away of a great and secret weapon for very small advantages. The argument has been rumbling on ever since that long-ago 15 September. Broadly speaking, the parties fall into two clearly definable groups – those who say the tank ought to have been kept secret until enough were present to make it decisive include all, or nearly all, the men whose duties about the business were performed in England: those who demanded its use were the men in the field. Before 15 September they had tried everything they could think of to break the German front, including Rawlinson's dawn attack with four divisions on 14 July. Only this trick remained, and the use by the Germans of armour-piercing bullets suggests that Charteris had a point and the great secret was not all that secret. Baker-Carr puts it crisply: 'There are exactly two

Above and opposite: *Tanks under construction at the Metropolitan Carriage Co.'s Birmingham works.*

people to whose views it is worth listening, those of Hugh Elles the first commander of the Tank Corps and Colonel J. F. C. Fuller, the first Chief General Staff Officer of the Tank Corps and probably the most brilliant thinker in the British Army today (1930). These two officers, both of whom had to deal not only with the Germans but with (a far more difficult business) the British, were definitely convinced that the benefits derived from the lessons learnt in battle more than compensated for the obvious disadvantage of "premature disclosure". The very secrecy, which was essential during the embryo period, militated against the highest standard of mechanical and personal efficiency. Everybody was groping more or less in the dark. Even Swinton ... was of necessity unfamiliar with the actual battlefields on which the tanks would be called upon to fight.' The worst aspect of this difference of opinion, sometimes intemperately expressed on both sides, was that it marked the opening up of a gulf, sometimes an abyss, between the men at home who designed and made the machines and those across the Channel whose business it was to command and fight them. Voltaire said it all, with '*Le mieux est l'ennemi du bien*'. In other words is an indifferent tank today more worth having than a better one six months hence? The question is, of course, purely rhetorical, but attempts to answer it were to cause the most serious trouble before the end came.

One ancestor, momentarily neglected, was brought back by Stern. Mr H. G. Wells was invited to visit a factory at Birmingham and to write something about it.

80

He gave full value. 'I saw other things that day at X. The Tank is only a beginning in a new phase of warfare. Of these other things I may only write in the most general terms. But though Tanks and their collaterals are being made upon a very considerable scale in X, already I realized as I walked through gigantic forges as high and marvellous as cathedrals, and from workshed to workshed where gun-carriages, ammunition carts and a hundred other such things were flowing into existence with the swelling abundance of a river that flows out of a gorge, that as the demand for the new developments grew clear and strong, the resources of Britain are capable still of a tremendous response.'

A few days later Stern received an official instruction from the Army Council cancelling the order for the 1,000 tanks. The fact that the ukase came from Sir William Robertson was all that it needed to raise Stern's temper to boiling point. He had put up with a great deal from Generals and the end was by no means yet. In May, 1918, he was to write a paper for the then Prime Minister, Mr Lloyd George, which included the words 'The programme for 1917 was muddled away'. This manifestation of it was not to be endured and, with his customary contempt for usual channels, he went straight to his old friend who was, of course, still Robertson's Minister. 'I told him that I had, with enormous difficulty, started swinging this huge weight, and that I could not possibly stop it now. I told him that he could cancel my appointment, but he could not possibly get me to cancel the orders

I had placed.' Mr Lloyd George was equally furious. 'When I was Secretary of State for War in September, 1916, I ordered 1,000 tanks to be manufactured. Sir William Robertson countermanded the order without my knowledge. Thanks to Sir Albert Stern (his knighthood, in 1916, was still in the future) I discovered this countermand in time, and gave peremptory instructions that the manufacture should be proceeded with and that the utmost diligence should be used in executing the order.' Stern had to explain in Robertson's presence what had happened and then tactfully withdrew. It is hard to understand what 'Wullie' was playing at. Mr Lloyd George, as well as being the responsible Minister, was President of the Army Council. If 'Wullie' thought he could sneak the business through he did not know Bertie Stern. Lieutenant-Colonels at the War Office were ten a penny, but this one was no ordinary middle-piece officer. The arbiters of the destinies of mechanical warfare were no longer friends of the tank. Even Butler, who claimed to be an enthusiast, was a secret enemy of Stern, as later events were to show.

The name of the Tank Supply Department was now dropped and Stern became Director-General of the Department of Mechanical War Supply, with Bussell, an Admiralty civil servant, and Captain Holden as his Deputies. It was a distinction without a difference. The War Office remained the customer and the Ministry of Munitions the shop. Tritton got a well-deserved knighthood early in 1917 but, though Stern tried very hard on his behalf, Wilson got nothing. Later he was given

A Mk I Tank ditched.

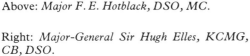

Above: *Major F. E. Hotblack, DSO, MC.*

Right: *Major-General Sir Hugh Elles, KCMG, CB, DSO.*

a CMG, the reward of the rear-rank diplomat. Stern pointed out in a letter that, in addition to being the technical brain behind the tank, Wilson had given up a lucrative engineering career for the pittance paid to a junior officer. The answer came back from the Admiralty on 20 March, 1917, that 'Sir Edward Carson is of opinion that there is no sufficient reason to give special prominence to Lieut Wilson's share in the design of the Tank'. He was given a half-promise of consideration for membership of the newly-created and widely despised Order of the British Empire. Wilson disdained money – he could have become a millionaire had he wished it – and had no ambition to become an OBE. Stern was given the more respectable CMG in the same list as Wilson. It probably amused him.

Swinton now disappeared from the scene, being posted back to the Committee of Imperial Defence; d'Eyncourt, with a KCB, became Chief Technical Adviser, jointly with Sir Charles Parsons of turbine fame. Tritton was director of Construction and Wilson Director of Engineering. Hugh Elles got the command in France and General Anley, an under-appreciated man who had commanded a Brigade at Mons, took over the tanks at home. It was Anley who moved the Corps from

Thetford to an unblasted heath at Wool in Dorset.

Stern was busier than ever. It looked as if he would never get a better engine for his tanks than the converted tractor affair that had been in general use so far. The other great difficulty was the transmission. Here Stern made a false step. He had been much taken by the petrol-electric system used in the French St Chamond machine, 'for it gave greater ease in changing speed, though at the price of greater weight'. Off his own bat he gave orders to the Daimler Company for the making of 600 sets, even though the thing was untried in England. The last months of 1916 and the first of 1917 were critical for the Heavy Branch. Whatever Sir Douglas might have said, the decisions did not lie with him and the tank had powerful enemies. Every time it seemed that a better engine might be available the Royal Flying Corps staked a claim on it and there was no denying that priority for the RFC came first. All the supplies of aluminium and high-tensile steel were earmarked for the flying service and Daimlers refused point-blank to take on any new designs. They were far too busy with more important customers.

The last public appearance of the tanks before winter closed in came in the middle of November; two of them were put in on the 14th to help with the attack on Beaumont-Hamel. Both got as far as the German front-line trench and there they stuck fast. As their guns were still able to bear they kept up a brisk fire until 400 Germans emerged with their hands up. They were rather an embarrassment until infantry arrived to take them away. Four days later, in the attack on The Triangle, an important lesson in direction-finding was rubbed home. Captain Hotblack, already a name of power in tank circles, had marked out the route overnight with white tape. By morning it was invisible under the snow. Hotblack calmly walked in front, bullets whistling and cracking round him, and led the solitary machine straight on to its first objective. That taken, he repeated the performance until the tank became bogged. Only Hotblack's nearly miraculous survival had made the task possible. In future a better way would have to be found.

Mr Tritton, meanwhile, had been busy with his drawing instruments. The first design must surely have been influenced by Stern. It was for a huge machine shaped like 'Mother' but carrying a dome of armour some two inches thick and driven by a pair of Daimler engines. Its estimated weight was something in the order of a hundred tons. Stern always thought big; in Hitler's War he spent a lot of time demanding that tankers displacing 100,000 tons be built. The 'Flying Elephant', as Tritton's new brain-child was nicknamed, never got beyond the drawing board. Which is hardly surprising. With the Elephant stillborn, he turned his attention to something entirely his own, a variant on his original trench-crosser. It was not, however, primarily intended to cross trenches, for it was something much lighter and faster than any of 'Mother's' brood. He called it the Chaser, for that was to be its function. The design was not of a rhomboid shape but resembled more closely the tanks of a later day. The tracks went only round the chassis and, as with the Elephant, each had its own engine. The choice fell upon the 50 hp Tylor, a well-tried piece of machinery much used in Army lorries and some LGOC omnibuses. At the rear end stood a small armoured shed from which three light machine-guns poked out. It was to be steered by a wheel, to carry a crew of three, to weigh only 12 tons – half the weight of 'Mother' – and it ought to manage a speed of 7 mph in reasonable going. The Chaser would be the new cavalry, not calling for a lot in the way of man-power but capable of moving fairly fast and hitting harder than any number of horsemen could do. Wilson reckoned it 'a sound job'.

The Heavy Branch had gone into the Somme battles with great reluctance. Only an unwillingness to let down the infantry at a time when they were taking a terrible hammering had persuaded the pioneers to let loose their young men at all on a venture that promised so badly. Nobody needed to be told that the Daimler engine, designed for quite different purposes, was not suitable. As it was the only kind available that was even worth trying they had put up with it despite all shortcomings; search for something better had never ceased but only in October, 1916, did some glimmer of hope appear.

Tritton discovered it, purely by accident. In the course of his pre-war commercial business he had made the acquaintance of a young engineer named Harry Ricardo who had invented a two-stroke motor, named the Dolphin, and had produced a number of them from a small factory at Shoreham. Ricardo, though barely 30, came from a long line of engineers, and was kin to the Ricardos of Gatcombe Park in Gloucestershire. As he himself put it, 'It had been my good fortune to have been on intimate terms with the petrol engine since its first appearance in England.' At the beginning of the war Ricardo had worked with Commander Briggs on engines for a flying-boat but Briggs' untimely death from pneumonia had brought this to an end. It was in the late Spring of 1916 that Tritton, knowing Ricardo to have had experience of railway work, sought him out to advise on a matter relating to the moving of tanks on to the railway trucks that had been designed for them. One thing led to another and Ricardo soon found himself an honorary member of Squadron 20. There he met Stern, whom he soon came greatly to admire, and the rest of the founder-members. In this capacity he attended a trial at Wolverhampton and was shocked at what he found. Apart from its insufficient power, the lubrication of the engine was very faulty; the troughs in which the big-ends dipped failed to produce any oil when cocked up at an angle. The sleeve-valve system furnished no means of spreading oil circumferentially and only by applying oil generously to the outer sleeve could it be prevented from seizing up. This process carried oil into the exhaust port; the consequence was smoke being emitted at all times with dense clouds emerging as soon as the engine was 'revved' up after idling. This, of course, made all efforts at concealment futile.

Everybody agreed that a completely new design of engine was needed; this would be easier said than done since all the regular motor manufacturers already had their hands full with work for the RFC on top of the ordinary lorry production. Ricardo, who had many professional friends, was sent to find out what help could be had. The great firms of Mirrlees, Bickerton & Day and Crossley both said that they could make a small number but that somebody else must first design the things. When Ricardo reported back, d'Eyncourt invited him to try his own hand at it. Ricardo was delighted; the subject was his absorbing interest and even though his

The Ricardo engine.

experience was limited his grasp of mechanical detail was equal to that of any man.

Mr Windeler of Mirrlees lent him two draughtsmen, named Ferguson and Holt, and the three got down to work in the office of Ricardo's grandfather's firm. Wilson, the transmission expert, advised that the existing clutches and gearboxes would not be able to cope with anything bigger than 150 hp. The firms approached by Ricardo when the engine design was ready - seven of them in all - said that they could between them put together two or three hundred. By Armistice Day they had made well over 8,000; not all, however, went into tanks.

At the beginning of October, 1916, while a few Mk Is were still floundering in the Somme marshes, the Mk IV was in existence as a prototype and the Mk V with Wilson's transmission and Ricardo's engine was on the drawing-board. Ricardo took a pre-war experimental engine of his own, employing a cross-head type piston which had proved very effective for oil control. The air on its way to the carburettors was made to circulate around the crosshead guides and under the piston crown, raising the air temperature around the carburettor just enough to effect proper carburation of the wretched petrol of about 45 octane that the tanks were obliged to use. By March, 1917, the first engine was running on the test bed. At the end of April Mirrlees had turned out the first production model; so well had his people done their work that it exceeded its designed 150 hp, putting out 168 at its governed speed of 1200 rpm and just over 200 at 1600 rpm. By summer the consortium was making about forty engines each week. Wilson had not yet completed his new gear-box and a few Ricardo engines were therefore put into existing Mk IVs. In the first half of June all the work was finished and the first Mk V was put through its paces at the Dollis Hill testing ground. It worked well, amazingly well considering the shortness of the time given to it. The only complaint was that much of the exhaust was inside the hull and that it grew excessively hot during running. A metal jacket was added and this seemed to work well enough during the routine tests carried out by Squadron 20. Much encouraged, Ricardo set to work on a 225 hp version.

However hopeful things might be looking in the factories and on the testing ground there was little cheer for what was called the Fighting Side in France as winter closed in and the Somme battles petered out. Nor were things going well for Stern. As already mentioned, he had been over-impressed by the petrol-electric system of the St Chamond. As he was not an engineer but possessed of daemonic energy he pushed ahead with other ideas on his own initiative and without the backing of the professional experts. Anything seemed worth trying, however long a shot it might be, for there was always the possibility that something might turn out better than expected. In addition to ordering the Daimler petrol-electric machine he approached Mr Mertz, the greatest authority in this country on electric traction, and demanded an attempt at a better means of propulsion based upon that used by the ordinary London tram. Vickers were pressed into service to build a Williams-Janney hydraulic transmission, the Hele-Shaw Company were told to produce something similar and Metropolitan to make, in addition to Wilson's gearbox, a multi-clutch device designed by a Mr Wilkins. These side-shows destroyed any chance there might have been of getting back again on good terms with Wilson.

In France the tanks had been removed from the Loop and given a home of their own in and around the empty château of Bermicourt near St Pol. Baker-Carr was invited to take command of one of the new tank battalions about to be formed and, his work with the machine-guns being pretty well finished, he accepted with delight. Elles, a couple of years his junior in the Army List of long ago, had twice formed up to Sir Douglas with the suggestion that Baker-Carr should command the about-to-be-formed Tank Corps with himself as chief staff officer. Sir Douglas, whilst appreciating his motives, was quite firm about it. Lieut-Col Baker-Carr had not been to the Staff College; there was, therefore, no more to be said about it. Baker-Carr, probably rightly, said that it was a good job. His forte was the making of something out of nothing and he was regarded in the higher circles as a buccaneer. Elles was a better organizer and doors at GHQ opened to him which would have been slammed in the face of the other. The two men got on extremely well together. One fortunate result of chivalrous behaviour was that it left the post of Chief of Staff open and the man who above all others was born to fill it happened to be available – Lieut-Col J. F. C. Fuller, commonly called 'Boney'.

All the same it is interesting to speculate about what might have happened had the command gone to Baker-Carr. Like Elles, he only held the rank of Lieut-Colonel

Lieut.-Col. J. F. C. Fuller,
CB, CBE, DSO.

but he was no run-of-the-mill professional field officer. His years in civil life had removed some of the scale that must form over the eyes during the encapsulated life of the regular soldier. Elles was young for his rank and had no particular claim to recognition. Baker-Carr knew, and was known by, all the important men and they had a wholesome respect for his tongue. Wavell, no bad judge, wrote of him as 'of very independent and outspoken views'. He would have been less trammelled by the fetish of 'loyalty', which so often means acquiescing in the decisions of a senior officer even when they are manifestly absurd; and nobody would have dared call him a 'croaker', not even 'Uncle' Harper. Elles, one may feel, was perhaps too disciplined a man to argue about orders for his tanks whatever his private reservations may have been. But this is, of necessity, speculation.

By November, 1916, the Heavy Branch had acquired some young officers of outstanding merit. Hotblack had given proof of the rarest kind of courage and was to do so over and over again. Captain Giffard le Quesne Martel was another such, but although a DSO and a MC testify to his gallantry it is as a thinker that he is remembered.

CHAPTER 8

Evil Days

THE PAPER, called *A Tank Army*, was written at Bermicourt in November, 1916, the same month during which Mr Churchill was setting out his own ideas in the more famous thoughts on mechanical warfare, *Variants Of The Offensive*. Though it went out over one signature the Bermicourt manifesto was actually the work of five thinkers, Elles, Fuller, Hotblack and Uzielli – head of Tank Corps 'Q' Branch – in addition to the signatory Martel. They prophesied as the shape of things to come Battle Tanks, Destroyer Tanks, Sapper Tanks and even Ambulance Tanks, all of them rattling along at 20 mph or better. The Battle Tank would carry nothing less than a 12″ howitzer and all would be not merely amphibious but screw-driven for river crossings. Fuller admitted, years later, that it was only done to clear their minds. Some of the prophecies were fulfilled during the prophets' lifetimes, but Martel, for one, was to modify his ideas as time went by.

While Bermicourt lucubrated, Stern was having his work cut out to keep up supplies even of the outmoded Mk Is. Constant demands from both sides of the Channel for changes in specification, some trivial but others quite important, kept the factories from maintaining the smooth production runs that the builders wanted to see. Squadron 20, still dressed as sailors and technically part of the Naval Air Service, was preserved in existence after the other original Armoured Car Squadrons were disbanded for testing machines as they came out of the factories and for shipping them to France; about half the Squadron became permanently based at Le Havre. The naval antecedents of one early optional extra for tanks suggest that the squadron had some hand in it. All larger warships were equipped with anti-torpedo netting which hung around them as farmers hang netting around their raspberries. The nets were carried outboard and supported on cigar-shaped wooden spars about six feet long; these, some minor genius discovered, could be attached to tank tracks and, thanks to the lozenge shape and lack of turrets, could pass right round the hull and give quite a lot of help when stuck in the mud. They became a standard issue; not an answer, but better than nothing. It was as well for the Heavy Branch that there was a lapse of months after Beaumont-Hamel until the next battle. Even if 'Uncle' Harper, now commanding 51st (Highland) Division, and his peers did not reckon much of the tanks, men like Hotblack were building up a tremendous esprit de corps inside the new arm of the service. Instead of dreaming about tank armies yet to come they trained their new crews extremely hard. Next time it would be different.

Stern went to and fro between London and Bermicourt, with visits to GHQ at Montreuil. He had a little to tell Elles for his comfort, but not much. By the end of November there wre 150 tailless Mk Is in being; the factories were working on 100 more, in addition to fifty of the Mk II, with spuds on the track plates, designed for but not fitted with better armour, and fifty Mk IIIs whose only difference was that the armour was slightly thicker still. The Mk IV, the subject of the 1,000 order, was in plan form. It looked much the same and had – for want of anything else – the same engine but there were important differences. The petrol tank was to be at the back, the shoes wider, the armour better and, above all, the sponsons were to be made so that they could be stowed inboard when travelling by train. Solomon's glories were abandoned for a mud-brown colour. It had a compensating weakness. Some expert – Stern calls him 'an officer of the Tank Corps who had once been in charge of the Lewis Gun School at St Omer' – insisted that the slim and light Hotchkiss gun should be supplanted by the tubby Lewis.

Apart from a bulkiness that limited its ability to traverse and was vulnerable to damage from small arms fire, the Lewis had a drawback that made it quite unsuitable for tanks. The ingenious and effective cooling system relies upon an aluminium radiator casing which maintains a steady flow of air during firing as the gases following the bullet are drawn from rear to front through the flanges. When the rear of the gun is mounted inside a hot, fume-laden tank the process goes into reverse, squirting a stream of burnt cordite gas straight into the gunner's face. Every tank man learnt this within a minute or so. Stern left it on record that 'The Tank Corps told us that they could not go into battle with the Lewis gun in the front loophole, and that until we could make the necessary alterations to put back the Hotchkiss gun no Tank actions could be fought'. Nevertheless the Lewis gun remained. One cannot help wondering what Baker-Carr would have done; probably a short drive to Montreuil to get Sir Douglas out of his bath if necessary.

The litany of hopes deferred went on. At the November, 1916, meeting, in the presence of General Davidson from GHQ, General Anley and Elles, Stern announced that the first Mk IV would be ready in January and, if the order were confirmed, the whole lot should be available by September. He then mentioned Tritton's 'Chaser', whose son was to become the famous Whippet. Davidson and Elles liked the idea; Stern asked for a quick decision so that he might order 500 engines. There seems no reason, apart from the usual blowings hot and cold by the War Office, why at any rate some Whippets should not have been at Cambrai. But Cambrai, in November, 1917, was a full year away.

On the last day of 1916 Colonel Elles, no doubt with the benefit of advice from Baker-Carr, Hotblack and Martel, wrote a long minute about the unsatisfactory situation: 'The fighting organization is under a junior officer who, faute de mieux, has become responsible for initiating all important questions of policy, design, organization and personnel through GHQ France and thence through five different branches at the War Office. In England administrative and training organization are under a senior officer located 130 miles from the War Office (Anley, at Wool) with a junior Staff Officer (Staff Captain) in London to deal with the five branches above mentioned.... In actual fact, the Director-General of Mechanical Warfare Supply, an official of the Ministry of Munitions, at the head of a very energetic body, becomes the head of the whole organization. This officer, owing to his lack of military knowledge, requires and desires guidance, which none of the five departments at the War Office can, and which the GOC Administrative Centre is not in a position to give him. In effect the tail in France is trying to wag a very distant and headless dog in England.'

January, 1917, was a month of great importance for the future of the tank. Stern, as has been mentioned before, had been much attracted by the petrol-electric transmission used by the St Chamond. Back in September, 'all the experts were against me, but later in the year GHQ made such urgent demands for Tanks that, in order not to lose time, I gave orders to the Daimler Company on January 5th 1917 for 600 sets of petrol-electric gear... The machine had not yet been tested, but this was to prevent any delay should the trial machine be a success.'

It was not. A test was carried out on 12 January 'and the result clearly showed that the Daimler Petrol Electric was unable to pull out of a shell hole except by a succession of jolts, produced by bringing the brushes back to a neutral position, raising the engine up to 1800 rpm and then suddenly shifting the brushes up to the most advantageous position.... All agreed that it was unsatisfactory. So after a great controversy and many tests the Petrol Electric engine was rejected as untrustworthy and all orders were cancelled.' Stern came in for bitter criticism from Wilson for having thus disrupted the entire year's programme. Wilson had been with him in France and had watched the show. His view was uncompromising: 'The large French machine (petrol-electric) could put up no performance whatever.' Had this happened a year earlier when Stern and Wilson were still friends the engineer would probably have been able to talk the amateur out of his over-enthusiasm. By December, 1916, however, they were hardly on speaking terms. Wilson seems to have felt that the responsibility lay with the Head of the Department and if he wanted to do something silly he could get on with it. Stern's cavalier behaviour of the previous summer still rankled.

Later in the same month Elles sent an officer to Stern in order to get firm figures of deliveries of new machines. Stern declined to be drawn; there were, he said, too many imponderables. Though he made no promises, he did give an estimate of twenty to thirty a week after the end of March. GHQ was now pressing for as many tanks as possible before May, adding that 'almost any design now is better than no tank'. Obviously some new battle was being planned for the Spring. Stern knew nothing of Haig's intentions but Bermicourt did. Elles sent for Baker-Carr in February and told him that 'there's going to be an attack by the Third Army in front of Arras about the 9th or 10th of April'. C and D Battalions, the Somme veterans, were to be made into the First Tank Brigade and Baker-Carr was to command it.

On 3 March, 1917, Stern put on another performance in order to show how much the tank had improved since 'Mother's' first appearance just over a year before. This time it was to be at Oldbury, Birmingham, and once again the arrangements were to be made by Squadron 20, now charged with the testing of every tank before it was shipped to France. About a hundred spectators were invited, including a strong French contingent under General (as he now was) Estienne. Seven machines were to be put through their paces. First came the standard Mk IV, the tank which would win immortality at Cambrai. It was not all that different from 'Mother' except for its thicker armour, shorter guns, and sponsons designed to swing inboard for rail travel. Top speed was still no more than 4 mph. Next to appear was Tritton's Chaser, the 12-ton cavalry substitute with a speed of $7\frac{1}{2}$ mph and a single light machine-gun. Wilson says that 'It put up a fine performance and showed a good turn of speed and quick manoeuvre'. Then came a Mk II fitted with the Williams-Janney hydraulic transmission which did away with the necessity for any clutch or gear-box at all. To quote Wilson again, 'This machine showed great ease of control, but could not be produced in quantity and developed some faults in continuous running that were not overcome until late in 1917.' It was not until 1918 that three British tanks, originally Mk IVs, were made to this specification by Brown Bros in Edinburgh; they were not a success.

There followed the star of the show, a Mk IV containing Wilson's greatest gift to mechanized warfare, the epicyclic gear-box. His comments are not vainglorious but strictly factual: 'It was obvious that this was the most practical solution of the difficulties and this machine ran the remarkable distance of 300 miles on test without serious mechanical trouble. This arrangement was adopted in the Mk V and all subsequent machines.'

The next performer was the one upon which Stern had misguidedly pinned his faith, the Daimler Petrol Electric. The power unit was 'a six-cylinder Daimler engine fitted with aluminium pistons and a lighter flywheel.' The transmission was described in the Programme: 'A single generator coupled direct with the engine supplies current to two motors in series. The independent control of each motor is accomplished by shifting the brushes. Each motor drives through a two-speed gear-box to a worm reduction gear and from thence through a further gear reduction to the sprocket wheels driving the road chain driving wheels. A differential lock is obtained by connecting the two worm wheel shafts to a dog clutch.' Wilson says dismissively that 'This machine had not sufficient tractive effort to pull out of shell holes.'

Of the last two competitors one, the Wilkins Multiple Clutch machine, 'had trouble and did not compete'. Charles Mertz's entry, the Westinghouse Petrol Electric, 'put up a good performance but the transmission was so heavy and occupied so much space that it was not a practical proposition.' Stern's effort to go it alone had failed. Mention has already been made of the notes made by Wilson in the copy of Stern's book that he presented to Major Buddicum. One of them, dealing with p. 167, reads thus: 'The History of design during 1917 is as follows. After the failure of the Daimler Petrol Electric and the cancellation of the 800 order for same (Stern says it was 600) which order was given against the advice of Major Wilson and Mr

Inside a nearly finished Mk I at the Metropolitan Works.

Tritton, the construction of Mk IV was hurried on; this was undoubtedly right as it was the only machine that could be constructed to be of any value in 1917, but a new design should have been prepared so that construction for 1918 could be commenced in good time.... A machine was designed by the Metropolitan Company embodying Wilson's epicyclic gear and the above conditions (machine-guns in preference to 6-pdrs). This machine was known as the Mk VI. A machine was also designed on the general lines of Mother, but using the epicyclic gear and other improvements in transmission and tracks and heavier armour. This machine was known as the Mk V. Mock-ups of both these machines were inspected at Birmingham on 23 June and met with general approval. Mk VI was inspected again on 13 July and passed but subsequently Col Stern and Sir Eustace d'Eyncourt expressed their disapproval of both machines and no further work was done on them.' Wilson does not explain the reason for this sudden condemnation.

'Requirements were completely changed and the general scheme of a small machine known as Medium B was drawn out and submitted on 30 July. No action was taken until 21 August when Mr Watson was placed in charge of the design of this machine.... Thus we see that in September, 1917, MWD had no designs embodying the improvements dictated by experience ready to place in the hands of the manufacturers. The position was still further complicated in that MWD was torn by internal dissension, the original members of the staff having unfortunately lost that great feeling of respect and admiration for Lieut [sic] Stern's energy and driving force with which he so inspired them in 1915 and the earlier part of 1916.' 'It was under these sad conditions that at last on the 5th October an order was placed with the Metropolitan Company to design under Major Wilson and construct a machine embodying epicyclic control and the 150 hp Ricardo engine, but it was then too late to embody all possible improvements as quantity production had to be commenced as each detail was decided upon, and over £2,000,000 of material ordered before the drawings were complete.... Although the order was only placed on the 5th October, 1917, the first machine was completed in January, 1918. Ten were completed in February and nearly 100 in March. This machine was known as the Mark V and proved of great service in 1918.' Had the designers and manufacturers been less rushed, a serious defect which will appear later might have been avoided. Stern came in for a lot of blame, but he seems to have been unlucky. He went back to France in April, lunching with Mr Lloyd George at the Crillon, and his diary for the 19th includes an entry saying, 'Spent Saturday at St Chamond and saw our Tanks, fitted with their petrol-electric transmission, ascend a hill of 55°.' It looked as if they really did manage some things better in France, but the machine was still not reckoned good enough and was swiftly dropped.

There was yet another lost opportunity. At the demonstration there was shown the first tank designed to carry a field gun or even a medium artillery piece, the model of which fifty had been ordered in June, 1916. Wilson remarks that 'It is of interest to note that when Major Wilson stated that either a 5-inch 60-pdr or a 6-inch howitzer cold be fired from this machine his assertion was derided by most of the members of the Ordnance Committee but both guns were successfully fired from the machine at Shoeburyness, the amount of movement being accurately forecast in both cases.' Self-propelled artillery would have been of enormous value during the last battles of 1918; thanks to the unbelievers it was never used. Nor was it in 1940.

Back at Bermicourt, having seen all these shapes of things to come, Colonels Elles, Courage, Hardress-Lloyd and Searle waited for the arrival of some more Mk Is or Mk IIs. It was the best they could hope for and whatever battles were to be fought in the Spring it would be these obsolete machines that would have to lead the way. They were not kept waiting long. The freezing cold and snow of March were followed by the freezing cold and snow of April at about the time the Mk IIs began to arrive. Joy soon gave way to horror. Not only did these lack the promised better armour, they lacked any armour at all. The hulls were of mild steel boiler-plate, incapable of keeping out so much as a pistol bullet. Some of the hulls had perforations for the fitting of a second skin at some future time, but this was never done. The explanation was pretty clear. U-boat sinkings had reached proportions that might easily have lost us the war. Every square inch of armour was needed by

Gun-carrying Tank equipped with the 60-pdr. medium gun.

Rear view of the same, with wheels. These were later removed.

the Navy to build new fast submarine-killers. Nor was this all. April, 1917, was the worst month of the war for the Royal Flying Corps. Before it was out 151 British machines had fallen to the guns of Germany's new Albatros and Halberstadt fighters. The RFC, whose pilots had an expectation of life then of twenty-one days, did at least have the consolation of knowing that the SE5 and the Bristol fighter, aircraft that would soon redress the balance, were coming into squadron service. The Heavy Branch seemed to be moving backwards. On the wider stage two events dominated. Russia, if not yet out, was down and only small German forces would henceforth be needed in the East. The strains of 'Over There' could, indeed, be detected on the west wind but Uncle Sam was virtually unarmed and his sons untrained. It would be long before they could much affect the military balance.

Meanwhile General Robert Nivelle had a plan. His *attaque brusquée* that had served so well at Verdun was going to be repeated on the grand scale towards the Chemin des Dames. The General had immense confidence in it, a confidence shared by nobody else. The British Army, having narrowly escaped being put under his command, was to contribute with an attack by Allenby's Third Army. In accordance with French practice exact details of the whole business had been broadcast through the customary network of wives and mistresses of those planning it. The fact that the Germans had withdrawn from the untidy positions which events had forced upon them, as it had also upon the Allies, to a new and carefully prepared trench system called the Hindenburg Line made no difference to Nivelle. Allenby was to strike first, on 9 April, his job being to take the entire line of Vimy Ridge. Sixty tanks, mostly survivors of the Somme plus the bogus Mk IIs which had never been intended for other than training, were to take part.

Unless Stern had greatly deceived himself, the use of these machines showed some lack of honesty at GHQ. On 12 March he had written to Dr Addison that 'I have persistently opposed the premature employment of Tanks this year. Also the employment of practice Tanks, i.e. Marks I, II and III in action this year. At the War Office Meeting last Sunday General Butler assured me that sixty machines of Mark I, II and III, which are being kept in France ready for action only as a temporary measure and which are really practice machines, will be returned for training purposes as soon as they can be replaced by the delivery of Mark IV machines. I consider it more than unwise to use practice Tanks in action under *any* circumstances. They have all the faults that necessitated the design of last year being altered.... Their failure will undoubtedly ruin the confidence of the troops in the future of Mechanical Warfare.' He was right.

Baker-Carr, who accorded Allenby an admiration he withheld from most Generals, was at the pre-battle conference. The tank part in it was necessarily subordinate to that of the traditional arms and once again they were to be employed in small packets. Given the equipment available it could hardly have been otherwise. Allenby took Baker-Carr aside after the others had gone and 'told me how confident he was that tanks would prove of great value'. Baker-Carr went the rounds of the Divisional Commanders and heard other views: 'Several seemed to think that tanks could travel at twenty miles an hour and, starting a long way behind the infantry, could catch them up before reaching the first objective.... One of them steadfastly refused to allow a tank to come within a thousand yards of his front line until zero hour, in case the Germans might hear it (amid the roar of a thousand guns, be it remembered) and suspect that an attack was about to be made.' Baker-Carr affected to agree but arranged that his tanks should actually move at the same time as the infantry. When all was over the General – he is not named – wrote to thank him.

Everything militated against a success for the Heavy Branch. To begin with it rained in torrents and bogged down all the machines waiting in the moat of the old Arras Citadel from which they were due to move off at 5.30 am. The materials ordered for construction of a causeway did not arrive. By superhuman efforts a number of tanks were got on to the start line; then it began to snow. By late morning the last had been extricated and they joined the infantry; this section did very useful work in clearing out German strong-points. Those allotted to the Canadians, however, achieved nothing. The ground leading up to Vimy Ridge was sodden by the rain and not a single tank out of the eight put in an appearance.

There were, however, bright spots. The Mk II tank 'Lusitania', commanded by Lieut Weber, having squashed one machine-gun nest, went on towards a German trench closely followed by the infantry; so closely indeed that Weber could not use his 6-pdrs for fear of hitting friends. It did not matter. The moral effect was enough and the occupants emerged with hands above their heads. 'Lusitania' then moved on to the Feuchy redoubt which it smashed up with gunfire as the enemy made off. They went to ground in a dug-out by a railway arch with Weber on their heels. Then came an odd incident. With shells, possibly British, falling all round them Weber sensibly decided to move back a little. This involved climbing a steep bank which the over-heated engine refused to take. The crew, drowsy with the fumes of cordite and petrol, took the opportunity of having a quiet sleep in the middle of the battle until the engine had cooled down. As soon as it started 'Lusitania' was off again, passing through the infantry, flattening more wire and chasing the garrison from another redoubt. Later in the day the magneto failed; by then it was 9.30 pm and the petrol was nearly exhausted. With shells dropping all around them and machine-gun bullets splashing uncomfortably close, Weber brought his crew out and joined up with the nearest infantry. In the morning he set out alone and returned with a new magneto, to be greeted by a battery commander apologizing for having fatally shelled his tank. So perished 'Lusitania'. Weber earned his MC and Sergeant Latham his MM.

Baker-Carr had had an abominable day waiting by a telephone for messages that never came or arrived garbled. 'In the small hours of the morning Elles and Fuller arrived with the appalling news that most of the tanks had got stuck whilst leaving their "lying-up" place. I do not know whether I wept, but I felt like it. It seemed so cruel after all the thought and care that we had lavished on our preparations.' It was not everywhere a tale of failure. Those messages that got through were for the most part encouraging: 'We have reached Z22 B64 and are going strong'. 'Have taken Tilloy village'; '900 prisoners scared and starved morale rotten'; a tank named Daphne claimed to have reached the Blue Line. Allenby's army had won a demonstrable victory and the Heavy Branch had certainly saved many infantry lives. One lesson had been taught: never to take unreconnoitred short cuts, no matter how alluring. One group of six machines made a path of railway sleepers and brushwood in order to circumvent what looked an unsafe way by the Crinchon stream. Underneath and invisible lay a morass into which all of them cascaded. It took many hours of blasphemous work to have them dug out, too late to play the parts given them.

Arras had been rather a poor day for the tanks but two days later came Bullecourt. This time it was the turn of 4th Australian Division to do the dirty work. To make it easier they were given eleven Mk I and II tanks, all of the kind described by Stern as 'practice'. The infantry commanders, after the last battle, were none too keen about it, for men unaccustomed to tank work had tended to bunch around them and had accordingly drawn very heavy fire upon themselves.

Not a single tank survived the opening attack. Dazzle painting had been abandoned as useless and all were now in the standard mud-brown. Against the snow it showed up admirably, from the standpoint of the German gunners. As they moved slowly forwards nine were picked off almost at once, one of them having come to a halt with clutch trouble. The armour in which they had trusted proved useless. Even small arms fire riddled the hulls. Two more disappeared into the blue heading towards Hendecourt with a party of Australians following behind. Neither tanks nor Diggers were seen again. Two tanks were trooped in slow time through Berlin shortly afterwards and they may have been these. It is hardly wonderful that the Germans were not moved to build tanks for themselves on the evidence of such death-traps. One tank, commanded by Lieut Money, seems to have reached the German wire before a direct hit from a field gun set it ablaze. All the crews who were not too badly wounded did as they always did on these occasions. They took whatever weapons they could find, Lewis guns or even revolvers, and joined up with whoever could make use of them. All the same, when an Australian Brigadier told Major Watson that 'tanks were no damned use' he could hardly argue. Still less could he explain how scurvily his Corps had been treated.

The strangest episode of all was at Monchy-le-Preux. The village, on top of a hill, was the target for six tanks in support of the 15th (Scottish) and 37th Divisions who were to move off at 5 am on 11 April. Two tanks broke down in the darkness, one became ditched but the remaining three ploughed on through the snow. Of our infantry there was no sign. As dawn broke and the ungainly shapes presented a perfect target for German gunners the three subalterns conferred. They must go either forward or back and it was surely right to go forward even though alone. The three drove into Monchy, shot their way down its only street and came out at the far end. Germans, seeing them to be unsupported, emerged from their hidey-holes and re-occupied the place. The tanks swung round to face a barrage of small arms fire and were also pelted with grenades. For an hour and a half they fought it out until a barrage came down and knocked out all of them. They were British shells. Nobody had thought to tell the tank commander that the attack had been put back by two hours. The infantry had to make a fresh start and had a hard battle to retake the place. Not to be outdone, a cavalry squadron, kept as usual for the 'breakthrough', staged a knee-to-knee charge. A little barbed wire and a few machine-guns cut them down. Colonel Bulkeley-Johnson was killed. No doubt it was the end he would have wished.

On 3 May came the last stab at the enormously strong Bullecourt position. This time the eight tanks employed all reached their objectives under very heavy fire. It was more than the infantry could manage to follow behind so few machines through such a barrage. One tank was riddled with armour-piercing bullets – it was, apparently, one of the training machines without proper protection – and five of the crew wounded. Five of the six Lewis guns were shattered, their big radiator casings being smashed. The remaining tanks turned round and came home. There was nothing more for them to do. Their brave and resourceful conduct brought the Heavy Branch another Military Cross, a DCM and a Military Medal.

One last, and significant, little action remained before the Arras battles passed into the history books. It happened at Roeux, a couple of miles north of Monchy where there stood a group of ruins called the Chemical Works. Guy Chapman, that fine soldier and writer, watched it. 'At every other hour, it seemed, a voice from division announced a further attack on the Chemical Works by the Highlanders. Each time they won it, and each time they were driven out. Our line lay waiting for them to finish. Every time they went in, they killed everything that was on the ground and each time, like dragon's teeth, the enemy sprang up again. The light died away without any alteration in the landscape. It had been another failure.' The Highlanders were 'Uncle' Harper's 51st Division. Baker-Carr's account is not quite the same: 'It was a hard-fought little battle and the infantry commanders were unable to speak too highly of the valuable assistance they received from the tanks. These reports were so eulogistic that I was much amused when the Divisional Commander in his report gave the entire credit of the successful action to the infantry and barely mentioned that fact that a tank had even been present. It was

The worst possible case. A Mk I firmly stuck.

not any lack of generosity that prompted this omission but "Uncle" adored his "Harper's Duds" and took good care that every single iota of praise should be bestowed upon them.' The 51st had been at Beaumont-Hamel before moving to the Arras front where they formed the left hand of the British attack; immediately on their own left was 4th Canadian Division. The Canadians complained afterwards that the 51st had failed to keep up with them, save for one platoon. This one remained all day attached to the Canadians while the rest of its brigade stayed in the wrong trench facing the wrong way, insisting all the time that it was in the right trench facing the right way. These things happen. It did not alter the fact that, to 'Uncle' Harper, everything 51st – 'my little fellers' he called them – did was perfection. Tanks, after what he had seen, were things they would have nothing to do with.

Ricardo meantime had been busy trying to improve their performance. One of the greatest handicaps was the low quality of the petrol allotted to tanks; they came last in the queue, after aircraft, staff cars and lorries. 'US Navy Gasoline', all that they were allowed, had what would now be called a 45 octane rating; this made it better than kerosene, but not much. Ricardo, invited to a high-level committee meeting on the subject, spoke of all this and asked whether he might have benzole. Asked why, he explained that it was not inclined to detonate, would thus allow him to raise his compression ratio and greatly improve performance. Nobody seemed quite to understand. The Chairman, Sir Robert Waley-Cohen, was Managing Director of Shell. He took Ricardo aside and asked for more information. The result was that half-a-dozen drums of petrol were sent from Shell Haven for Ricardo to test. They all seemed much of a muchness except for one that was far and away the best. Further examination showed it to contain an exceptional proportion of aromatics, which explained its good performance and high specific gravity. When Shell were asked about it they found it to come from an oilfield in Borneo; because its specific gravity was so high it met no specification and tens of thousands of tons were being burned to waste in the jungle. Waley-Cohen soon put a stop to this, but it would be a long time before the tanks got a superior brand of fuel.

Arras had, at least, been better than the Somme. Allenby issued a special Army Order praising the Tanks; Sir Aylmer Haldane, whose good opinion was worth having, even though he consistently refused to allow a rum ration and whose Corps had been the most closely connected with the operations, was 'outspoken in his gratitude'. Only Sir Beauvoir de L'Isle (now GOC 29th Division) was against them. In his opinion – and it was an informed opinion – if infantry once became used to tanks they would refuse to fight without them. This could not be dismissed.

The bits and pieces of the First Brigade moved back to Wailly, to refit and rearm in readiness for whatever might be around the corner.

General Nivelle's offensive, which began on the 16th, ended in utter failure. A noticeable part of the French Army mutinied or came very near to mutiny. Nothing beyond clinging to existing trenches could be expected from that quarter for a long time to come.

CHAPTER 9

Mud and Blood

IT WAS TIME ONCE MORE to take stock of the position and status of the tanks. On 24 April, 1917, Stern had another of his meetings with Sir Douglas Haig and General Butler, this time in the garden of a house in the Rue Gloriette at Amiens. They talked for half an hour. Stern, fresh from Paris where he had seen Mr Lloyd George – now, of course, Prime Minister – and General Estienne at the Quai d'Orsay had a good deal to say about production problems. He found a sympathetic audience. Sir Douglas said that he would do anything to help, for he reckoned a division of tanks worth ten divisions of infantry. Stern was to hurry up and send to France all the tanks he could muster. He was 'not to wait to perfect them but to keep sending out imperfect ones as long as they came out in large quantities especially up to the month of August.' Tanks, after aeroplanes, said the Field-Marshal, were the most important arm in the British Army. They were 'such a tremendous life-saver'.

Stern spoke of his difficulties with the War Office. Who, demanded Haig, was there in Whitehall who did not believe in tanks? Stern gave a straight answer: 'The Adjutant-General's Department.' It was agreed that this must be stopped. Nobody tried; presumably the futility of any attempt was too well recognized.

Lack of enthusiasm was not limited to the War Office. The histories of most of the Divisions engaged in the battles of early April are pretty dismissive, and they run to a pattern. The 9th (Scottish) tells how 'the four tanks allotted to the Division were very unlucky. Two were put out of action at the start by artillery fire. A third broke down about 200 yards from the railway on the front of 27 Brigade and the fourth failed to reach the railway after the officer in command was killed.... South of the Scarpe a Tank did good service by helping to clear the Railway Triangle which had caused a great deal of trouble to the Fifteenth Division.' The 15th – also Scottish – make no mention of this; merely that 'a tank, whose commander's name does not appear in any Diary, was very skilfully and gallantly handled and was of great assistance in the capture of (Monchy).' The 12th, whose chronicler was its own GOC, General Scott, merely observes that 'the tanks which had been detailed to assist in the capture of (Feuchy Chapel Redoubt) were out of action, two having been set on fire by the enemy's guns and two having stuck in the mud.' Some histories do not mention tanks at all. No battle plan had depended upon them; they, if they turned up at all, could only be reckoned as a kind of bonus.

The best account of Bullecourt is to be found in Appendix XXIX to Major-General Sir Edward Spears' *Prelude To Victory*, written in 1936. Spears, in his liaison capacity, saw as much of the wide field of operations as one man could and reports of what he did not see came in to him. His views are firm: 'The extraordinary optimism of the tank commanders was undoubtedly an important factor in (Allenby's) decision (to attack). They apparently believed that orders could be issued, the ground reconnoitred and the machines brought up in the short time available before daylight next day; nor did they doubt the ability of the eleven tanks to open a way for the attacking infantry.' He speaks of 'uncertain monsters whose commander was as inexperienced as they were themselves unreliable at this stage of the war'. Birdwood, commanding the AIF, objected to the business, says Spears, but was over-ruled by the C-in-C. There was a false start; very early on a freezing morning the Australians of 4th Division moved out into the open and lay there waiting. No tanks arrived; only an exhausted officer to say that they were still an hour behind. The infantry moved back in the dawn light like a crowd leaving a football match. When the tanks did arrive their task was hopeless. 'While it was still dark their outline, it is said, could be seen by the sparks from the bullets that hit them. As soon as daylight revealed them stark and black against the white background every German gun concentrated upon them. They resembled moles scattered on a marble slab.... The tank crews had totalled 103 officers and men. Of these fifty-two were killed, wounded or missing. It is probable that with the possible exception of the tank that penetrated the Bullecourt defences, every one of the machines had been put out of action by 7 am.... The gross incompetence with which the tanks were handled was a serious and unjustified set-back to the new arm, for the Australians attributed their failure largely to them, a judgment true as regards this battle but misleading as a generalization.'

Spears tells of the tank crews. 'Bravery of a very high order', he calls it. 'They were the targets for every hostile gun, to such an extent that their neighbourhood was an inferno from which the infantry fled; the sides of their machines were pierced by armour-piercing bullets (one had seventy such bullets in it); they knew there was every prospect of burning like torches at any moment; yet they held on their way until their iron prisons broke down or caught fire. Of the eleven machines engaged nine received direct hits and two were missing.' It is hardly to be wondered at that 'Uncle' Harper and several of his peers wanted nothing more to do with tanks.

All this was mulled over again and again at Bermicourt. Bullecourt had been a disaster, but it was no fault of the Heavy Branch. Gough was widely, and on the whole justly, blamed for it. The irony of it all is that had the battle been fought a year later with a dozen Mk V tanks it would probably have been a famous victory and the General would have been lauded as the first man to understand the truth about mechanical warfare. The position was the same as if the *Merrimac* had been rammed and sunk by a wooden frigate and the inference drawn that ironclads were no good. It was all very well for GHQ to demand lots of tanks no matter how obsolete. This was not what the Heavy Branch had been created for. Martel's *Tank Army* paper of November, 1916, and Winston Churchill's treatise on mechanical

At Wool Training Centre. A ditched Mk I. Note discarded spar, soon replaced by unditching beam.

warfare, written at almost exactly the same moment, showed what ought to be done. It was not the provision of more moles on more slabs.

All Bermicourt could do was to ram home to the authorities at home what the Fighting Side needed. So far as Stern was concerned this was pushing on an open door. No man could have applied more pressure where it was needed, but results were slow to appear. By the end of April, however, the first Mk IVs began to trickle in.

This was the tank destined to carry the burden of battle all the way through until the end of the March Retreat in 1918. In appearance it was much like its predecessors, using the same Daimler engine because nothing better was available and the same clumsy transmission. Despite all that, it was a far more serviceable piece of equipment. The sponsons were so constructed that they could be pushed inside the hull during railway journeys, and this saved much labour. Track rollers and links, the causes of so many breakdowns, had been redesigned and were much heavier and stronger than before. The dangerous inside petrol tank had been transferred to the outside and was well armoured. It was, indeed, in its armour (produced by Hadfields) that the Mk IV was so much the superior of the old machines. Its range of action on a tank of petrol was still only about fifteen miles.

The Germans, it will be remembered, had captured two tanks at Bullecourt. This could hardly have been more advantageous to the Heavy Branch had they arranged it on purpose. The German 'K' bullets, henceforth to be issued to every foot-soldier and machine-gunner, would go through the sides of a Mk I or a Mk II with ease. When it came to hit the Mk IV it bounced off. Not only was this helpful to the occupants but it did nothing for the morale of men who confidently expected to be able to stop the monsters in their tracks. It was disheartening to find that the trusted 'K' rounds were useless.

At Bermicourt a Second Brigade came into being under command of Lieut-Colonel Anthony Courage, a forty-year-old cavalryman and, like so many others associated with the early tanks, an Old Rugbeian. Courage had been in France from the beginning, had been wounded at Second Ypres and had just finished a year on the Staff at GHQ. No better choice could have been made. The men for his new command were got together in the same way as before and it might be convenient to take a look at them in their early training.

General Anley had set up the depot for the Heavy Branch at Bovington Camp, near Wool in Dorset, where it still remains. The original A, B, C and D Companies had long since gone to France and from them came the first four battalions. The name 'Tank Corps' was not officially granted until July, 1917, but it had for some time been used in colloquial speech and may as well be adopted now. E and F Companies remained at Wool and, with the passage of time, grew into five more battalions. It had all begun in great secrecy, arrivals and departures all being by night until the visit of a neighbouring farmer spoilt everything. He explained that for the last couple of days he had been looking after a tank; it had broken down and he had towed it into his yard with his horses. Not that he was complaining, but the Army might like it back.

This was the place to which all aspirant officers were sent and where they were put through a pretty rigorous course of training. It was not always easy to assimilate the new skills; several classes in the internal combustion engine were held close to each other in the echoing hangar and, with several instructors trotting out their 'what we are going on with now is ...' simultaneously, it could be confusing. Especially to those who, as yet, did not know a magneto from a carburettor. All were, of course, taught to drive. The standard pleasantry when the novice, faced by a be-wildering assortment of levers, lost his head and pushed or pulled everything in sight was 'This is a tank, not a bloody signal-box'. One who was there has left an account of first impressions: 'After a time the prospective landship commander found his sea legs and began to know his way about his strange craft, and that same evening at twilight he had his first view of tanks returning after a day's work. It was a most impressive and fearsome sight. Over the brow of the hill, dimly outlined against the dusk, loomed a herd of strange toad-like monsters. The noise of whirring engines and the weird flap-flap-flap of the tracks, like the padding of gigantic webbed feet, filled the air. The vast snouts went up and up, and then suddenly dipped down abruptly as the creatures made for home. They made one shiver: they were so

Sponson with 6-pdr. gun dismantled for instruction.

repulsive, so inhuman, so full of menace. Even though there was no danger one felt fear creeping through one's veins. The impulse was to turn and run for dear life, but instead one stood there rooted with horror and admiration.'

Once inside it seemed another world. There was nowhere to stand up, and just room to move down the narrow gangways each side of the engine. When this had been cranked up, a job that took three or four men on the big starting handle, the din was beyond description. So was the smell. The strangest thing was to find that when everything was running nicely and the tank moving forward at a brisk pace men outside could be seen walking unhurriedly past. It was bad enough for the men in front; the gearsmen could see nothing, had no idea of what was happening or about to happen and soon learned that a careless grab for safety might be of a red-hot exhaust pipe. Like everything else in this world, people became used to it.

The pressure was merciless. The driver would be made to climb up what seemed a perpendicular cliff, stall his engine and restart by sliding backwards with the gears in reverse. They followed slalom courses marked by tapes, all turns, bends, climbs, drops and sunken road for good measure. Last came the 'swallow dive', a harsh test of nerve. The tank was driven up a small incline; at the top it rocked gently on the verge of a precipice. 'Now look down,' said the instructor. There was nothing to be seen but an apparently bottomless pit. Having digested that, the driver was told to back a little, change gear and go over the top. 'Keep your hand on the throttle, and don't forget directly you feel yourself falling, throttle down. Don't open out until the tracks hit the ground.' The instructor then climbed out.

'Slowly the tank went forward, inch by inch it crept over the top of the incline.... Suddenly the nose of the tank tilted forward and the huge machine went down, and down, and down. He had the sensation of dropping gently through space. The throttle was almost closed, the engine ticking over: without warning the tank plunged violently downwards and, with a terrific bump the snout struck the ground. The tank, for a second, practically stood on end. One of the gearsmen in the rear, taken unawares, was hurled clean out of the sponson door. The others clung wildly to anything within reach, their feet sliding and scraping over the steel floor. Grease drums, oil cans and stray tools shot forwards in a clattering mass, landing on the driver's back and spraying him with oil. The driver himself was at such an angle that he looked straight into the earth a couple of feet in front of his face. But the throttle was now opened out full and, as the engine raced, the caterpillar tracks gripped firmly and foot by foot the tank crawled up to the top of the crater. Then, slightly shaken but triumphant, the driver got out to watch the next tank go over.'

It was a relief to march in squads to Lulworth Cove for gunnery exercises. The targets were set up on the land side of a cliff and bombarded from across a valley. All was ingeniously worked out. The tank drove up and down with the gunner at the 6-pdr, his eye glued to its telescopic sight. Flashes, indicating battery positions, were made to come from the target area and it was the gunner's job to hit them. Add to this much map and compass work and the making of the kind of reconnaissance report that had once been a cavalry job, instruction in that handy but sometimes dangerous to friends weapon the Webley Mk VI ·455 revolver and much PT, and at the end you have a young officer trained to a degree that makes it hard to believe how the completely green crews managed the Somme battles as well as they did. Their skills may not have been great but their courage and determination shone like a beacon for the new men.

A month or so after the First Brigade had gone home, moderately well satisfied with its performance, it became clear that something was up. A detachment of tanks was set to practice climbing up what was demonstrably the model of a sea-wall. The explanation was that it represented a segment of the fortifications of Lille and few people bothered to question this. Unknown to most, a large contingent from 1st Division had been withdrawn from its positions around Nieupoort and was being introduced to the same thing. All the problems that were to bedevil the planners of D-Day presented themselves in the summer of 1917. Landing craft were built, ramps designed and the Belgian architect who had designed the sea defences between Nieupoort and Ostend was dug out and pressed into service.

The spot chosen for the attack was near Middlekerke. All the infantry battalions of 1st Division were moved back to a camp in the dunes at Le Clipon and wired firmly in, 1944 fashion. A number of pontoons 600 feet long by thirty in beam were built to Admiral Bacon's design; the plan was that these should each be pushed by a pair of shallow-draft monitors which should also act as troop transports. The architect explained that his concrete sea-wall had a gradient of one in two with an overhang at the top. Undeterred, the planners had a concrete model made at Merlimont, near Le Touquet. A few tanks were fitted with large wooden 'spuds' and each was given a detachable ramp on girders, carrying a pair of wheels. The ramp was to be lowered, pushed forward until the wheels touched the concrete and then heaved up against the coping and detached. That done, the tank would climb up it and head for the open country with foot and guns following behind. When they had collected themselves they would, in conjunction with an attack across the Yser by XV Corps, take over enough country to enable them to bombard Zeebrugge and deny its use as a submarine base. It was all a deadly secret and, for a change, it remained one.

The tanks proved capable of doing what was asked of them, at any rate in the absence of opposition. 1st Division trained hard and seriously but were never called upon to show what they had learnt. The rain pelted down, as it seemed to do throughout the awful year of 1917; on 10 July the Germans mounted a spoiling attack and the advance along the Pilckem Ridge which was to have sparked the operation off became bogged down. The scheme had to be abandoned. Knowing what we cannot help knowing about Dieppe it may be that we should not regret this. It would have been a very hazardous business and, as the St George's Day storming of Zeebrugge in 1918 was to show, the place was not all that important to the U-boat service. In addition the whole area was open to the traditional defence, inundation by breaching the dykes.

The First Tank Brigade continued at its home called Erin, just by Bermicourt, though the detached tanks did not rejoin until October. The next battle would give Second Brigade, still untried, a chance to show what it could do.

At home it was business as usual. Stern, having discovered Ricardo, wanted him to make 700 engines. General Henderson, for the RFC, demanded that this be stopped. Stern said acidly that he was bespeaking them in advance of requirements precisely in order to avoid being caught out with a shortage of engines for tanks 'such as they were now experiencing for aircraft'. The committee sided with Henderson. Stern took no notice and doubled his order. None had yet been tested but he had great, and justified, faith in Ricardo. A month later there was another conference at the War Office at which it was agreed that the Tank Corps should be increased to nine battalions with seventy-two tanks each; another 352 for first reinforcements would bring the total up to the thousand.

He was at Bermicourt on 13 April as news of the battles became clearer. Colonel Fuller gave a lecture, emphasizing the supply difficulty for tanks in action. They had, he said, been obliged to bring up 20,000 gallons of petrol, to have four dumps and to have needed two lots of 500 men each merely for carrying parties. Next day, with Elles, Wilson and others, Stern went for a walk over the battlefields. Then he dined with Allenby who said 'he had not believed in Tanks before but now thought it was the best method of fighting and would not like to attack without them'.

For the next ten days Stern and his party attended conference after conference. At Marly with the French technical people, at Paris with Mr Lloyd George, Lord Esher, Hankey and General Maurice, Director of Military Operations at the War Office. Finally, at Amiens, with Sir Douglas and his entourage. Stern, manfully,

HOW THE TANKS WENT OVER.

——:o:——

BY OUR SPECIAL CORRESPONDENT,

Mr. TEECH BOMAS.

——:o:——

In the grey and purple light of a September morn they went over. Like great prehistoric monsters they leapt and skipped with joy when the signal came. It was my great good fortune to be a passenger on one of them How can I clearly relate what happened? All is one chaotic mingling of joy and noise No fear! How could one fear anything in the belly of a perambulating peripatetic progolodymythorus. Wonderful,. epic, on we went, whilst twice a minute the 17in. gun on the roof barked out its message of defiance. At last we were fairly in amongst the Huns. They were round us in millions and in millions they

died. Every wag of our creatures tail threw a bomb with deadly precision, and the mad, muddled, murderers melted. How describe the joy with which our men joined the procession until at last we had a train ten miles long. Our creature then became in festive mood and, jumping two villages, came to rest in a crump-hole. After surveying the surrounding country from there we started rounding up the prisoners. Then with a wag of our tail (which accounted for 20 Huns) and some flaps with our fins on we went. With a triumphant snort we went through Bapaume pushing over the church in a playful moment and then steering a course for home, feeling that our perspiring panting proglodomyte had thoroughly enjoyed its run over the disgruntled, discomfited, disembowelled earth. And so to rest in its lair ready for the morrow and what that morrow might hold. I must get back to the battle   TEECH BOMAS.

seems to have said no word about the misuse of the training tanks. It was all past now and there was much more to be said about the future. He left with Butler the design for a Mk VI and an opinion that 'we could probably produce 300 a month of the Heavy Tank, and that 1,000 ought always to be kept in commission as war establishment. The Mk VI was Wilson's own idea. Like everybody concerned in moving tanks to and from railways he hated the clumsy sponsons. His new design did away with them altogether. With an epicyclic gearbox the driver alone could control the tank and the commander was freed from the duty of working the steering brakes. In the new Mark he would be given instead the handling of a 6-pdr firing straight forward between the 'horns' while the rest of the crew would work in an elevated structure in the middle. The design meant much rejigging in the factories, among other things requiring that the entire engine be shifted to one side. This would have been more than a mere hiccup and no Mk VI was ever made.

The pace of things at home was gathering speed. Stern asked Sir Douglas to write to the War Office officially asking that the Tank become an established unit of his armies. Haig obliged and a high-level meeting took place at the War Office on 1 May. Lord Derby, Secretary of State, presided. It was a long business; the end product was a decision to set up a Tank Committee; the Chairman should be a

General with recent battle experience; the Members two from the Ministry of Munitions, one from the War Office and one from the Tank Corps, this last another General. Stern saw Derby privately and protested. This was worse than ever.

The scheme, produced by two weak Ministers, could never have worked well; under another Chairman it might have limped along in some fashion but the moment Stern and Major-General John Edward Capper came face to face it died in its tracks. They detested each other on sight. Stern, not unjustly, was convinced that all wordly knowledge about Tanks (he always spelt the word with a capital T) belonged to him and his trusty band. There were, no doubt, Generals of supple mind who would have accepted this and have been prepared to take instruction from a civilian disguised as a Lieutenant-Colonel. This was not General Capper's style, nor should he be blamed for it. His more famous brother, Thompson Capper of 7th Division, had said that in this war it was an officer's duty to be killed; he had been, at Loos. The Cappers were of a hard race. This one's credentials were certainly impressive. Starting his service as a Sapper officer, he had carried out public works in India, had been Commandant of the Balloon School, Commandant of the School of Military Engineering and, at 56, he had lately commanded 24th Division in the fighting around Arras. The Division had been on the left of the Canadians, in the Lens area, where no tanks had been employed. He can hardly have been unaware that, because of the failure to give them any help, tanks were not highly regarded by the Canadian Corps. It is also fair to assume that Capper had reached what Lord Montgomery would have called his 'ceiling'. In his Diary Sir Douglas constantly complains that many of his senior formation commanders were not up to their jobs. Had Capper been fit to command a Corps, GHQ would never have allowed him to go. Stern says disdainfully that until his appointment Capper had never seen a tank. This may have been literally true, but he had certainly seen and heard reports on them. In December, 1916, the *BEF Times*, later re-named *The Wipers Times* and practically the official organ of 24 Division, had published a news item that its General could hardly have helped seeing. It appears opposite. Capper intended to introduce proper military discipline to a Department run far too long by civilians. The War Office representatives, Lieut-Colonels Keane and Mathew-Lannaw, could be counted on to back him up. Capper belonged to the 'In And Out'. Stern preferred his Garrick Club. Their styles are not the same.

Relations with General Furse, lately Colonel Churchill's Divisional Commander, got off to a better start when he took over from von Donop as Master-General of the Ordnance, as a very civil letter shows: 'My dear Stern, I tried to get you on the telephone this evening to tell you how delighted I was to hear that those extra plates have been pushed off to France today for the Mk IVs. This is really a fine performance, especially in this filthy time of strikes. Bravo.' Furse was, of course, a Gunner and the British artillery was now a huge and powerful force. Tanks were still merely ancillaries. It would not have been reasonable to expect him to devote too much time to them.

Stern addressed the meeting on the Committee's first appearance rather as a lecturer than as what Capper would have called a subordinate temporary officer. He

spoke of Haig's talk with him – no harm in making the point that he had Sir Douglas' ear – and gave some figures: 'In 1916 we produced 150 Tanks; in 1917 we shall produce 1500 Tanks; in 1918 we can produce 6,000 Tanks.' He then tore into the arrangements that brought the War Office in as a fifth wheel to his coach: 'What possible advantage can accrue from the passage of ideas and requirements through numerous Departments of the War Office?.' Then, fully alive to the fact that there was no chance of him being appointed dictator of all tank affairs, he made a proposal, though it must have been a painful one: 'I wish to suggest that the rapid development can be achieved by the appointment of a Director-General of all military Tanks in England and abroad, solely responsible for everything to do with Tanks, except when detailed for action in the field. Major-General Capper has already been appointed General in Command of Tanks, but to my mind he requires these powers. His position as regards Tanks should be similar to the position which Sir Eric Geddes held in England and abroad with regard to railways.' The reference to Geddes may have been deliberate, for on the face of it it was tactless. Geddes had gone straight from his railwayman's business suit into the uniform of a Major-General; this was bitterly resented by the Regular Army but the army's resentment was mild compared to that of the Navy when the same man appeared shortly afterwards camouflaged as a Vice-Admiral. Capper would not have found the comparison

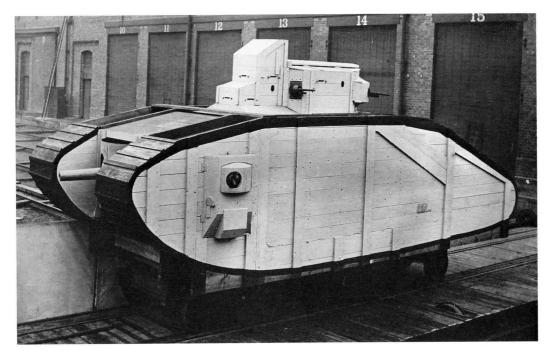

Above: *Wooden mock-up of a Mk VI Tank. None were built.*

Opposite: *Major-General Sir John Capper, KCB, KCVO, at a post-war inspection.*

flattering. Anyway, the Army worked through Committees; jumped-up civilians could not be expected to know this.

Tritton's Whippet tank was ready to go on to the production line with two 50 hp Tylor engines. Ricardo had designed an engine giving 168 hp, had the firm of Peter Brotherhood at work on the first forty of them and had arranged contracts with Crossley, Napier and Vauxhall, with Mr Windeler of Mirrless, Bickerton & Day – the leading firm in industrial diesels – coordinating arrangements. Wilson's epicyclic gear, which did away with the need for gearsmen, was waiting to go into production. This was a masterpiece of ingenuity which enabled the torque to be shifted from one track to the other without any great effort on the part of the driver. There was no obstacle, from the manufacturers' point of view, to the immediate production of the Mk V Tank. Had the business been left to the professionals both Mk V and Whippet might have been at Cambrai. What this could have meant we shall see presently.

It soon became obvious that under the new dispensation these things were not going to happen. Stern and d'Eyncourt drew up a long remonstrance, copies going to the Prime Minister as well as to the Minister of Munitions.

It began with a sweeping denunciation of the military authorities who had not grown up with the tank and failed to grasp the possibilities; what they could, and did, do was to disregard more and more the opinions of those who did know. First came the old sore, the machine-gun. The Hotchkiss had not been selected arbitrarily but after careful thought, once it had become clear that there would be no Madsens. On 23 November, 1916, the military authorities, against advice, had ordered that it be replaced by the Lewis. Six months later the military authorities had bowed to pressure and agreed that a change back be made. 'The result is that this year's Tanks will carry converted Lewis gun loopholes and Hotchkiss ammunition in racks and boxes provided for Lewis guns.' As the Lewis gun carried its rounds in drums and the Hotchkiss in strips this was more than just inconvenience. The litany went relentlessly on. Originally it had been decided that equal numbers of males and females be made. In the winter of 1916-17 the military authorities suddenly changed this to one male to two females. Then to three males for two females. Apart from the alterations needed, there were not enough 6-pdr guns.

Then came the training tanks. Because the War Office had insisted that it must have a hundred of each in France and England they had been made and supplied, although both the Tank Committee and the Prime Minister had strongly questioned the need for so many. Sixty unarmoured tanks had been sent into battle. The excuse was that the real tanks had not arrived when they should. The War Office, ignoring arrangements made with the Tank Supply Committee, had taken away many of their skilled workmen to make aeroplanes and guns. Tank builders were still not given the same exemption from call-up as were the others. It took the personal intervention of Sir Douglas Haig, obtained by Stern at the 24 April meeting, to have this put right. There was much more of the same kind. Spare parts, training, repair facilities and many other things were dealt with, complete with evidence of how War Office meddling had made things far more difficult, and later, than would have happened under business-like arrangements. It ended with a detailed exegesis of what needed to be done: a five-man committee, all full-timers, with the Chairman having a seat on the Army Council. The distribution of duties is set out, Capper recommended by name for the top job, and no mention made of any part for the War Office in day-to-day business.

'If these recommendations are approved, I can see every hope of carrying out the big programme which is on order this year, and the programme which has been foreshadowed for next year, but unless the new organization is formed on these lines, with the flexibility suggested, I see no possibility of carrying out either this or next years programme.' The paper went out over Stern's signature; d'Eyncourt added his as concurring.

The row that this stirred up made all previous ones as zephyrs to a tornado. First to march in was General Capper, fresh from Tank Corps HQ at British Columbia House in Kingsway. He had seen the CIGS, Sir William Robertson, who ordered that the paper be withdrawn. Stern, as befitted a man who had negotiated big loans to the Young Turks, was having none of that. Only when Capper gave 'Willie's' personal assurance that all the things criticized would be altered did Stern agree. Two months later, nothing having been done, Stern returned to the charge.

The document was withdrawn at the end of May. The next round was fought at the end of July. In the meantime the Tanks had fought another battle, this time using Courage's Second Brigade.

Seldom, if ever, can a battle have been prepared as thoroughly as was Messines. More guns had joined the barrage at Arras than at the Somme. Still more – 1500 field pieces and 800 medium and heavy – were available to General Plumer. No longer was there a shortage of shells; the worry now was that the guns would be worn out by such intensive use. Stores and dumps were scattered everywhere. The new port of Richborough, at the mouth of the Kentish Stour by Pegwell Bay, now came into use and large shrouded objects on flat cars embarked at the custom-built train ferry en route for Bermicourt by way of Le Havre. In the short darkness of summer nights they were unloaded at advance railheads and the new Mk IVs, the first genuine armoured fighting vehicles, clanked to their allotted places. Men spoke of them in awed whispers. The German guns were no less active and all the back areas came under steady shell fire. For eight days the artillery thundered away; from the British side 2,374 guns, on a front of 17,000 yards sent out 92,264 tons of high-explosive and shrapnel, thickened up by 70 tons of poisonous gas. This was war on the grand scale at last.

At 3.10 on the morning of 7 June, 1917, just as the darkness was beginning to thin, it happened. Nineteen great black pillars rose quietly into the sky; before anybody had time to wonder what they were came the rumble and crash of the greatest explosion since Krakatoa went up. It was the climax of the work of years. Plumer's Tunnelling Companies – surely the least enviable job of any – had burrowed their way under the Messines-Wytschaete ridge and had now touched off nearly 500 tons of ammonal. The Spanbroekmolen crater had a diameter of 140 yards. As the earth went up the barrage came down. The tremors were felt in Kent and the thunderous crash was clearly audible in London. It was a copy of the method used by Grant at Petersburg in 1864 which had, until now, been the classic of its kind. Grant had used four tons of black powder: Plumer 470 of high explosive. The result had been much the same. 'Set piece' is an expression often used for battles. Only for Messines is it really apposite. General Nugent of 36 (Ulster) Division said that he had seen 'a vision of hell'.

It was the day of the tunneller rather than of the tank, but Courage's men were no mere spectators. The seventy-two Mk IVs were there, ready and willing, with a dozen Mk Is and IIs converted to supply machines. It was reckoned that each of these could do the work of about three infantry companies. The start was more disagreeable than usual as the Germans had soaked the rear area with lachrymatory gas and respirators had to be worn. The night being very dark, commanders and drivers had had to take theirs off with the consequence that they went forward coughing and spluttering and with tears rolling down their faces. Twelve Mk IVs went to Morland's Xth Corps at the north end, sixteen more in the centre under IX Corps (Hamilton-Gordon); the last twenty were sent to IInd Anzac Corps (Godley) at the southernmost end, their objective being the pastoral-sounding Fanny's Farm.

Once again, parts of the attack by tanks were excellent. On IX Corps front, a little short of the Oostaverne Line, the last objective, stood a placed called Joye

Farm. The three tanks of 'A' battalion were not needed for the assault – possibly just as well since it took 100 minutes to cover two miles in such going – but they mopped up some machine-gun nests and put out a patrol in front whilst the infantry got themselves consolidated. As night began to come down all three were ditched. Because there was no point in trying to unditch before daylight they remained embedded. On emerging just before dawn to extricate themselves; the crew observed that the Germans were massing for a counter-attack. Being fortuitously in a 'hull down' position they took every advantage of it. The Lewis guns proved their unsuitability for tank work by being unable to traverse sufficiently; the crews took themselves off to convenient shell holes, the guns with them, and set to work as infantry. The 6-pdrs were better placed. As the Germans moved along the Wanbeke Valley towards them they opened up, the Lewises joined in and the attack was halted. Streams of armour-piercing bullets were directed at the hulls but none penetrated them. This went on for five hours, the 6-pdrs doing excellent service, until the message got through and the Royal Artillery took over. The counter-attack was discontinued. The tanks, however, were stuck fast. No amount of effort could dislodge them from their muddy beds and there they remained until the salvage men came for them. All went well on the Anzac front. By 7 am both infantry and tanks were lodged in Fanny's Farm.

On X Corps front things were less successful. The History of 47th (London) Division says, laconically, that 'A section of tanks was allotted to assist in the capture of the Damstrasse and the White Château and stables. Of the four tanks actually engaged, one was ditched 200 yards North of the Château, and two others near the stables.' No mention is made of No 4. The Ulstermen of 36th Division were better served. 'The 10th Inniskillings were held up by a machine-gun. A tank was just in front but the occupants apparently could not see the gun nor could the infantrymen attract their attention to it. A sergeant of the Inniskillings ran up to the tank, beat upon its side with a Mills bomb, and so gained the attention of the crew. The tank then bore down upon the machine-gun and put it out of action.' Later comes Ulster's verdict: 'The tanks had been a success. They were useful in incidents such as that which has been described and they probably saved the infantry some casualties on the top of the ridge.'

More praise, though still something short of ecstatic, came from 25th Division, on the Ulstermen's right: 'Difficulty had been anticipated in the employment of tanks on (this) front, owing to the marshy nature of the ground on the line of the Steenbeeke. This proved well-founded, as three out of the four allotted to the Division were ditched before crossing the enemy's front line in the initial attack. The fourth, commanded by 2nd Lieut Woodcock, got safely through. The four others detailed for the subsequent attack on the further line overcame the difficulties of the journey and were of some use to the 11th Cheshires and the 8th Border Regt, though little opposition was encountered. The Tank commanded by Lieut Tuit materially assisted the latter with its machine-gun fire in the capture of the position and some prisoners. The high percentage of casualties sustained by their personnel are a sufficient indication of the difficulties of their work.' The last word, however, must go to that prince of 'G' Staff officers, General 'Tim' Harington: 'Tanks were started from behind the infantry assembly trenches and followed the infantry advance; the success of the infantry, however, did not afford many opportunities for effective action by tanks before the first objective lines had been gained. Fifteen out of forty tanks were able to reach their objectives near the Damm Strass and east of Wytschaete and afforded moral as well as material support, besides drawing on themselves hostile fire which would otherwise have been directed against the infantry.'

Taken in the round it had not been a bad day; better certainly than Bullecourt. The supply arrangements had worked well, each old Mk I having five 'fills' aboard. A 'fill' was a complete set of everything a tank needed, from a full load of petrol to a complete refill of ammunition. There were no obvious lessons to be learned; nobody needed to be told that Flanders mud was a far more deadly enemy to a tank than anything the Germans might think up. They had indeed made one discovery. The 'K' bullet was useless against a Mk IV. The most likely antidote would be a few field guns carefully sited in the forward infantry positions. Henceforth they would always be there.

CHAPTER 10

Trouble up at Plant

AS THE CHRONICLES OF THE TANK have to deal with activities in several places at the same time it is not possible to set them out in a straight chronological form. For the moment we must leave the Tank Corps, justly proud of its new name, to its own devices. For the most part, during the weeks immediately following Messines, these consisted of anxious consultations between Elles, Fuller, Baker-Carr, Courage, Martel and their battalion commanders led by Charrington and Hardress-Lloyd upon the single subject of unditching. We shall see presently what they contrived.

Back in London very important things happened during the month of July, 1917. First amongst these was the return of a pioneer. Colonel Churchill, reverted at his own request to plain Mr, came back into power as Minister of Munitions, succeeding the ineffectual Dr Addison. There was a howl of protest from the ultra-Conservatives; Mr Lloyd George showed commendable courage in bringing back a man with so many enemies but he had to stop short at returning him to the Cabinet. This was to have serious consequences. As a mere Departmental Minister, and one not universally trusted, he had nothing like the free hand he needed in order to do the things he believed to be right. His function was that of a mere purveyor and when Admiralty or War Office made demands upon him it was his duty to comply with them, however strongly he might disapprove.

After reducing some fifty committees to a more manageable ten, Mr Churchill addressed himself to the neglected subject of mechanical warfare. His worst enemy was the Admiralty. Nobody grudged their Lordships a privileged position, for if the Navy could not beat the submarine nothing else would matter. Their Lordships, however, presumed heavily upon it. One instance, typical of many, must serve for all. When the Navy demanded potato-peeling machines for the Grand Fleet, skilled men engaged in making range-finders for anti-aircraft guns were taken off their work. The Navy had vast supplies of armour plate but would part with none of it. Mr Churchill set himself to glut them to such an extent that they could no longer protest.

Tanks were well to the front of his mind. While he had been away 'they had been consistently misused by the generals and their first prestige was markedly diminished'. This was beyond argument. The Press had long ceased to write about tanks walking down streets with an army cheering behind. Nor was it only the Press that had become disenchanted. 'In the fight to secure a handful of steel plates for the tank programme we encountered at first the odious statement: "But the Army doesn't want any more: GHQ does not rank them very high in their priorities: they have not done well at Passchendaele; they cannot cope with the mud, etc.".' This was the voice of 'Wullie' Robertson and his cronies in London. Privately the Minister took a different view. None the less, the War Office was the Minister's customer and the customer is always right.

One of the first letters seen by the new Minister had been sitting in the 'In' tray for some time; it was dated 18 June and came from Major Wilson: 'Officially I have nothing but a title, Director of Engineering. I have no authority, no responsibilities and am in a purely consultative capacity to give my opinion only when asked. Practically, by courtesy of the Metropolitan Company and with assistance of their drawing office staff, I have got out all the designs of the Mk V and Mk VI ... also, in conjunction with Major Greg, all the designs for gun carrying machines.... The position is so unsatisfactory and the results obtained within the last nine months so poor that I must ask you seriously to consider the change in the organization in the technical side of the MWSD. I append a letter showing the organization I suggest.... I have had twenty years' experience in responsible positions but have never worked under such conditions as I have for the past 18 months. I would not have tolerated such conditions for one moment had I not believed my services were of special use to the country in time of war. I have twice been dismissed by Colonel Stern but have refused to go but I now think the interests of the country will best be served by asking you to accept my resignation unless a working organization can be made.' Admiral Moore was deputed to smooth Wilson down and he was, in November, appointed 'Chief of Design'. It was a distinction but without a difference. All the same it shook Mr Churchill's confidence in Bertie Stern.

He and d'Eyncourt, for their part, were keeping up the steady bombardment of the Ministry. On 24 July another letter was placed in front of Mr Churchill, a copy having gone to the Prime Minister. It treated of the folly in using landships in places where they could not possibly do what they had been designed to do. Stern reminded his readers that 'the military authorities had agreed to make it a rule that they would not use Tanks where the weather and ground conditions were very bad. In spite of this, in spite of the fact that the designers and builders had told them that over very heavily crumped, soft, muddy country Tanks were practically useless, they had been using them in the mud and now it seemed likely that the Army would cancel all orders for Mechanical Warfare.' After a recapitulation of all that had happened so far, Stern set out what he thought ought to be done: 'Accumulate Tanks and continue to do so until you have thousands, well trained and well organized tactically into an efficient self-contained mechanical army.... Several types of Tank will have to be incorporated as the different new designs are introduced. Finally this great force would consist of brigades of Tanks of different designs, each organized for its own particular role: all organized under one head, who would be responsible for a Mechanical Army (trained with its complement of artillery and infantry etc until ready to complete its task) and to win a decisive battle.' With it went a copy of a letter from 'a very important Staff Officer'. The style suggests Fuller. It was in some ways prophetic: 'There are two theatres to consider: Flanders and Cambresis. The first has mud and the second wide and deep trenches. As I cannot imagine anyone choosing Flanders again, our difficulties may be spanning power. This requires very careful consideration. The mud here is beyond description. I have never seen anything like it either on the Somme or the Ancre.'

As no reply was received by 27 July d'Eyncourt and Stern went on strike. 'The three military members, who a month before had never seen a Tank, laid down all rulings even with regard to design and construction. They were in the majority and we could do nothing.' Though Stern does no more than imply it, the impression sticks that he was given the *de haut en bas* treatment. He was, after all, a Director-General and such appointments carried the rank of Major-General. His credentials were not less than those of Major-General Eric Geddes and in a paper written soon afterwards he complained that he had requested time after time that proper ranks should be given to Holden (his Deputy), Wilson and Syme. Two were only Captains and Wilson, a Major, had entered the old 'Britannia' only three years after Beatty. 'The War Office refuses and General Capper refuses them all promotion.'

Stern, very much the senior banker and not at all the junior officer, wrote direct to the Prime Minister. The letter began dramatically with 'A crisis has arisen in the relations between the War Office and the Ministry of Munitions re the progress and development of Mechanical Warfare.' The first complaint was that, since no Department of Tanks existed at the War Office, which refused to have such a thing, he was obliged to trail from one department to another, with predictable results. Then came more charges of ignorant interference with tank design and production: 'All the experimental work and testing etc is done by Naval men lent by the Admiralty. *The War Office refuse all assistance.*' Furthermore the War Office, while demanding complete co-operation with Bermicourt, 'make it practically impossible for me to send technical men over by refusing commissions and suitable rank to those who hold commissions'.

Sir Douglas, possibly taking his tone from General Kiggell, Chief of the General Staff, was no longer the enthusiast of the 'Go back and make as many tanks as you can' days. On 27 August, 1917, he put his revised feelings on paper: 'The Tank, at any rate in its present state of development, can only be regarded as a minor factor. It is still in its infancy as regards design. It is of uncertain reliability.... As time goes on and the designs improve, the tank will very probably become a more important factor in the choice of the battlefield, but under present conditions it must be, as I have said, a minor factor.'

On 16 September Stern wrote to Mr Churchill, with a brusquerie more appropriate to a customer exceeding his overdraft. Having asserted that 'lack of action and lack of decision will most assuredly ruin the chances of mechanical warfare for 1918', he reproved the Minister for not having kept his promise, made after the July letter, to investigate the position. It ended with 'Immediate action must be taken'. The tone was not that to which Mr Churchill was accustomed; not as recipient.

'Wully' Robertson was given a demonstration of the Mk V. After that another letter, dated 21 September, went to Mr Churchill. 'After a lengthy discussion I gather that he (Robertson) agrees that the science of Mechanical Warfare has reached a point when mechanical cavalry in large quantities, in conjunction with other arms, have a better chance than any known weapon of winning a decisive battle. We believe that we have the design of such a machine.' 'Willie's' standard answer to such as this was 'I've 'eard different'. And so he had, even though Stern said in the letter 'I gather he agrees'.

Stern's optimism was misplaced. Whether he knew it or not his following had deserted him. Wilson, in his notes to Stern's book, wrote that 'This belief existed only in the minds of a few and this was the root cause of many of Col Stern's troubles'. When 'Bertie' looked for somebody to hold his coat no one was there.

Even had he known of this Stern's attitude would not have changed. His civilian experience had taken in a country with far greater potential for manufacture than that of Britain. 'Now I suggest a still greater effort,' he wrote; 'let a great General organize our effort in conjunction with the Americans and the French.' It is possible that Mr Churchill was beginning to feel a little irked by Stern and to think that perhaps there was something to be said for the Generals. On 29 September there was a great colloquy at the War Office, with all the Imperial General Staff and all the Tank Commanders present. The bomb was planted by Butler. Sir Douglas, he said, could only find 18,500 all ranks for the Tank Corps. As few Whippets as possible should be made but he wanted the Mk IVs replaced by Mk Vs without loss of time. He would probably want some supply tanks also but Butler did not know how many. They would meet again on 10 October.

Stern was horrified. In his last letter to the Minister he had reckoned that by 1 July, 1918, England could produce some 2,000 tanks, America about 4,000 and France 500. Now it looked as if the entire order of battle of the Corps would be about 1,000, including those already in service. He sought out Sir Arthur Duckham, the oil man, who was one of Mr Churchill's Commissioners. The paper that went to Mr Churchill over Duckham's signature was short and to the point. The men who knew most about tanks were at Bermicourt; those nearest to them in knowledge were Stern's people, including Squadron 20 which tested all new machines at its Dollis Hill grounds. Last came the War Office, constantly meddling. A new Committee, of Capper, Elles, d'Eyncourt and Stern, would be better by far than the present arrangements. Mr Churchill agreed. Stern took General Foch to Dollis Hill and showed him the Mk V and the Gun Carrier. 'You must make quantities and quantities,' said the General. 'We must must fight mechanically. Men can no longer attack with a chance of success without armoured protection.'

A day or two later Mr Churchill told Stern that the army did not want quantities and quantities. It only wanted a total of 1350. Stern exploded. 'This I determined to fight with every means in my power and I told Mr Churchill so.' Men have been given VCs for less. From the Hotel Metropole Lieut-Colonel Stern walked round to the War Office and bearded General Sir William Robertson. 'I told him that the proposed preparations for 1918 were wholly and entirely inadequate.' 'Willie', keeping his temper, replied that that was pretty straight. 'I replied that it was meant to be straight.' This merited a bar, but 'Sir William Robertson was extremely polite and shook hands with me when I left.' 'Willie' pretty certainly knew this to be his valediction.

On 11 October Mr Churchill saw Stern at his own request. Stern related his own history in tank matters and asked whether he still enjoyed the Minister's confidence. Mr Churchill answered that he himself had complete faith in his Director-General but the War Office 'wanted a change made'. 'The War Office,' Stern wrote later, 'accused me of lumbering them up with useless Tanks at the Front and of wasting millions of public money. Here I asked him to go slowly as I wished to take down his astounding statement.' In the opinion of the War Office, he said, there had been a total failure in design, no progress had been made, all the money spent on Tanks had been wasted, and the belief in Mechanical Warfare was now at such a low ebb that they proposed to give it up entirely. Stern once more went over the history from the beginning. It may have eased his feelings – very possibly Mr Churchill shared them although he could not say so – but the deed was done. He was offered some sort of honour but declined it furiously. A few days later Sir Arthur Duckham told him that three Generals at the War Office had demanded his removal.

The whole trouble was that he had pressed for 4,000 tanks at a time when the War Office had lost its nerve. Mr Churchill did concede that privately he shared the view that quantities of tanks would be needed for 1918 but as Minister he could not argue with the Generals. This could not be gainsaid. Months later Stern put his views on paper: 'On the demand of Generals Capper, Furse and Butler I was removed from the position of Director-General of Mechanical Warfare. Not one of these Generals had ever heard of mechanical warfare until the pioneers often endless experiments succeeded in producing these weapons. Why? ... I fought for standardization of mechanical warfare against continued changes of design. Because I refused to be bribed into silence by the promise of honours and to allow inexperienced officers to ruin the one development of this war in which we have outstripped the Germans. This new development instead of its continuing its healthy growth under imaginative practical men has been placed under the heel of elderly servicemen with the usual results.' Stern never seems to have realized that he had lost the backing of the other pioneers.

Shortly after he had seen Stern, on 21 October, Mr Churchill submitted a paper to the Cabinet; its subject was the Munitions Programme for 1918. It was a long paper; only when one reaches paragraphs 30 and 31 does it become clear that the Minister's views are still those of the battalion CO. This war would have to be won by machines. On 6 November he produced the Munitions Budget for the forthcoming year. Para 14 deals with tanks. They had never been used in sufficient numbers nor were they reliable enough. Because of that the army would not go beyond the figure of 18,500 men. 'This limits the number of fighting tanks required to an establishment of 1080 with ample maintenance and a certain number of supply and gun-carrying tanks.' There was a coda: 'The new designs will not be available in full numbers until July, 1918. Thereafter considerable expansion would be possible.' The useless cavalry remained at about 32,000.

The customer had changed his mind. Whatever Sir Douglas may have said to Stern in the past he wanted no more Mk IVs. When the shop could offer him Mk Vs he might be in the market again. Until that day talk of tank armies and such-like had better stop.

A new Director General, Admiral A. G .H. W. Moore, was soon appointed. No possible criticism could be made of him. He had never seen a Tank. Stern, possibly because he had been standing before the picture for a long time, could never bring himself to believe that anybody who had missed the Greenhithe Trials or the debut of 'Mother' could possibly have anything to contribute to the Mechanical Warfare philosophy.

CHAPTER 11

'Did we really send men to fight in that?'

SIX VALUABLE WEEKS PASSED between the end of the Messines battles and the opening of the next series. The Germans wasted none of them. A lightly-held outpost zone lay in front of a proliferation of pill-boxes. With a water table only just below the surface it was not the country for digging trenches and deep shelters in the Somme fashion.

Harsh things have been said of Sir Douglas Haig about his decision to attack over this part of Flanders. The unhappy man was under much pressure from outside. From Jellicoe at the Admiralty came the cry that unless the Belgian sea-coast was cleared the U-boats would win the war for the Kaiser in a very short time. From Pétain came another cry, nearly though not quite as urgent. The French Army was in a state of mutiny and might disintegrate if attacked. The duet demanded that the Field-Marshal do something to prevent these unthinkable things from happening.

Stand, if you have not already done so, at Tyne Cot Cemetery on Passchendaele Ridge and look towards the middle of the saucer upon whose eastward rim you are. There, at what seems only a drive and a chip shot from you, are the ramparts of Ypres and the towers of its now restored buildings. Between is a formless network of drainage ditches. It used to be the law, very probably it still is the law, that any farmer who neglected these would be brought before the magistrates and fined. They alone prevent the country relapsing into its ancient wetland. Not far away, almost exactly six hundred years before Plumer's and Gough's battles, a French Army under Louis X had arrived to chastise the recalcitrant Flemish weavers. His horsemen sank into the mud under the weight of their armour before a blow was struck. Look across at Ypres through the light mist that is usually about and you will stand amazed that any soldiers could ever have crossed such a place and wrenched the heights under you from a brave and competent enemy.

Baker-Carr, his brigade unused at Messines, was told before he left the Arras front that an attack around Ypres would be made in July. He was horrified, for 'it was inconceivable that this part of the line should have been selected. If a careful search had been made from the English Channel to Switzerland, no more unsuitable spot could have been discovered.' The drainage system had, for obvious reasons,

Mk IV Tank awaiting orders during the Menin Road battle, August 1917.
The tracks are 'spudded' for better grip.

been untended for a couple of years and the near-polder land had been comprehensively shelled by both sides. 'The result was that many square miles of land consisted merely of a thin crust of soil, beneath which lay a bottomless sea of mud and water.' It would be a thousand times worse when the stupendous bombardment being planned had stirred it around. 'I never met one single soul who anticipated success, with the exception of GHQ.' At that rarefied level there was some optimism, for Brigadier-General Charteris had many incontrovertible facts proving that the Germans were in far worse case than the French and would certainly disintegrate if roughly handled. The Germans did not know this. Sir Hubert Gough did. 'I have just come from an interview with the Commander-in-Chief and he tells me that everything points to a complete break-down of the enemy morale and that one more hard thrust will crumple up his defences.' Not once but many times did Gough begin his conferences with these words. Nobody believed him, but nobody can contradict an Army Commander. Nobody, that is, who wants to keep his job and not be sent home as a 'croaker'. Baker-Carr was flown over the prospective battlefield; it looked even worse than from the ground. 'Everywhere it was churned up by shell-fire and had the semblance of a face badly pitted by small-pox. All the craters were half-filled with water and it looked as if there was as much water as land.'

It may be that the decision of GHQ to begin the Third Ypres battles and to continue them as long as it did can be justified. This is not the place to judge it. What cannot possibly be justified is a decision to put tanks into action in conditions which must be fatal to their success, even if the enemy were to be no more than spectators.

The Tank Corps had done all that men could to fit itself for battles in which landships would have to live up to their name. A training school had been set up at, of all places, Agincourt. The memory of what had happened there long ago, when armour had for the last time crashed to defeat against resolutely handled missile weapons, did not weigh heavily. Colonel Searle, Chief Engineer to the Corps and a man who has never received anything like proper recognition, had made from nothing a very considerable repair and maintenance organization at Bermicourt. By midsummer 1917 the Central Workshops at Teneur, a couple of miles away, were well stocked and organized; the stores covered seven acres of railway sidings and another six of buildings. All this was Searle's kingdom and he ran it with relentless efficiency. It was from here that came the first of the improvised contraptions that brought tank work in mud just within the realms of the possible. The torpedo-spar had not been much of a success. To replace it there came the 'unditching beam', a great baulk of teak, wider than the tank it was to serve, shod with iron at the ends and carried athwartships just clear of the tracks. Heavy chains were provided with which it could be firmly attached to the tracks, carried forward and downwards until, when underneath the tank's belly, it gave something upon which it could get a grip. It was still necessary for members of the crew to go outside and deal with the

A Mk V Tank in France, showing the unditching beam.

The Mk IV. The victor of Cambrai.

The German A7V of 1918. The first of the Panzers.

The Medium A, or Whippet, Tank of 1918.

fastenings but, so long as they were not picked off, the beam gave some chance of the machine hauling itself out on to firm ground. If the mud was too deep the beam simply travelled with the tracks underneath the tank and up again. Too often the mud was of such quality that a tank would thrash away, the beam travelling round and round, until the engine boiled over and it was stuck for good. All the same, it was, as Williams-Ellis says, 'pretty effective and but little could have been done in the Ypres fighting without it'.

There had been other small improvements. The leather helmet had not lasted long and crews wore the customary steel one. The nuisance – sometimes the danger – caused by 'splash' and splinters was still serious; a mask, closely resembling the mediaeval visor, and made of chain-mail was provided for the use of drivers and commanders but, with the Germans using gases of all kinds as never before, it usually had to give place to a respirator. The glass prisms through which men looked forward had proved too dangerous; at the usual tank speed any competent rifleman could hit them and a burst of machine-gun fire sent them in shards straight into the driver's face. Out they went, to be replaced by a pattern of tiny holes, all about the size of the letter 'o' in this print. It provided less of a view, but it was a lot safer.

Three brigades, totalling 216 machines, were at the disposal of GHQ for the battles compendiously known as Third Ypres. Sir Douglas had, of course, known the place at the time of the first battle when he had gained admiration by riding slowly down the Menin Road with his Staff around him at the moment of greatest crisis. Ypres had changed in the three years since then and GHQ staff was very different from that of First Corps. Few, if any, of the senior men had seen the Salient since Plumer had become Warden. It is hard to believe that anyone who knew the area in its 1917 state would have dreamt of putting a tank anywhere near it; the memories of Arras and Messines were recent enough. But GHQ so decided. There was nothing that could have been called a Tank Plan, unless parcelling them out to formations could be dignified by that name. Elles made what seems a curious remark in his Introduction to Williams-Ellis' book: 'It was our fate up to the first Cambrai battle to "chip in when we could" in conditions entirely unfavourable. The employment of Tanks in Flanders has often been criticized, without intelligent appreciation of the fact that had they not fought in Flanders they would probably have fought nowhere. Better, therefore, that they should fight and pull less than half their weight, and still save lives, than that they should stand idle while tremendous issues were at stake.'

Elles is entitled to a fair degree of sympathy. Amongst the red and gold of GHQ he was a very junior officer and lacked any great record of achievement that might have commanded respect out of proportion to his rank. Had he refused flatly to put his tanks into the mud-bath he would have been returned to the Sappers in short order. Then one of two things would have happened. Either somebody more biddable would have been put into his place or the entire tank concept would have been dropped as an unprofitable nuisance. There would have been no Cambrai, no Hamel, no Amiens, and the assailants of the Hindenburg Line would have been armoured in serge rather than steel. A sacrifice to ignorance and stupidity was demanded. Elles was the chosen officiant, the Tank Corps the Victim. The High Gods of Montreuil were appeased and the tank was permitted to live.

Baker-Carr, not looking forward to the coming battle with any excess of optimism, remarked on the weather once again taking a turn for the worse: 'A wind, bringing mist and fine rain, blew steadily from the west. It was the last piece of ill luck required to complete the tale of our misfortunes.' The previous six weeks had been of beautiful summer days. He mentioned another misfortune. His brigade was sent to work with a Corps of Gough's Fifth Army: 'This . . . was during the height of the "Gough tradition", and Sir Hubert had been specially selected to direct the offensive on account of his audacity and dash – save the mark! Gough's command was, at that time, to the Army what the 'K' Class was to submariners – something to be avoided if at all possible.

Matters began badly for the First Brigade. The tanks were railed to a special siding in Oosthoek Wood, near Ypres, and moved to what was then called a 'tankodrome' nearby. Soon afterwards the place came under uncommonly accurate shell-fire by day and bombing by night. It was subsequently discovered that the gaff had been blown by a Sgt Phillips, variously described as a Welshman or an Irishman, a prisoner or a deserter. Williams-Ellis calls him 'a garrulous fool or a very treacherous knave'. The story of his treason was read out in orders to all tank units, with a promise that his account would be settled at the end of the war.

At midnight on 30 July the first wave moved off. Each tank was at last fairly well equipped. The pigeon basket usually had to be put on top of the engine, but there was for everybody a decent compass, two cupboards where the petrol tank had been for rations and whisky and, of all grotesque things, a handsome brass carriage clock. One can only assume the maker to have had a friend at the Ministry. As soon as an issue of chocolate and fruit arrived the crews knew that they were in for a long haul. Elles and Hotblack, the Reconnaissance Officer, walked forward to see what happened, accompanied by Baker-Carr. The night was muggy, the drizzle incessant and very soon they met the gas shells. There were tracks in the mud leading to the causeway across the Ypres-Comines canal but not a tank to be seen. They returned to their HQ to wait.

Before long the first pigeons fluttered in: 'Hopelessly ditched behind our own front line'; 'Direct hit on tank by field gun. One killed two wounded'; 'Ditched in German front line. Being heavily shelled'. Time passed, and slightly more encouraging news came in from the Flying Corps. Tanks were in action in 'comparatively advanced positions' and several infantry battalions were loud in their praise. Sir Ivor Maxse, the Corps Commander and one of our best Generals, was generous with his. But the swamp still seemed to be winning.

Baker-Carr once more got into trouble for speaking his mind. Ten days after the attack began he was summoned to GHQ to give a lecture. It was broadly hinted that his comments were influenced by the failure of the tanks; at this Baker-Carr flared up. 'It was not a question of tanks being unable to fight, but a question of anybody being able to fight under such conditions. . . . The battle was dead as mutton and had been so since the second day.' General 'Tavish' Davidson, DMO, sent for him. 'I am very upset by what you said at lunch, Baker. If it had been some junior officer it wouldn't have mattered so much, but a man of your knowledge and experience has no right to speak like you did.'

'You asked me how things really were and I told you frankly.'

'But what you say is impossible.'

'It isn't. Nobody has any idea of the conditions up there.'

'But they can't be as bad as you make out.'

'Have you been there yourself?'

'No.'

'Has anybody in Operations Branch been there?'

'No.'

'Well then, if you don't believe me it would be as well to send somebody up to find out. I'm sorry I've upset you, but you asked me what I thought and I told you.'

The battle went on until November. There were plenty of instances of sheer herosim by tank crews and names like 'Fray Bentos', 'Cape Colony', 'Cyprus' and 'Culloden' have their place in the Tank Corps roll of honour. Apart from these isolated actions only one operation could have been called a success. On 16 August, the weather being slightly less vile, General Maxse despatched a dozen tanks of

Baker-Carr's brigade to help out the infantry on the Langemarck–St Julien road. All became bogged before coming into action. The infantry in turn were held up by a line of pill-boxes to the north-east of St Julien. All these tough little fortresses were hidden in the ruins of farms, Mont du Hibou, the Cockcroft, Triangle Farm and Hillock Farm. It was reckoned that the cost of capturing them could not be much less than a thousand men.

Baker-Carr, unflappable as ever, undertook to General Maxse that if he were allowed to do the business in his own way he would guarantee to take the pill-boxes at less than half that price. Maxse took him at his word. There was to be no shelling, only a smoke barrage. A hard road from St Julien to Poelcapelle ran behind the pill-boxes roughly parallel with their line. There were corduroy roads leading to the main roads but their use had, for obvious reasons, been forbidden to tanks. The Divisional commanders were sceptical but Maxse ordered them to do as Baker-Carr wished. A composite company of tanks under Major Broome moved over the corduroy roads during the night of 17/18 August and lay up in the ruins of the village of St Julien until dawn on the 19th. Then, a pair of tanks detailed for each of the five pill-boxes with the last pair in reserve, they clanked up the main road as the smoke came down. The garrisons of the first two forts took to their heels as soon as the strange shapes loomed out heading for them; the pigeon with the news – pigeons have to be thrown downwards to let their wings work – came in at 7 o'clock. The next arrived soon afterwards; the 6-pdrs had made short work of Mont du Hibou. It happened by a rare stroke of luck. One of the pair, a male, became bogged about fifty yards from the two-storied pill-box with one six-pounder pointing straight at the back door. Forty rounds were pumped in as quickly as the gunners could work their piece; the garrison shot out like rabbits, to be caught by a waiting infantry platoon. Triangle Farm alone fought it out, the Germans standing to their weapons and giving as good as they got. They had little chance between the guns of two tanks and another platoon waiting outside. It was here that the only tank casualties were taken.

The Cockcroft was attacked by a lone female, her companion having ditched. The garrison was not to know that she had suffered the same fate when within biscuit-toss of them. The Lewis guns rattled away, the garrison lost its nerve and ran for it. The tank commander promptly made the agreed signal by waving a shovel through the roof aperture but the infantry commander was an unbeliever. When the tank sergeant arrived on foot to assure him that the place really was empty he was nearly enough called a liar. It took a visit from the subaltern in command to the infantry colonel to persuade his men that it was a true bill and the Cockcroft was their for the occupying. One should not criticize the infantrymen too harshly; the idea of a hundred German soldiers firmly ensconced behind eight-foot thick walls taking off at the sight of a single firmly wedged tank defied all experience.

The unditching beams served their purpose just in time. As the last tank finished extricating itself and ambled back the way it had come a heavy German barrage crashed down. It did not worry the infantry who were by then more comfortable than they had been for a long time. Their casualties were not a thousand killed but just fifteen wounded. The crews suffered worse, with two dead and fifteen hurt. It was a lesson in how tanks ought to be used and it was not wasted. When GHQ asked Maxse how the thing had been done he answered monosyllabically 'Tanks'. The neat piece of work probably saved the Tank Corps from disbandment. Even 'Uncle' Harper who had been at the pre-battle conferences and, 'though inclined to belittle the tanks did not fail to put in a claim for a far greater number of the machines than that to which he was justly entitled', could not have failed to notice it. 'Uncle', however, took the view that one swallow does not make a summer. This had been a fluke and was unlikely to be repeated.

The remaining machines were kept at it throughout September and October, still in the old futile way. There is little object in following them all. 'Baker-Carr's battle' - the words are Maxse's - apart, there was nothing to inspire confidence in landships or mechanical warfare.

As if the Field-Marshal had not trouble enough already with the Admiralty and the French, another burden had landed on his back. The Italians had been routed at Caporetto in October, he was obliged to send them what succour he could and the first German divisions had started to arrive from the now defunct eastern front. They had to be hit before they could themselves organize a full-dress attack out of their strong Hindenburg positions. Another old-style battle was out of the question. All other things apart, the Cabinet would not stand for it. It was time to find out whether there really was anything in Mr Churchill's *Variants On The Offensive*. The Tank Corps Staff were quite convinced that there was and that the choice of battle-field almost made itself. The downlands of Cambresis, in Sir Julian Byng's bailiwick, might have been designed for the purpose. Lieut-Colonel Hardress Lloyd was deputed to put the matter to Byng; he was a 17th Lancer, Byng a 10th Hussar. Horse-soldier could speak to horse-soldier as no Sapper or Rifleman could. Sir Julian listened attentively.

CHAPTER 12

Enter Uncle Sam

STERN'S ABRUPT DISMISSAL and the barely credible reason given for it shook some of the pioneers badly. Murray Sueter wrote that 'It was a very real grief to me when I learnt that Colonel Stern had been suddenly hurled from the high post he had obtained.... Very often I have wondered whose path Colonel Stern was standing in.' It was all most confusing. Mr Churchill's letter of dismissal was dated 16 October. On 13 October Sir Douglas, importuned by that new friend of the tanks Sir Julian Byng, had agreed to a great attack by them in Cambresis; Butler, the one-time enthusiast, was still Deputy Chief of Sir Douglas Haig's General Staff; his immediate superior, Sir Launcelot Kiggell, was not well-informed about the subject.

Mr Churchill was playing a deep game. The War Office Generals were a combination that he could not beat but there were other ways of forcing variants on the offensive. The same letter that gave Stern his *congé* opened up wider vistas: 'I shall be glad to hear from you without delay whether those other aspects of activity in connection with the development of Tanks in France and America, on which Sir Arthur Duckham has spoken to you, commend themselves to you.' The reasoning behind it is clear. America was the most mechanically-minded nation in the world and would not welcome Sommes and Passchendaeles of its own if tanks could replace masses of half-trained infantry. France had a tank programme in being, even though the French Tank Corps had little enough to show for its efforts at this date. Stern, though not even a small General, was to be Churchill's Commissioner for Mechanical Warfare (Overseas and Allies). 'It seems to me that your first duty will clearly be to get in touch with the American Army and discuss with General Pershing or his officers what steps we should take to assist them with the supply of Tanks.'

Stern, having delivered his usual Cassandra warning about the War Office, accepted. With his overseas banking experience on top of his tank knowledge he was the only possible man for the job.

America had, so far, proved a disappointment to Mr Churchill, who had expected the build-up in France to be far more rapid than it had been. Sir Douglas had met General Pershing at Montreuil on 20 July and had taken a liking to him, being 'much struck with his quiet, gentlemanly bearing'. He had also made a mental note of Pershing's ADC, Captain George S. Patton, Jr, who was 'a firebrand and longs for the fray'. To long for the fray cannot be other than commendable in a soldier but the US Army was not yet fit to take on experienced Germans. It had no tanks; indeed it had little enough of anything. Every aeroplane and every gun used by the Americans had to be supplied by Britain or France. It was Stern's job to see what could be done about this.

The French, thanks to General Estienne, were another matter. When, at the end of 1915, Estienne had been CRA of a Division he had, on a visit to the British sector, seen a Holt tractor at work towing a big gun. The conclusion he reached was the same as Swinton's. In December, as 'Little Willie' was being discarded, he went with Joffre's blessing to have a talk with the great Schneider engineering works. There a plan was sketched out before Estienne returned to his command at Verdun. The French War Office placed an order for 400 Schneider tanks and followed it up in April with another for 400 of the St Chamond type. Up to then British and French had kept each other firmly at arm's length. The Schneider looked much like 'Little Willie' with loopholes and a lid. St Chamond was a bigger affair, resembling a 'soixante-quinze' on a Holt tractor, the whole wrapped about with armour plating. By April, 1917 – the Nivelle month – nine companies of Schneider and one of St Chamond were ready for business at Champlieu, on the southern end of the forest of Compiêgne. Franchet d'Esperey had pleaded – something he did not do easily – with Nivelle for their use in his attack across the Aisne around Berry-au-Bac, but had been curtly refused. Later Nivelle, much pressed, changed his mind. Eighty tanks, all Schneiders, went into action on 16 April. As the French cavalry always

A French Tank. The St Chamond.

French Schneider Tank moving up on the Oise.

festooned their horses with bales of hay so did their Tank Corps hang reserve petrol cans all over the outside. They drew a fire that Spears, never a man for purple prose, calls 'hellish' and the cans served only to cremate the brave crews. On V Corps front, by Pontavert, another group of forty-eight made for a bridge over the German front-line trench. The Genie had not finished it. One by one the Schneiders ditched and the German guns turned on them. The reserve petrol cans caught fire and, Spears says, 'in a few seconds they were red, glowing masses of metal, incinerators of their roasted crews. The exits were too small in most instances for them to escape.' Thirty-two of the forty-eight were destroyed in this way. On 5 May two Schneider and one St Chamond Companies took part in a sketchily planned operation on the Sixth Army front. The St Chamonds were lucky; all but one broke down before contact was made. The Schneiders had a small success, capturing a mill. That was the sum of it all. Between May and October several more attempts were made in the general direction of the Chemin des Dames with much the same results. When the Schneiders and St Chamonds wore out, which they did quickly, they were not replaced.

General Estienne had come to England in June, 1916, and was taken to see a Mk I at Birmingham. This, he reckoned, would do as an infantry tank once its initial wrongs had been put right but it was not all that he wanted. Cavalry tanks, in large numbers, were the thing. In all 3,500 of the little Renaults were ordered before the summer was out. There is a well-known French small car which is known to the ribald as 'the Paris pissoir on wheels'.* The Renault FT 17 tankette, though painted *bleu d'horizon*, looked much the same on tracks. But, like all Renault products, it worked. The order went out that thirty battalions of them be formed. The amount of munitions made by France, in spite of the loss of all her coal mines and much manufacturing capacity, was amazing. Not only did Madame la Republique equip her own huge forces, she armed Greece, and contributed substantially to the arsenals of Italy and America. This additional task would be too much even for her.

Futile experiments continued with bigger and worse St Chamonds and Schneiders. A 40-ton affair was built in December, 1917; one of 70 tons was seriously projected. Stern's task was to help co-ordinate all these wayward imaginings. It would not be easy.

Stern, rather against his wishes, was elevated to Sir Albert, KBE. This, like many people, he did not regard highly; the Most Excellent Order of the British Empire was Mr Lloyd George's creation and was widely derided, especially by Owen Seaman with his *Punch* poem entitled 'A Large Order'. Stern was no stranger to the Americans, for as long ago as June, 1917, he had arranged a demonstration at Dollis Hill for their benefit. Ambassador Walter Hines Page, Admiral Sims and Admiral Mayo had all been there and were suitably impressed. Mr Page had promised to cable President Wilson to say that 'he considered it a crime to attack machine-guns with human flesh when you could get armoured machines, and machines, too, which he would never have believed capable of performing the feats actually carried out that day before him.'

On 11 November Stern took his letter of introduction from Mr Churchill to General Pershing. The General seemed enthusiastic and named two officers, Majors Drain and Alden, as his tank representatives. Drain was a businessman of experience who had relinquished a much higher rank in the National Guard in order to get to France with the US Ordnance Department. He and Stern took to each other at once. Within a few weeks an Anglo-Franco-American Commission had come into existence charged with the duty of producing the best possible tanks for use by all three armies in common. M Loucheur represented France. Very soon the question of engines came up. Stern had said at a tank committee meeting some time previously that although America made the best lorries in the world 'her big engines and flying engines were not sound enough for our special purposes'. This, of the countrymen of the Wright brothers, might have sounded strange, but it was true. Plans were put in hand for a low-compression engine of 300 hp, to be called the Liberty, which could serve both for tanks and aircraft. All the the big names in the business led by Packard and General Motors, would be put to work and a super-tank would be built to house it. Major Alden would collaborate with Tritton and the others over design.

---

* Otherwise 'Vespasienne'. The Flavian Emperor has his memorial.

French St Chamond Tank at Marley-le-Roi, December 1916.

Stern set himself up in an office in Paris, for the plan envisaged a great factory somewhere in France where 1500 tanks should be built at the greatest possible speed. Loucheur could not help. France, hardly surprisingly, had neither men, machinery nor material to spare. Nor, one may fairly suspect, had she much enthusiasm for tanks. The Americans were whole-hearted in their agreement and much consultation followed upon the questions of which country should supply what.

As they deliberated, news came in of a great tank battle having been fought.

Renault FT17s in the Victory Parade.

CHAPTER 13

The Day of the Cataphracts

I F SIR DOUGLAS HAIG had known what a junior member of his Staff had been forbidden to tell him there would probably never have been a battle at Cambrai and the tank idea might have withered away. Major (in due time General Sir James) Marshall-Cornwall was GSO2 under Brigadier-General Charteris in Intelligence. Charteris, of course, has gone down to history as the man who was constantly assuring his Chief that the German Army was about to collapse at any moment. Why Haig believed him against all evidence remains a mystery. A week or so before the assault was due to take place Marshall-Cornwall found out from prisoners – he spoke fluent German – and from captured documents that three fresh Divisions had just arrived from the Russian front to reinforce that part of the Hindenburg Line exactly where the blow was planned to fall. Charteris had stated baldly that no reserves were there. He assured his junior that all the facts he had discovered were no more than bluff. 'If the C-in-C were to think that the Germans had reinforced this sector it might shake his confidence in our success.' Marshall-Cornwall was so horrified that he formed up to Major-General Davidson, DMO – the same Davidson who had reproved Baker-Carr for pessimism at Ypres – and said that he could no longer serve under a man who was suppressing vital information to suit his own ideas. Davidson ordered him to stay at his post and hold his tongue.

Sir Douglas, misled into believing that the enemy was weaker than he was, agreed to the attempt at a new kind of battle: as on 15 September in the previous year, he badly needed a victory. Seldom had so much concentrated thought gone into preparation. Byng, successor to Allenby at Third Army, had a visit from Elles at Albert in September. Both were thinking on the same lines, of a swift armoured raid designed not so much to occupy territory but to kill and chivvy – Williams-Ellis's word – Germans. Fuller had been at work on it for some time.

Whatever other people might think, the German High Command had not been captivated by the tank. Probably, even more than the War Office, Hindenburg thought it unsoldierly. He had led his company up the slope at St Privat in 1870 against the massed Chassepots and that was the proper way to conduct a war. At about the time of Third Ypres General von Freytag-Loringhoven was writing disdainfully about the subject: 'The English and the French sought to prepare the way for their attacking troops by the employment of battle-motors – the so-called tanks.'

In his book *Deductions From The World War* the Baron makes no other mention of them. Gas, of course, was quite another matter. All the same somebody had measured the captured ones, found out that their trench-crossing maximum was ten feet and had widened the Hindenburg Line throughout its length to twelve. The last letter Stern had had from Elles before his dismissal had said, 'We are very anxiously depending on you to solve two main conundrums that confront us. (a) A device to get the Mk IV and Mk V Tanks over a wide trench and (b) some very simple dodge by which we may be able to put on the unditching gear from the inside of the Tank.' Stern's people were working on these things; Squadron 20 usually had ideas. So did Colonel Searle at the Central Workshops.

As with the tank itself, mediaeval history came to the rescue. For many centuries besiegers everywhere had had to think out the best way of crossing unbridged ditches. The school solution had been worked out long ago and had probably been as familiar to Archimedes as it had been to Wellington's Colonel Fletcher. The only difference was in size. Fascines – the very word recalls the lictor's bundle of rods – would probably serve nicely, provided they could be made big enough. The British-occupied area of France abounded with saw-mills, mostly worked by steam traction-engines, which were reducing woods and forests to gun platforms and trench revetments. Colonel Searle set his Labour Corps to work. There was a particularly large saw-mill by the side of the St Pol road, very near to Bermicourt, and arrangements were made for great quantities of brushwood to be made available. Squadron 20, always willing helpers to their own landships, were sent in search of chain, from the Navy or from anywhere else that it might be found. In all 21,000 bundles of brushwood were put together. That done, eighteen tanks were used for making

Central Workshops, Teneur. The engine shop.

bigger bundles out of the bundles, some sixty or seventy to each fascine; the chain fastenings were pulled tight by the simple expedient of making each end fast to one of two tanks which then drove slowly off in opposite directions. The finished article weighed a ton and a half. So great was the pressure that, months later, an unsuspecting infantryman in search of firewood was killed by the sudden springing open of one of them after he had filed through the chain. 350 of these aids, along with 110 sledges were turned out by Central Workshops in time for the battle. Though it took twenty strong men to roll a fascine through the mud, these were at last available. In August, 1916, the British Military Attaché at Peking, Lieut-Colonel David Robertson, had suggested that some arrangement might be made with the Chinese Government for the employment of civilian labourers to work in France, mainly on the very important business of road-making. The War Office, liking the idea, sent an official representative to the Chinese capital; the result was that, with powerful help from the authorities in Hong Kong and Weihaiwei – then a British Protectorate – together with that of the local missionaries large numbers of men were engaged and shipped off. By the end of the war, which China joined in August, 1917, 96,000 Chinese were in France. They soon won high praise for their work and good conduct. One of the largest camps was at Houdain, no great distance from Bermicourt, and Colonel Searle gladly employed as many as he needed. It became apparent that many of the labourers were fit for better things than pushing and shoving; a good number – exact figures are elusive – came to work in the Central Workshops as fitters and proved themselves excellent at the job.

Fuller, Martel and Hotblack worked out a simple drill based, according to Fuller, on one used by the Persians of antiquity. Once a fascine had been dropped it was gone for good and there were three trench lines to be crossed. The tanks were likewise mustered in groups of three – always a number of mystic significance to Fuller – each bearing a fascine on its roof. On hard chalkland there was no need for unditching beams. The job of No 1 was to trample through the wire as far as the parapet of the front line trench; this was not to be crossed. The tank would then execute a left wheel, move along a prescribed length and shoot up everything it saw. Thus protected, Nos 2 and 3 would move up, each aiming for the same spot. No 2, the left-hand tank, would drop its fascine in the trench, drive over it and then would itself swing left and use its guns to thicken up the fire of No 1. No 3 would also cross on the same fascine and head straight on. When it came up to the second trench it would drop its fascine, cross on it and treat the second trench as No 1 and 2 were treating the first. As soon as No 1 saw that No 2 was over and shooting it would come back, cross both trenches and head for the third line into which its fascine would go. Then it would resume the business of shooting anything in the trench that moved. The infantry were similarly told off in three groups; Trench Clearers, who would go in immediately behind the tanks, Trench Stops to net the rabbits and Trench Garrisons to take over captured positions. It was simple and sensible, though there was little enough time for rehearsals.

The artillery would stay silent, not even being allowed to register from its new positions. As the tanks arrived on their first objective down would come the barrage,

Central Workshops, Teneur. Men of the Chinese Labour Corps hosing down a Tank.

much thickened up by smoke. Since GHQ had insisted that this must be more than a raid and the usual cavalry breakthrough was anticipated with the customary confidence a proportion of the tanks was kitted out with grapnels; these were to be trailed behind, pulling away the wire like balls of knitting wool and making nice wide pathways fit for horses. The original plan had, by early November, snowballed into a combined affair to be undertaken, at the start, by five full Divisions.

One of the Divisions to take part in the initial assault was 'Uncle' Harper's 51st Highlanders. At the pre-battle conferences Fuller's plan, which had already been approved by General Byng, was carefully explained. The infantry was to follow the tanks in single file, keeping as close as it could for protection. 'Uncle' Harper was at least honest. While every other Divisional General nodded and agreed to give the plan a try, 'Uncle' flatly refused. He knew all about tanks. They broke down. Always had done. He was not going to see his 'little fellers' stuck out in the open under fire from everything behind a lot of useless lumps of metal. He would cross his start line an hour after everybody else. When the conference ended he buttonholed Baker-Carr and denounced it as 'a fantastic and most unmilitary scheme'.

'Uncle' had the measure of his Corps Commander. Sir Charles Woollcombe was in his 62nd year and, although he had been commissioned as long ago as 1876 he had not seen a great deal of active service. Although he had a reputation for keeping good discipline, Woollcombe had only been in France for a short time. Whether Harper protested at the Conference or whether he kept quiet, privately resolving to do things his own way, is uncertain. Probably the latter. An experienced General, such as Maxse or Haldane, would have wrung from him an acknowledgment that he knew what he had to do and would comply. Woollcombe seems to have let him get away with it. The relatives of some tank crews might justifiably have said that he got away with murder. The Division neighbouring the 51st, the 62nd, good West Riding Territorials, were under Major-General Braithwaite; in 1907 he and 'Uncle' had been Instructors together at the Staff College. Eight years later, as CGS to Sir Ian Hamilton, he had come near to following his Chief into oblivion. Hamilton had written of him that 'by the Lord they shan't have the man who stood by me like a rock during those first ghastly ten days'. Braithwaite survived, and for his penance was given command of this second-line Division from which nobody expected spectacular performance. He made it into one of the best in the BEF, before he was, deservedly, promoted to command a Corps.

Cambrai developed from the designed land-borne commando raid into another ten-day slogging battle. There is no shortage of accounts of it but here it is only possible to tell of the work of the tanks. Three hundred and seventy-eight fighting machines were allotted to Divisions, roughly the tank strength of $1\frac{1}{2}$ armoured divisions of 1944. In all, the Tank Corps fielded about 690 officers and 3,500 other ranks. The disparity between numbers of men and numbers of vehicles demonstrates how complex were the arrangements before and behind. Hugh Elles, as everybody knows, issued his Special Order No 6. In soldierly language he reminded his crews that everything depended upon their judgment and pluck. This was not hyperbole. Had either failed there would have been no Tank Corps by Christmas.

General Elles led the attack, as an Admiral of landships should, standing in a tank called 'Hilda' wearing his red hat and carrying on the end of his ashplant a flag of his own devising. He and Hardress-Lloyd had had it run up from materials they had bought at a little shop in Cassel. The choice of colour proclaimed a primitive heraldry. Mud, blood and grass green for the fields beyond. There could be no harm in a little panache to colour a war lacking in such things.

When Baker-Carr had protested that if his commander could ride into battle like Chandos or du Guesclin he could do the same, Elles threatened him with 'terrible things'. A commander's place, he said, was at his own HQ. For his part he compromised, riding defiantly on Hilda's bridge, following tapes painstakingly laid out by Hotblack and the others until she had crossed her first objective. Then, much to the crew's relief, he dismounted and walked home, impatiently pushing aside groups of German soldiers anxious to surrender themselves to him. The going, across chalk downland uncrumped by shells, was excellent. The Tank Corps, well prepared for what it had to do, was in high spirits. This, at long last, was the opportunity to show what it could achieve.

Spot on 6 am on that memorable 20 November the whisper went round, 'Here they come'. As groups of tanks moved forward, led in the early stages by their subaltern commanders on foot through a dawn mist, a thousand silent guns bellowed out as one. Down came the barrage with a roar that made the earth quake underfoot as the infantry, all save Harper's 'little fellers', rose up and followed the Mk IVs. To begin with it resembled a ceremonial parade, all hands keeping their exact distances. Each section of tanks moved off in arrowhead formation, a hundred yard perpendicular between apex and base, itself a hundred yards across. At the same distance behind the two rear machines followed a platoon of infantry in extended file. This was the kind of thing Mr Churchill and Colonel Swinton had long envisaged and it worked.

Belts of barbed wire, skilfully erected at leisure by Germany's abundant slave labour, of a depth and thickness that no British soldier had seen before and much of it on reverse slopes that no gun could reach, were trampled down as gumboots trample nettles; here and there they were forcibly pulled out and cast aside by the grapnels. The battle drills so carefully worked out by Fuller and the others did everything that was expected of them. Trenches reckoned to be takeable only at the price of great losses fell for half-a-dozen casualties. The cavalry performed its now customary function of cluttering up all the roads in rear that were urgently needed for the passage of supplies and ammunition. One Canadian squadron did some useful work during which most of its horses were killed, but, apart from that, it was an idle day for horsemen. Why they were there at all has never been satisfactorily explained. Baker-Carr's 1st Brigade had obeyed orders and cleared a way for the 2nd Cavalry Division of Major-General Mullens ('Gobby-Chops' to his many unfriends). All he saw of them was a single liaison officer who repeatedly took back messages that all was clear; by the end of the day he was almost in tears.

Only at the crucially important village of Flesquières, Harper's first objective, did the plan fail and that because no attempt was made to carry it out. Sixteen tanks duly arrived on the ridge. Ahead of them lay Graincourt and beyond that the ultimate objective, Bourlon Wood. The Highlanders, who should have been on the ridge within a couple of minutes, were not to be seen. The tank crews, having nothing else to do, wandered around in awe looking at the great works they had captured by their own efforts. Then the German artillerymen recovered themselves and began to fire from a nearby orchard over open sights. With no infantry to help them the Mk IVs dodged the shells as best they could, but with the complicated business of drivers signalling to gearsmen and waiting for them to do their parts this was pretty ineffective. One by one they were picked off and smashed. When the 51st finally arrived they had a far harder time of it than would have happened if their GOC had obeyed orders. There was no longer any question of storming Bourlon Wood. The adjacent 62nd Division had done wonders in taking all its objectives and had outflanked Flesquières. When General Braithwaite offered to enfilade the place Harper refused his help.

Only on the right was success less than complete. The bridge across the Scheldt Canal at Maisnières had been partially destroyed by German sappers and, as everybody concerned knew, this was the key to the very important Rumilly-Seranvillers ridge. The commander of the leading tank, under no illusions about his chances, went for it bald-headed. The gamble nearly succeeded, but not quite. The tank reached the half-way mark but then the last steel girders buckled and snapped, gently lowering the machine into the water. As other tanks arrived they did what they could by providing covering fire, but it was too late. The Germans had time enough in which to fall back on the half-complete Maisnières-Beaurevoir Line. 'Bald-headed' suggests the Marquis of Granby but it is not inapt here. The Tank commander lost his wig in the canal.

By tea-time on the 20th the battle was over for most of the Tank Corps. Losses had been heavy, mostly from field guns used in an anti-tank role. The advance, however, had been something without parallel in this war, about eight miles on a front of 13,000 yards; 8,000 prisoners and more than 100 guns had been taken. The supply tanks had done what they were needed to do; wireless tanks had passed messages swifter than the best of pigeons. The sum total of casualties did not exceed 1500. In England church bells rang, though the ringers were soon to regret it. Colonel Swinton, far away from the battlefield, received a telegram. 'All ranks thank you. Your show. Elles'.

The next couple of days saw the end of the Armoured Division style of battle and a reversion to the penny packet. Composite companies were quickly put together but there could be no repetition of Day 1. The infantry were physically exhausted and the new formations unpractised at working with armour. 'Consequently,' says Williams-Ellis, 'many strong points, though they were finally captured, gave us more trouble than they should.' Thirteen tanks of B Battalion smashed their way into Cantaing and two more drove the Germans from Noyelles, no losses being suffered in either operation. Twelve more, from H Battalion, were ordered to make the long slog of six miles across the open to see what they could do about Fontaine Notre Dame, the furthest point reached by anybody. They got there at 4.30 pm, had a battle lasting an hour and handed the village over to the infantry, who were themselves driven out next day. On the 23rd the tanks came back, twenty-four of them. A full day had sufficed to make the place inexpugnable; every building was a fortlet and in the narrow streets it was impossible to bring the guns to bear. The clumsy Lewis had a very small traverse; it might have been another story given either Madsen or Hotchkiss. As it was, the crews were lucky that November days are short and that darkness gave them a chance to withdraw.

On the same day thirty-four tanks of 1st Brigade supported 40th Division in their brave attack on Bourlon Wood and village. They drove through the wood but once again the village was prepared to receive them and the infantry were worn out. Fontaine and Bourlon remained in German hands.

Hankey wrote in his diary for the 21st: 'The great event today is the full news of the great tank attack near Cambrai, where 400 tanks have burst right through all the German lines of defence and let through the cavalry. It is in a sense a great personal triumph for me, as I have always since the first day of the tanks advocated an attack on these lines.' Then came the counter-attack, bolstered up by the divisions from Russia whose presence had been kept from Haig by his own Chief of Intelligence. By the end of the month losses and gains of all kinds about balanced out.

The Renault FT 17 Tank of 1917. Still in use in 1939.

Vickers Medium Mk 2. For years the backbone of the RTC.

The Tank Corps had an unexpected epilogue. Colonel Courage's 2nd Brigade, on the right-hand end of the front, had been reduced to about thirty effectives and had been doing fine work in helping to hold up the German onrush. Baker-Carr, his end being fairly quiet, paid a visit to Third Army HQ where he met Major-General Vaughan. The withdrawal was a disappointment, Vaughan said, but he hoped that all the tanks would get out all right. Baker-Carr, knowing nothing of this, pressed for information. Apparently orders had been sent to Elles that the line was being pulled back to the original one and that all tanks had to be behind it by 11 o'clock. By inspired staff work the message had been addressed to Elles by name and sent to the low-grade cabaret in Albert which was serving as Tank Corps HQ. Elles was at GHQ; the order lay unopened on his table. With so many hours lost and with tanks littered about the old battlefield either under or awaiting repair there was no possibility of compliance. A number of tanks had to be left stranded in territory that would soon be occupied by the Germans. Frantic efforts were made to blow them up but some were bound to be in a state capable of being put back into service. As they were – by the Germans.

General Woollcombe was removed from his command. The discerning reader will have guessed the name of the man whose superior philosophy demanded his advancement. 'Uncle' Harper got his Corps. 179 tanks were out of action, though only sixty-five of them by German fire, before Bourlon Wood was reached.

At GHQ there were also changes. The ebullient Charteris and the lugubrious Kiggell – so unsuitably called Sir Launcelot – both had to go. Kiggell, best remembered for his 'Good God, did we really send men to fight in that?', left as his opinion that Cambrai had been all very well but such an operation could never be repeated. Sir Herbert Lawrence who replaced him was a man of other mettle. Butler also was removed by popular demand. Sir Douglas, who had a high opinion of his capability, tried to have him promoted to Kiggell's old position but anti-Butler feeling was too strong. He was given instead the chance to show what he could do as a commander. General Pulteney, creator of IIIrd Corps, had not come too well out of the new style of warfare and was replaced by the former Deputy Chief of the General Staff.

Bertie Stern, never the most patient of men, was left to meditate what might have happened had a few companies of Whippets replaced many regiments of horses. Had he only been given his head, with the powers promised him by Sir Douglas so long ago, it could have been arranged.

CHAPTER 14

Present Tense: Future Imperfect

UPON THESE THINGS Stern pondered at Rue Edouard Sept, numero deux, in Paris, the office he had procured for the Anglo-American Commission. Before setting himself up there Stern had had a meeting with Mr Churchill; it took place in London on 26 November, a day that saw the last few surviving tanks of F and I battalions still working away at saving the lives of men of the Guards Division and Braithwaite's 62nd. It was also the eve of the great German counter-thrust. Stern, forgivably, gave a reminder that it was only a month since he had been convicted of piling up useless machines.

Mr Churchill was a very worried Minister, and that with good reason. U-boat sinkings had drastically reduced the flow of iron ore from the Spanish Biscayan ports; Passchendaele and its associates had drastically reduced the number of effective fighting men in France. The Americans had not yet arrived in significant force, whereas the German army in the west was gaining strength every day. The French army was on the ropes, though by no means out of the fight. His own vision of the mechanized battle had never wavered and he made some calculations of his own. Infantry strength was greatly reduced, though artillery remained tremendously strong. He put each arm about 40% of the total. The RFC he reckoned at 10%; the cavalry, although two Indian Divisions had gone east, still made up $3\frac{1}{2}$%; another 4% went to the Machine Gun Corps and $\frac{1}{2}$% to the Gas experts. The 2% remaining was the Tank Corps. A long and carefully thought-out plan went to the Cabinet proposing a cutting-down of foot and guns, the reduction of horse to $\frac{1}{2}$% and the increase being in aircraft, machine-guns, gas and the tanks. These last would be multiplied four-fold. The date of the paper was 5 March, 1918. The events of 21 March overtook it.

Early in December, less than a week from the anti-climactic end of Cambrai, Mr Churchill had, however, done something to ensure victory in 1919 despite all the gloom. The Anglo-American Commission was set up, with Stern and Drain as Commissioners, charged with building great numbers of a tank superior even to the Mk V which would be made with British hulls and the Liberty engine. The Commissioners would build a factory in France capable of producing 300 tanks a month to begin with and rising to 1200. In 1918 there would be 1500, with a distribution of bits and pieces carefully set out. All this was incorporated in a formal Treaty, signed on 22 January, 1918, by Ambassador Page and Arthur Balfour. France made available a site at Neuvy-Pailloux, a couple of hundred miles south of Paris and within easy reach of the American-used ports of St Nazaire and Bordeaux. Annamite labour in sufficient quantity would also be found by France.

All this lay in the future and there were pressing problems nearer home. Tank production, largely because of steel shortage, had fallen below the 200 a month that had been achieved during 1917. Stern continued to badger, blaming all this, perhaps not entirely fairly, on the War Office. As he had the ear of Mr Lloyd George far more frequently than did General Capper, he managed to get the matter raised in Cabinet with useful results. There was much gloom in London in early December, 1917. GHQ was distrusted as incompetent and Mr Lloyd George would gladly have sacked Haig had he only dared. GHQ, with Mr Churchill as ally, complained that something like a quarter of a million troops who ought to have been in France were kept at home for specious reasons connected with invasion threats. Manpower was running very low. When the Navy demanded 90,000 more hands the Admiralty received its first rebuff for years. Sir Douglas was ordered to take over more of the French line, taking his right down to Barisis on the Oise. It was in a shocking state of disrepair and demanded much labour to make it anything like defensible. He was told, though not in so many words, that the men who should be working on it were rotting in their muddy graves by Ypres.

The immediate business of tank people was to get rid of the Mk IVs and bring in Mk Vs and Medium 'A's, alias Whippets. A trickle had begun in the autumn but it was woefully insufficient. The Cabinet's new Tank Board looked promising. General Seeley was President with Mr Maclean (the civilian successor to Admiral Moore) as his Deputy. 'Boney' Fuller was a member, along with General Furse, d'Eyncourt and Stern. Elles was added later, along with that founder member, Ernest Swinton. With men of this quality at work it is not remarkable that things got on the move again. Their programme of 5,000 modern machines during 1918 began to look possible.

In France the building of the Neuvy-Pailloux factory was handed over to the English firm of Holland & Hannen, with its supervision entrusted to Sir John Hunter of the Ministry of Munitions. Stern was not among his admirers, and it seems to have been mutual: 'All through the early months of the year Sir John Hunter objected to any advice or help on our part,' ran one of his letters to Mr Churchill. Furious telegrams complaining of delay and mismanagement flooded into Whitehall over the signatures 'Stern and Drain', It sounded much like '*Sturm und Drang*'.

Relations with General Capper had not improved. A report on the tank operations at Cambrai was drawn up fairly quickly and submitted to the Ministry of Munitions. Stern asked for a copy and was brusquely told that he could not have one. As usual he went back to Mr Lloyd George – something that the General would have furiously resented – and Capper was ordered to hand it over. Cambrai had been fought during a fortunate interval in time. The Mk IV, because of its clumsy ancillary gearboxes – which often stuck in moments of stress – was a sitting duck to any sort of field gun, as the Germans were beginning to realize. Tests carried out in France for Stern's committee by an engineer named George Watson suggested that it might be even worse than was generally thought. His report, dated 26 September, said that he was convinced of the Mk IVs inability to be driven up a gradient of more than 35° from horizontal and in 2 to 3 feet of soft ground he was doubtful whether it would climb anything at all. In several parts of the Hindenburg Line, he pointed out, the relation of width, depth and height of parados was such that the angle might be as steep as 50°. The drivers and reconnaissance officers at Cambrai must have been uncommonly skilful, uncommonly lucky or a bit of both. In any case the Mk IV must not be used again in an important attack.

On 8 January, 1918, Stern sent the Prime Minister a detailed appreciation of the war situation. Lay it alongside Mr Churchill's Munitions Estimates for 1918 of a couple of months later and it would be hard to tell who had written which. Free from War Office interference their minds had met completely. But the War Office still had shots in its locker.

Between Cambrai and the March Retreat the Tank Corps had time for rest and retraining. All the battalions were withdrawn to the sea coast around Le Treport. Everybody knew that they were in the eye of the hurricane and that they must prepare themselves for battle of a kind not previously experienced. The tank in defence was a new concept. The battered Cambrai veterans, about a third of those which had gone over, were thoroughly refurbished and with new arrivals from home the total of Mk IVs came up to 320. From Squadron 20 at Le Havre came also the first fifty Medium As. The Whippet, as everybody called it, was Tritton's Chaser brought up to date. Twenty feet long, nearly nine wide and turning the scales at fourteen tons, it looked much more like the tanks of today. Each track had its own engine and it was steered by varying the speeds. A cab was perched on top of the tail end, with three Hotchkiss guns inside, and it could manage a top speed of 8 mph. Much was expected of the Whippets, but they were the new cavalry and cavalry was not designed to hold positions. It did, however, show to frustrated men that better tanks were on the way.

It was impossible to put any sort of date on when they might arrive. Stern continued to pester Mr Churchill; when rumours reached him of the tanks being built by Germany he pestered the War Office also. Finally he pestered the Prime Minister, to whom he had already sent a long paper setting out his own *Variants On The Offensive;* having had more experience than other men, he wrote the most practical exegesis of the whole business. His reward, if such it can be called, was that a Cabinet on 8 March decided to adopt an immediate programme of building 5,000 tanks. Mr Churchill, not a member though lunching at least once a week with Mr Lloyd George and F. E. Smith, was told to see to it.

It was on 8 April that Lord Milner, now Secretary for War, visited Stern in Paris and much had happened between these two dates. Stern returned to the charge. There ought to be a central authority to develop Mechanical Warfare 'untrammelled by all the vested interests of all the established branches of the War Office. In this

Two views of a Medium A Tank, the Whippet.

way, a highly technical development could be carried out by a practical man with the advice of the military authorities.' Modesty forbad him to name the most practical man, but he made it very clear to Milner that, had he been given his head, the original figure of 5,000 tanks for 1918 would never have been cut to 1350 and the Army would now have had far more in service than it did. Stern begged Milner to talk to d'Eyncourt. Apparently he did, for 'from this data a new era of progress started for Mechanical Warfare at the War Office'. It was only just in time. The war might easily have ended with a German victory soon after 21 March.

Dawn on 21 March, 1918, saw by far the greatest attack in the old style. The Kaiser's armies had at last been able to mass an enormous superiority in guns and men with which they were determined to fight and win the last and decisive battles. They came very near to doing it. Six thousand guns lashed a forty-mile front with gas and high explosive under whose cover three-quarters of a million trained men advanced to the assault. Most of this fell upon General Gough's makeshift defences and, despite much unrecorded heroism by men who died where they stood, the surge came dangerously close to Amiens.

This was not the kind of battle upon which 370 tanks, most of them worn out, could have much effect. Most of the Mk IVs fought their last fight until they had to be abandoned for want of petrol or were picked off by German field guns. Many crews removed their Lewis guns and joined with the nearest infantry as a welcome reinforcement. Only about 180 ever got into action and even Clough Williams-Ellis could not find out enough to tell a coherent story of the doings of all of them. The Whippets, apart from one piece of misfortune, did far better. They had recently been issued to the 3rd battalion at Bray-sur-Somme, a camp that was destroyed early on in the fighting. Several Whippets were temporarily out of action with engine troubles of a minor kind; as spares could not be got forward in time they had to be blown up. Those that remained proved excellent value and far more reliable than anything used before.

According to his own account, 'Boney' Fuller sat upon the top of Mont St Quentin, just outside Peronne, and watched the Army fall back. There he put to himself the question 'Why are our troops retreating?' and answered it with 'Because our command was paralysed'. Fuller's thoughts were always in a rarified atmosphere. The simple explanation that Gough's army was in the position of a bather on the shore engulfed by a wave of gigantic size, was too simple by half for him. His physical resemblance to the Corsican was misleading, for this 'Boney' never subscribed to the belief that 'In war, moral considerations make up three-quarters of the game; the relative balance of man-power accounts only for the remaining quarter'. Fuller had never, apart from some scrimmages in South Africa, commanded even the smallest number of men in battle. His article of faith was the antithesis of this one: material, not morale, wins wars. He had been told about a light tank, not yet in existence, which could manage 20 mph and with this he reckoned the tide could be turned; not perhaps in 1918, which must look after itself, but in 1919 or possibly even 1920. It was against this discouraging backcloth that he mused upon his Plan 1919. Much the same idea seems to have occurred to Sir Henry

Wilson a few days earlier. March, 1918, however, gave little scope for 'psyching out' the German army.

On 26 March two companies of Whippets did sterling work; once again it was 'Uncle' Harper who made it necessary. The blow had fallen on a Thursday. On the following Monday, in Gough's words, 'The Third Army gave up Bapaume and fell back behind the Ancre and north of it, a distance in places of over 10 miles. A very dangerous situation developed on its front during this afternoon. Its IV Corps (General Harper), although it consisted of six Divisions, left a gap of four miles in its line, from Hamel to the north of Puisieux, which was some twelve miles north of the left flank of the Fifth Army. Into this gap the Germans had penetrated to a depth of three miles, and had seized Colincamps before nightfall. Colincamps is barely nineteen miles north-east of Amiens.'

Two companies of the 3rd Tank Corps arrived at Mailly-Maillet about noon on

A Whippet at Mailly-Maillet during the March Retreat with men of the New Zealand Division.

the 26th. The village stands about a couple of miles due south of Colincamps. Nobody had the slightest idea of what was going on, bar the fact that infantry were still retreating and the Germans could not be far away. Three hundred of them soon arrived, in close formation, and were met head on by the leading Whippets as they rounded the corner of a wood. The Hotchkisses opened up briskly; the Germans, those who survived, either fled or surrendered to the infantry who were following behind.

As the retreat went on a job of sorts was found for those tanks that were still in business. Very often it was impossible to tell who, for the moment, owned any given village. It cost far less in lives to send a tank to find out than to put in a platoon of foot-soldiers. Several times the tanks found villages hostile and fought it out for an hour or two. With guns red-hot and petrol almost exhausted they then tried to make their way home. More often than not they had to be abandoned for lack of fuel and efforts were made to blow them up.

Much the same thing happened during the German offensive on the Lys. These

Another Whippet. Red and white stripes were used for identification after the Germans began to use captured machines.

were not tank battles, at any rate not with the few veterans that were still operational. It was at Villers-Bretonneux on 24 April that a milestone in history was passed. A section of three tanks, a male and two females lay up overnight in a gas-drenched wood behind the little town among the swollen bodies of dead horses and 'birds with bulging eyes and stiffened claws'. At dawn on the 24th two German aircraft spotted them and dropped flares. A deluge of shells, many of them being asphyxiating gas, crashed down into the wood. The crews, choking into their respirators, climbed back into the machines and moved a little to the rear. Wounded men and stragglers drifted back; Mitchell, the subaltern in command of the male, agreed with a nearby battery commander that when the Germans arrived his tanks would take them on over open sights. Several members of his crews had to be taken out, overcome by gas and hors de combat. Eventually an order arrived: 'Proceed to Cachy switch-line and hold it at all costs.' The three Mk IVs crawled off, passing right through the German barrage at the best speed they could manage. All of a sudden an infantryman appeared, waving his rifle and yelling 'Look out, Jerry tanks about'. Captain Brown disembarked hurriedly and ran across the shell-swept field to warn his females.

Lieutenant Mitchell opened a loophole and looked out. 'There, some three hundred yards away, a round, squat-looking monster was advancing; behind it came waves of infantry, and farther away to the left and right crawled two more of these armed tortoises.' Mitchell's tank zigzagged between the trenches and turned left. His gunners fired several rounds without scoring a hit. Then came the sound of hail on a tin roof, accompanied by showers of splinters that rattled off their helmets. The Germans were using machine-guns with armour-piercing bullets. The Mk IV continued to dodge, the gunner on the left side, one-eyed as a result of the gas, firing often but still hitting nothing. Near Cachy Mitchell saw the two females, limping away with great holes in their sides. Another swing nearly brought his tank into a trench manned by our own troops; an armour-piercing bullet went through both legs of a Lewis gunner. The 6-pdrs still banged away, scoring many near-misses but no hits. Mitchell took a desperate decision. He brought his tank to a standstill in order to give his gunners one last chance before they too were scuppered. The one-eyed gunner scored three bulls in rapid succession. The monster halted, keeled over and its crew emerged through a door.

The Lewis gunners gave them a drum or two for luck and then they went in search of the others, the 6-pdrs firing case-shot – the modern version of grape rejected by the War Office in 1916 – into the German foot. The German tanks, seemingly, had had enough; one by one they backed away and made off. Mitchell's troubles were by no means over. A German aircraft bombed him from less than a hundred feet, blowing the tank clean off the ground. 'We fell back with a mighty crash, and then continued our journey unhurt.' A few minutes later they dropped into an unobserved shell hole; the driver quite rightly revved up the engine and, just as their nose was protruding, it stalled. Every German gun within miles seemed to concentrate on them. At such an angle all the efforts of the crew to swing the huge starting handle got them nowhere. The driver, well trained at Wool, did the only thing left; he allowed the tank to run back in reverse, let in his clutch and the good Daimler engine started up again.

As they climbed out Mitchell saw that the German infantry were waiting for him and were about to attack with bundles of lashed grenades capable of blowing off a track. Then he saw something more cheerful: 'Seven small Whippets, the newest and fastest type of tank, unleashed at last and racing into action. They came on at six to eight miles an hour, heading straight for the Germans, who scattered in all directions, fleeing terror-stricken from this whirlwind of death.' The Whippets, manned by twenty-one crew, routed some 1200 Germans, killing at least 400. A fourth German tank appeared but did not linger.

Nemesis followed hubris. A shell finally hit a track and blew it off. No 1 Tank of the 1st Section of A Coy had got its quietus. It was a glorious swan-song for the Mk IV. Never were decorations – Mitchell got an MC, his sergeant an MM – better earned. The German tank, 'Elfriede' by name, was salvaged with much difficulty. It carried a crew of eighteen but, apart from the luxury of a sprung track, it had nothing to teach the British designers.

A few days later the Mk Vs began to come along in numbers and the penny-farthing era was over. Factory workers, put on their mettle by the losses during the retreat, had been working as they were not to work again until 1940. New Mk Vs had been piling up and were now being shipped across as fast as could be managed. It was just as well. Apart from the Whippet companies the Tank Corps had almost ceased to exist.

The Landship conception was not yet history. Lieut Mitchell, captain of HMLS A1, solemnly and in due form submitted a claim to the Admiralty for prize money, he and his crew having captured SMLS Elfriede. Their Lordships, never over-swift to know that their legs were being pulled, passed it to the War Office. The reply does not say in so many words that Landships had ceased to belong to the Navy. It merely asserts that there was nothing doing, 'there being no funds available for the purpose of granting Prize Money in the Army'.

CHAPTER 15

The Pendulum begins to Swing

THE MK Vs, shipped from Richborough by Squadron 20, were received with enthusiasm. Wilson's epicyclic transmission, once it had been mastered, made all the difference in the world and not for the drivers alone. With the ancillary gearboxes gone two men were freed to give all their attention to fighting the ship while the driver could manoeuvre it single-handed with a far better chance of dodging shellfire. A kind of conning tower in the roof not only gave far better vision for the commander but at last made it possible to fix the unditching beam from inside the hull. Ricardo's engine, made without the use of either aluminium or high-tensile steel, gave the necessary extra power and was entirely dependable. Using Shell No 1 Aviation Spirit the tank could cover 25 miles on a single fill, could amble along at 5 mph and could change direction whilst mounting a slope, something beyond the powers of the Mk IV. The Lewis gun had been returned to the infantry where it should have been all along, and each Mk V was kitted out with three Hotchkisses, the third being a stern-chaser. Fuel was delivered by an Autovac and the petrol tank was divided into three independent compartments, each capable of delivering even if the others were holed.

There were, however, two serious defects. First, the ventilation was extremely bad. Everybody knows the heat that hits you when entering an ordinary car that has been standing in the sun. Thin sheet metal holds a great deal; armour plate is far worse. A belt-driven fan circulated the hot air and expelled some of it through the roof but it was far from being effective. Nor was this the worst of it. Ricardo's engine ran very hot and most of the exhaust system lay inside the hull. Quite soon after starting the pipes glowed red; after an hour's running they became white-hot and the metal buckled, discharging raw exhaust gas into the interior to mix with cordite fumes, esprit de corps, and, sometimes, with the chlorine or phosgene gas loosed by the enemy. Sheet-metal cladding was added as a desperate expedient but it made little difference. In the summer days that lay ahead the capabilities of the Mk V were to be limited by the capacity of the crew to endure these conditions rather than by anything mechanical. It became a very serious matter. The Whippet did not suffer from an inefficient exhaust system but it was even more vulnerable to

A Mk V Tank at Bovington.

extreme heat. All of these chasers were concentrated in a single Brigade – Hardress-Lloyd's 3rd – and much was expected of them. The 3rd Battalion's History is eloquent: 'On a hot summer's day one hour's running with the door closed renders a Whippet weaponless except for revolver fire. The heat generated is so intense that it not only causes ammunition to swell so that it jams the gun, but actually in several cases caused rounds to explode inside the Tank. Guns became too hot to hold, and in one case the temperature of the steering wheel became unbearable.' It is well to remember these things. Tank Corps crews, by long experience, were able to live on a blend of exhaust fumes, cordite and phosgene gas rather than air, but human endurance has its limits. The Mk V Star, an elongated version weighing 35 tons to the Mk V's 29, was designed to carry almost a platoon of infantry on to its objective; conditions inside, however, were so abominable to the unaccustomed that the passengers arrived sick and fainting. The time for troop-carrying had not yet arrived. In addition, the extra 6 feet of length made the Mk V Star less manoeuvrable and a better target.

Stern, whom Ricardo called 'the most active driving force behind the whole project,' was working very hard at this as well as other things. His relations with the Americans were excellent, for Colonels Drain and Alden were both of the same way of thinking. With the French the best that can be said is that he got on well with the military men. M. Albert Thomas (described by Haig as '39 but he looks older. He is so covered with hair and spectacles') had complained officially about his bullying manner but General Estienne took him to dine with Pétain on 24 April; Pétain, despite the Schneiders and St Chamonds, was a believer. He asked Stern to try and get authority from his Government to form a central school and training-ground for an Inter-Allied Tank Army at Chateauroux. Foch, he said, was of the same mind. Stern took this seriously enough to go straight to London and seek out the new CIGS,

Henry Wilson, who had taken 'Wully' Robertson's chair. Wilson, about to set out for France, said that he would recommend the idea to GHQ. For a start an Inter-Allied School of Tactics was opened at Bourron, south of Fontainebleau, and each of the three powers sent a tank battalion there. General Estienne, liked and respected by everybody, was the first and last President.

Things were looking up for Stern. At a meeting of the Tank Committee at the War Office on 25 June General Capper resigned. He and Stern had quarrelled fiercely. On 7 May a letter from Stern had gone to Frances Stevenson saying that 'All my efforts to coordinate Mechanical Warfare are stultified by this unbusinesslike somersault of the authorities. Both the American and French authorities are aghast at these incomprehensible methods. Every year the same muddle goes on and if we lose this war I for one can give complete and conclusive reasons in my Department for the causes of such an overwhelming disaster. Will you please put this before the Prime Minister. The Programme for 1917 was muddled away, and the same for 1918 occurred. I am determined that it shall not occur for 1919, of which there is great danger.' Already a similar one was on its way to Mr Churchill: 'The French and Americans are now informed that the representative of the Ministry of Munitions as far as Tanks are concerned on questions concerning the Allies is General Capper. This already has produced a feeling of blank astonishment.' Capper's last throw had been to ensure that GHQ refused Stern and his people the passes they needed to travel freely in the British Army area. Clearly there was not room for both of them. Stern, the more valuable, stayed; Capper, at a War Office meeting on 25 June, resigned. Later on, when the war was over, he became Lieutenant-Governor of Guernsey. In 1923 he was appointed to be the first Commandant of the Royal Tank Corps.

Stern seems to have become reconciled with Admiral Moore, for when the suggestion was floated that a new Tank Board be set up at the War Office they formed up together, along with d'Eyncourt, to General Seeley, now Deputy Minister of Munitions. Seeley, during his command of the Canadian Cavalry Brigade, had received a report from Haig that he was not fit to hold such an appointment. As a Minister, with Plumer's old Chief of General Staff 'Tim' Harington at his elbow, he managed things better. The new Board contained the men who knew about tanks. Seeley was President, with d'Eyncourt as his Deputy; Fuller, now at War Office, spoke for the General Staff, Furse for the Army Council and Stern for Overseas and Allies. Later on Elles and Swinton were added. The Admiral bowed out, but Admiral Bacon came back in. A programme of 5,000 tanks, to be made in England, was agreed without argument. A further 1500 super-tanks would come from Neuvy-Pailloux with British hulls and American Liberty engines.

It was not only the Tank Board that watched the slow progress of the Liberty. Sir Hugh Trenchard had been promised it for the big Handley-Pages of his Independent Air Force that was going to bomb Berlin. When it finally arrived the war was over; so good was the engine, however, that because of a shortage of Rolls Royce Meteors a number of specimens were disinterred in 1942 and put into a tank for Hitler's war called the Centaur. It was not the worst tank of that era. The first Mk

Wilson's Medium B Tank.

VIII hull was sent to America in July. Ricardo designed an engine of the same power, 300 hp, and the factories began to work on it. In addition to the Mk VIII there was to be a Mk IX, unarmed save for a machine-gun but capable of carrrying a full platoon of Vickers gunners, complete with machine-guns and impedimenta in reasonable comfort. M Renault was, meanwhile, churning out his tanklets by the hundred.

The American Army took to tanks like ducks to a pond. A US Tank Corps, under Brigadier-General Samuel D. Rockenbach, was early formed; a battalion, the 301st, was sent to Wool to learn its trade in Mk IVs under British instructors whilst the remainder were cantoned at Langres awaiting the arrival of the Renaults. One battalion commander there – soon to be a brigade commander – was the 33-year-old George Patton, already glimpsed by Haig as Pershing's ADC. Though the outward forms of discipline manifested by the 301st were not those of the Tank Corps they proved first-class material, every man being a trained mechanic.

The British battalions in France could not say the same. Losses during the March Retreat and on the Lys had been heavy, most of them incurred when tank crews were serving as infantry Lewis gun teams. The critical need for more foot-soldiers was plain to see; nor was it all that surprising that word went round yet again of plans to disband the Tank Corps. Oddly enough, although the German cavalry had not surged through the breaches during the Retreat – in fact they had hardly been seen at all – nobody had the temerity even to think of laying hands on

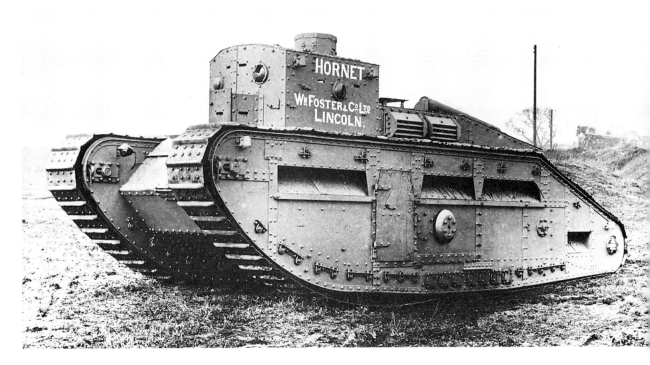

Tritton's Medium C Tank.

General Kavanagh's troopers.

The horsemen had fought manfully but, as at First Ypres, they did their work on foot, using their mounts merely to move them from one part of the field to another. Their fire power, because of the number of horse-holders needed, was very small. A cavalry regiment could put about 400 riflemen in the line, immobile and fit only to hold a position until they were shelled out of it. The same number of men could have crewed well over a hundred Medium As, bringing down the fire of three Hotchkiss guns each and with the ability to move about counter-attacking the German masses whenever the chance came. One cavalry General, placed in command of 14th Division, went off his head with the strain, as Gough reported to Haig. If Stern and his people had been given their heads a mosquito fleet of Whippets, though they could not have stemmed an advance so massive, could have influenced events far more than three Divisions of cavalry. Raids upon German communications, always their most vulnerable areas, might have slowed things down and the cost would have been far less. All this had been thrown away, so he reckoned, because Generals lacked faith in the New Model Army. He could only hope for better things, perhaps later this year, perhaps in 1919. At least an order had been placed with Mr Docker's Metropolitan Company for 450 Medium C tanks, a super-Whippet tentatively called the Hornet and Tritton's work; whether it would put in an appearance during 1918 was another matter. Wilson was working on a similar machine, to be called the Medium B. He was not in the best of tempers, for his design for a Mk VI, a tank

Twilight and dawn. Cavalry ride past a Mk V Tank.

without sponsons but having a 6-pdr firing directly ahead, had been rejected by d'Eyncourt on the grounds that the muzzle must inevitably dip into the mud.

It is fortunate for the Tank Corps that in 1918 it contained at least one officer who did not equate discipline with blind obedience. Baker-Carr, as soon as the rumour of disbandment reached him, sought out Elles and demanded a few days' Paris leave, darkly observing that it would be better for his commander not to know why. On arrival, 'I rang up an old and trusted friend, one of the British officers attached to the Supreme Council at Versailles, and asked myself to lunch with him.' The friend arrived at the Ritz complete with a French Cabinet Minister. This statesman was sunk in gloom. According to him the French army 'was in an appalling condition and on the very verge of mutiny'. There was much more to the same effect. This finished, Baker-Carr managed a private word with his friend whom he calls W. W was deeply perturbed for even then a counter-offensive was on the planning board with much work for the tanks to do. He went away and came back in a few minutes with 'a French officer who stood extremely high in Marshal Foch's confidence'. Baker-Carr explained his presence; the Frenchman undertook to pass on everything he had said direct to the Generalissimo. A few days later GHQ received a polite request from Foch that as many tank units as possible be brought into being at the earliest moment. There was more than a little of Nelson in Baker-Carr; or it may have been that service under Kitchener in the Sudan had taught him useful things. Be that as it may, no further word was heard about reduction, let alone disbandment, of the Tank Corps.

Soon the lessons of the Retreat became understood. The factor that had made it peter out was not so much British resistance as German staff incomprehension. Apart from the fifteen fighting tanks like Elfriede that Daimler Benz and two other firms had made, and a score or so captured Mk IVs, the German army had no form of transport capable of working away from roads. Thus, as divisions became gummed up in the abomination of desolation that were the old Somme battlefields, they could not get their supplies through and for want of them the very successful break-through ran out of steam. This was a mistake that Sir Douglas would not make when his own hour came. Every decrepit tank that could move, even including a few Mk Is that had somehow survived, was made roadworthy and kitted out with as many sledges as they could haul. Next time tanks would not merely cross and smash trenches or pulverize pill-boxes; they would be the indispensable blood stream of an army moving forward.

CHAPTER 16

The End comes in Sight

ON 27 MAY THE GERMAN ARMY enjoyed its last success of the war. Led for the first and only time by tanks of its own it smashed through on the Chemin des Dames against some very indifferent French generalship. Five battle-worn British Divisions, sent there for a rest, formed the hard core of the defence. The thirteen-mile advance drew more salients on the map, as such advances always did, before the momentum flagged. The next assault, in mid-July, though it employed the biggest concentration of guns ever heard before and probably since, was a demonstrable failure. Even the mighty German Army could not now win the war by the old methods, no matter how large they might be writ. By midsummer the pendulum had reached the end of its swing and began to move in the opposite direction.

May and June were busy months for the tanks. Every battalion, except for some in Baker-Carr's First Brigade, was now equipped or equipping with Mk Vs, Mk V Stars or Whippets. A few even bigger troop carriers called the Mk V Two Stars began to appear, though none came in time for the last battles. In addition a battalion of armoured cars arrived. This owed nothing to memories of Samson at Dunkirk but came into existence almost by accident. The Imperial Russian Government had ordered a number from the Austin factory. They bore little resemblance to the elegant converted Rolls-Royces used by Samson and T. E. Lawrence. The Austins were more plebeian, solid-tyred, weighing just under six tons and capable of 18 mph flat out on a hard road. Behind the driver's cab stood two turrets, closely resembling great armoured dustbins each with a Hotchkiss gun poking out of it. The revolution in Russia left them on the hands of the British Government which decided that a use could be found as auxiliaries to the Tank Corps. Events were to show that the decision was amply justified. When the time came it was the 17th (Armoured Car) Battalion that led the British Army across the Hohenzollern Bridge into Cologne. But much was to happen before that memorable day arrived.

The main thrust of the British-Canadian-Australian-New Zealand Armies remained, on its southern flank, in the capable hands of General Sir Henry Rawlinson. His last personal experience of tanks had been almost exactly two years before and in almost exactly the same place. In 1916 he had been little impressed by them; in 1918 he was a convert, with all a convert's zeal. His plans for hitting the Germans

The Austin armoured car. A late model with pneumatic tyres.

as they had never been hit before depended largely upon the new arm.

There were others yet to be converted. Since Bullecourt no Australian soldier had ever spoken of tanks but with contempt and loathing. This was hardly remarkable. Bullecourt had been the only battle in which they had lost many men as prisoners. All the same, before offensive operations could begin the Australian Corps would have to accustom itself to new ways. Their commander, Sir John Monash, was a civil engineer in private life and he saw the potentials of the Mk V and the Whippet more clearly and sooner than did most men. With his cordial encouragement Tanks and Diggers met again in order to get to know each other better. They were not so much demonstrations as parties. Courage's Fifth Brigade put its Mk Vs through all their tricks, allowing the Australians to travel on them and even on occasions to drive. Then challenges were issued. Let the Australians prepare the strongest works they knew how to make and the tanks would set about them. Wire, trenches and redoubts were all flattened as a man grinds his boot heel into a wasp's nest. Australia, ever a sporting nation, admitted the bet lost. From then on Five Brigade and the Australian Corps worked as one.

There were other little rehearsals during June. Stern, with his French and American colleagues, was working hard to build an Allied Tank Army. For this to become a reality the three armies concerned must learn each other's ways. There had been a few chance-medleys at the end of April where French formations had found themselves encadred with the remains of British tank Battalions and the crews had earned much praise in little scrambling fights. The Armoured Car battalion first saw battle with the French First Army on 10 June at Belloy. Five females of the 10th Battalion took part in a night raid – the first in which a tank was featured – at Bucquoy on the same day. The American 301st Bn, equipped with the latest Mk V Stars, trained at Wool and on arrival in France became part of the tank force of the British IX Corps, of Chemin des Dames fame.

The Hotchkiss gun which all tanks now carried was better for its purpose than the Lewis but efforts were once more made in June to obtain the best light automatic of them all. The Marquess of Salisbury, in a Lords debate on the 6th, said that he had tried out the Madsen and found it to be 'enormously superior to any other gun in existence'. Lord Charles Beresford, who had seen the Gardner jam when the square broke at Abu Klea, called it 'the most wonderful machine of its kind ever invented' and Lord Moulton, most scientific of Peers, pointed out that its construction was so simple that stoppages simply did not occur. This could never have been said of any other machine-gun, not even of the Vickers itself. More tests had been carried out in May but in spite of all efforts no more could be got out of Denmark. It was a great pity, for this was the perfect tank weapon.

Rawlinson and Monash, men who got on well together, worked out details for a curtain-raising operation before the power of the Allied armies should be fully extended. It was not all that important to drive the Germans from Hamel, a short walk from Villers-Bretonneux, but it was as good a place as another for a dress rehearsal. This is strange country, a little to the south of the canalized Somme with the marshes stretching away from the bank. It is curiously up-and-down, little chalk ridges and little chalk depressions tossed about haphazard. Local people call it 'the silent land' and certainly the acoustics are freakish. In many spots a noise made nearby can hardly be heard though it can be picked up loudly half a mile away.

Since the attack was planned for 4 July Rawlinson decided to use, as well as tanks and Australians, the US battalion that had been sent to be trained by Fourth Army. When forbidden to do so, he turned a deaf ear. The plan, conceived mainly by Monash, depended almost entirely upon that forgotten element, surprise. On the first night of July a flight of RE8s, a particularly noisy kind of aeroplane, flew up and down in order to drown the sound of tank engines. Sixty Mk Vs moved furtively into position, forty-eight fighting tanks for the first stroke followed by a dozen more heavily laden with everything an infantry soldier could want. At 3 o'clock on a summer morning they moved off, the infantry leading. Every one of Ricardo's engines ran as sweetly as a crew could wish. Two aircraft circled overhead, watching every German movement. As the barrage came down, so close that men could almost lean on it, tanks and infantry went in together, sometimes one ahead, sometimes the other. Only the German machine-gunners, the best men the Kaiser had, stayed to fight it out; it was a one-sided business. The Mk Vs used little ammunition but, with their superior manoeuverability they crushed the nests, crunching them into the ground as they turned and turned again on top of them. Only five machines were damaged and all were rescued. The Tank Corps losses amounted to thirteen wounded. The Australians were as pleased with the tanks as the tank men were captivated by the splendid dash of the Diggers and the Doughboys. More than 200 machine-guns were squashed, 1500 prisoners shambled off to the cages and the Australians unpacked their stores. Later the RAF, for the first time ever, dropped further supplies of ammunition. Another shape of things to come; General Slim's Fourteenth Army, twenty odd years later, made it standard practice.

Hamel, though on a much smaller scale than Cambrai, was technically far in advance. After 4 July battle plans did not end with 'And, by the way, you've got some tanks in your sector. Mind you, they probably won't turn up'. Henceforth tanks would be reckoned as reliable as artillery, machine-guns or anything else. Mr – later Sir Harry – Ricardo and Major Wilson had good cause for pride.

Next, after Hamel, it was to be the turn of General Estienne's Frenchmen. A fortnight after Hamel 375 of the little Renaults burst out of the forest of Villers-Cotterets, the spearhead of Mangin's eighteen divisions that were to fight the second Battle of the Marne. They were undeniably funny-looking little objects, especially when set alongside a Mk V, but each carried either a 37 mm gun or a light automatic in a rotating turret. The Germans did not find them amusing. With no Hindenburg Line to be crossed and the going easy, the Renaults had a field day. France, hard hit and shorn of some of her fairest land, was at last effectively striking back and the savage Mangin was just the man to lead her soldiers. The presence of strong, fresh

Demonstration of fire and movement aided by Mk V Star.

American divisions, each double the size of a normal one, heartened all hands. Germany had nothing similar to cheer her tired men.

On 23 July there came an interesting combined operation. At Mailly-Raineval, hard by the little River Avre, stood several troublesome German batteries. The French intimated that some tanks would be helpful to the four battalions they had detailed for the assault. Brigadier-General Courage was despatched with the 9th Battalion to see what could be done. It turned out to be much like Hamel but without the opportunity of the careful preparation that Monash always demanded. The positions were taken and the batteries smashed, but at a price. Of thirty-six tanks engaged fifteen were knocked out by shell-fire and fifteen more so knocked about that they were beyond salvage. Almost worse was the loss of a Mk V, hit while trying to tow away a captured gun. It may have been damaged beyond repair for, unlike some of the Mk IVs taken at Cambrai, it was not seen again under the Iron Cross. The French were well pleased; 1,800 prisoners, five field pieces, forty-two trench-mortars and 276 machine-guns were a haul not to be despised. General Debeney issued a very handsome 'Ordre du Jour' and presented the 9th Battalion with the badge of the French 3rd Division, to be worn on the sleeve evermore.

Baker-Carr's First Brigade, in Sir Julian Byng's Third Army, was not engaged in any of these affairs. To his chagrin he still had only Mk IVs, though Mk Vs were beginning to dribble in. Nor was his life easy, for his Brigade was in IV Corps area. 'Uncle' Harper, 'after his experience with tanks, first at the Arras battle, then in the Third Battle of Ypres, and finally in the Cambrai battle, felt that he knew more about tanks than any living man and, at his Corps Conferences, had no hesitation in

Hamel, 4 July, 1918. Australians with a knocked out Mk. V.

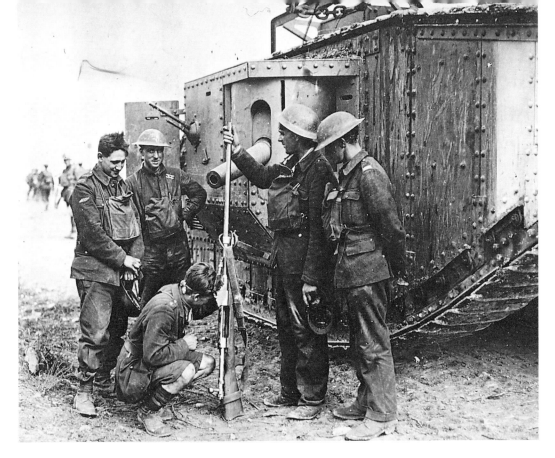

Mk V at Amiens with captured German anti-tank rifle.

saying so. "I know far more about tanks than anybody, Baker," he usually began, "and this is what you are to do." He then proceeded to outline a scheme which was utterly impossible to carry out. Such trivialities as time and space were completely ignored and the tanks were ordered to dash about a battlefield like a terrier in a cornfield catching rabbits. Only on one occasion did he prove obdurate to my arguments and I was forced to appeal to higher authority.' Baker-Carr and 'Uncle' Harper had by no means seen the last of each other, quite apart from the incident when one of the Americans, sent to First Brigade for instruction, amused himself by loosing off a captured German machine-gun and nearly decapitating a senior member of IV Corps Staff. Baker-Carr submitted meekly, for him, to a cursing on the subject of 'your barbarians'. Yet everybody still liked 'Uncle' Harper.

Sir Henry Rawlinson mulled over his plans for the first punch in the battles of the hundred days which would bring the war to an unexpected end. Under his command was a big and highly efficient Armoured Corps: fourteen battalions, two Whippets and the remainder all Mk V or Mk V Star, plus the Armoured Car battalion and a company of gun-carrying tanks converted for the occasion to supplying infantry with all kinds of explosive; Tank Salvage Companies followed close behind them all. The Fourth Brigade, under Brigadier-General E. B. Hankey, would go to the Canadian Corps; Courage's Fifth, of course, would stay with the Australians. One battalion, the 10th, should belong to Butler's IIIrd Corps and the remainder, Hardress-Lloyd's 3rd, which included the two Whippet battalions, would help the Cavalry Corps in yet another of its attempts at a break-through. The odd

Another view of the Renault FT17 long-lasting machine.

unit, the 2nd battalion, would remain in GHQ Reserve.

Sir Henry Rawlinson was the embodiment of the Old Army. The thirty years of service now behind him had taken him to India as ADC to Lord Roberts, chasing dacoits in Burma, up the Nile with Sir Herbert Kitchener and to Ladysmith with Sir George White. He had commanded a Mounted Infantry regiment in South Africa; years later, after a visit to Russia, he had written to Lord K saying that 'my old 8th MI could run rings round any number of Cossacks'. More recently he had been in every battle since First Ypres, beginning as the first Commander of IV Corps and his experience was unmatched in the BEF. His meticulous preparation for the battles that began on 8 August could hardly have been bettered. There was, for one thing an elaborate deception plan involving dummy tanks, British troops far from Amiens masquerading as Australians and Canadians, and spoof wireless traffic; all expedients to be repeated in 1944, with variations. The tanks this time worked to a plan and not as mere gate-crashers. The distribution was deliberate, the bulk of them on the south of the Somme where the going was easy and only a few in the far more difficult north.

Every tank officer was, at last, given precise orders, not padded out with masses of typed matter with which he had nothing to do. Most of them were taken to examine from hilltops the places where they would be doing their work, and the infantry with whom they would be cooperating knew it just as well. It was a kind of mutual benefit society, the tank men saying, in effect, 'I will make you a path through the wire and squash any machine-guns that may try to knock you about';

A Mk V Tank at Peronne.

the infantry reply was, 'You do that and I will keep you heading in the right direction; what is more, my snipers and Lewis gunners will take care of any anti-tank guns that may want to take a hand.' The gunners would drop their barrages at such times and places that German artillery would not be in any shape to interfere. There was no need now for the man metaphorically carrying a red flag to walk in front. More often than not a couple of infantrymen travelled on the roof to do any guiding needed. It worked very well.

The attack, of course, was not yet on the main Hindenburg position. This battlefield was an old one for both sides, the one from which the Fifth Army had been driven in March. It held no secrets from the attackers, though the Germans had made the most of everything available to them.

Early on the morning of 8 August Rawlinson's guns, all 2,000 of them, bellowed out as one. Infantrymen and Mk Vs moved forward through what General Maurice calls 'a friendly mist', with the RAF weighing in from above as opportunity offered. The German army, while still an uncommonly good one, was not that of 1916. By the same token, nor was the British; it lacked some of the dash of the first Somme battles, but it was a lot more artful. This was just as well, for the supply of men was running very low. It is often said that the effect of the tanks on the Kaiser's war was mostly moral; how wire is flattened and machine-guns screwed into the ground by moral suasion is not explained. All the same it is more than a copy-book heading. Ludendorff himself admitted later that he had underestimated the tank; probably the capture of the early marks had done the Allies more good than harm. The

Officers of the Central Workshops.

Germans did begin a tank-building programme of their own but it came too late. Only fifteen Elfriedes ever turned up and they did not prove formidable.

There is no doubt but that by August the bulk of the German infantry when confronted by tanks or rumours of tanks quickly developed the condition known to soldiers as 'wind up'. The turn of other armies was to come years later. Anti-tank weapons were strangely slow in arriving. Oddly enough it was the British Army that laid the first mine-fields, very ad hoc and made out of artillery shells; the only German anti-tank weapon apart from the field gun was an enormous rifle firing large-calibre bullets; nobody fancied using it for the kick would dislocate a man's shoulder. Large numbers were captured, mostly unused. It was nearly as futile as the Boys rifle of a generation later.

The battle of 8 August went much like a sand-table exercise. Ricardo's engines purred happily, Wilson's epicyclic gear did everything its inventor expected and bullets rattled off Tritton's strong hulls.

Only the Whippets had nasty experiences. The idea of combining them with horsed cavalry was not clever; possibly the old forces were too strong even for Sir Henry Rawlinson. On the approach march the tanks could not keep up with the horses, fresh after long inactivity. Once the start line was crossed and a machine-gun or two began to fire, the horses could not keep up with the Whippets. The result was that two valuable battalions were kept from doing what they had been designed to do simply because of the presence of masses of incongruous animals. The armoured cars, however, had a field day. There is an excellent Roman road running in a dead straight line from Villers Bretonneux to Peronne. As there seemed no obstacles on it after the tanks had moved some felled trees, the cars drove along the road, catching up with masses of fugitives who were running away from the Australians. The cars sped them on their way with machine-gun fire. One section got as far as Framerville, nine miles from the front line, caught a German Corps

Experimental Mk V Star with trench-crossing bridge.

Headquarters at an unguarded moment in a farm-house, grabbed every document in sight, shot up the Staff officers, the Corps Commander being absent, and drove back home with valuable booty – complete, detailed plans and photographs of the main Hindenburg position.

It was not all like that. A company of gun-carrying tanks, converted for the occasion to supply tanks, had been hidden in an orchard at Villers-Bretonneux where it was loaded up with petrol, mortar bombs, gun cotton and the like. On the evening of 7 August a single shell hit one of them and set it on fire. The flames could not be

Mk V Two Star with Majors Buddicum and Wilson and Mr Ricardo.

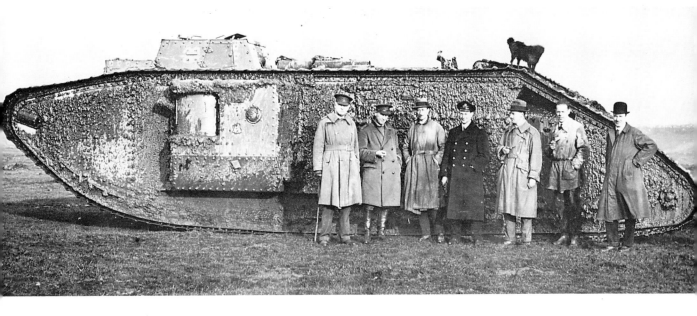

hidden and for several hours German guns searched the area. Every tank was destroyed. Then the shelling stopped. Nobody knew how it had happened.

Nor should the impression be given that 8 August was a walkover. When the sun dispersed the mist and a fine warm day followed, the German gunners got to work. A good many tanks were knocked out after the first four hours of the battle, the Canadian sector being hardest hit. Nevertheless the third and last line of objec-

Mk Vs of 10th Bn. Tank Corps with New Zealanders. Grevilliers, 25 August, 1918.

tives, the Red Line, had been everywhere reached before the day was over. Those of the Whippets not tied to the cavalry had made piratical raids well into the rear areas. Lieutenant Arnold and his 'Musical Box' are among the Tank Corps immortals. Nor was it only the German gunners who held back the tanks from doing all that they had planned. The defective ventilation system of the Mk V made ovens of them as the sun rose. One report, from a battalion with the Canadians, says that, 'With the prolonged running at high speed the interior of the Tank rapidly became unbearable through heat and petrol fumes and the crew were forced to evacuate it and take cover underneath. At this moment two of the crew were wounded, one was sick, one fainted and one was delirious. Fortunately, before the enemy could take advantage of the lull, two Whippet Tanks and a body of cavalry came up and the enemy in the valley began to retreat over the hill.' Around Beaucourt-en-Santerre nine out of eleven tanks of A Company 1st Battalion were knocked out by a field battery firing over open sights.

The Mk V Star had proved not up to the job for which it was designed. Passengers unaccustomed to the fumes and motion became so very sick that, wherever possible, they were allowed to get out and walk behind. When fire compelled them to get back in they became so ill as to be useless for anything for the next couple of hours. Stern and the Americans were working on this. The Mk IX was now on the drawing board. In the Spring of 1919 hundreds of them would be carrying fifty men each in Pullman car comfort by comparison with that offered by the Mk V Stars. That, at any rate, was the hope. In sober fact, on the authority of Wilson, the machine designed by d'Eyncourt and Lieut Rackham, 'developed considerable mechanical troubles and only a few were completed before the Armistice'.

With the Mk IX the wheel would come full circle. The very first report of the Landships Committee, delivered to Mr Churchill in June, 1915, had told how 'these Landships were at first designed to transport a trench-taking storming party of fifty men with machine-guns and ammunition; the men standing in two ranks at each side and protected by side armour of 8 mm thickness and roof armour of 6 mm. These vehicles were 40 feet long by 13 feet wide.' They had never got beyond the stage of working drawings, much modified as time went on and the near impossibility of the plan became clear. Now, in little more than three years, the thing had been done and the first intentions of the founding fathers had taken tangible shape. Until the Mk IXs appeared, however, the Mk V One and Two Stars had to do the best

Men of 5th Australian Brigade with Mk V Star. 8 August, 1918.

they could. More often than not they were used either as fighting tanks or as freight rather than passenger carriers. This was the best use that could be made of them; a Canadian soldier described his journey in one as a 'sort of pocket hell'.

The next morning, the 9th, found 155 tanks still going about their business. It was another successful day, even though it cost eight machines to the German artillery at Lihons and five more around the awkward Chipilly spur to the north of the river. 'The Whippets' action, in as far as they were billed to act with the cavalry, was disappointing. By some fault of liaison they were kept too long at Brigade Headquarters,' said Williams-Ellis. By 10 August the number of effective tanks was down to eighty-five, of which twenty-five were to receive direct hits during the day. On the 11th only thirty-eight, each in dire need of overhaul, went back in. On 12 August the last six were engaged and before the day was out the Tank Corps had been withdrawn in its entirety.

Death came suddenly and messily to many tank men during the sunny August days. Quite apart from those who had to be buried in sacks there were men decapitated and men roasted alive in addition to the Reconnaissance Officers who went ahead and were killed in the customary ways. Most of the damage was caused by a single battery in a wood near Le Quesnil. As the French had not kept up with the Canadian right a gap existed from which the Germans could catch the tanks in enfilade as they crossed the Sancerre plain. They did not waste their opportunity. Word spread among the infantry that life in the Tank Corps was not the reserved occupation that some people thought; all the same volunteers still came forward. They were needed. By the autumn Elles was obliged to report that he had tanks enough to see him through the year; it was shortage of trained crews that would limit his operations.

Sir Douglas Haig, though not the expert 'Uncle' Harper was, had learned much about what tanks could and could not do. As the line was coming up to the formless moonscape of the old Somme battlefield, he pulled them out and sent them north of the river to help Sir Julian Byng take Bapaume. Baker-Carr's First Brigade, already in Third Army, still had a fair number of Mk IVs on his strength, the last ones left as fighting machines. The morning of 21 August promised a fine sunny day, the usual mist hanging low until close upon noon. Many a tank crew member wished it would freeze. It was wretchedly bad luck that conditions inside Mk Vs and Whippets were so affected by heat for this was about the first long bout of decent weather since Mons. One hundred and ninety tanks of all three kinds took part in the battle for Bapaume. The moral effect was satisfactory, large bodies of enemy appearing only too anxious to be packed off to the prisoner-of-war cages. The first line fell with almost suspicious ease. Then at about 11 o'clock two things happened at once. The mist rose and the leading tanks found themselves on or near the embankment of the railway from Albert to Arras. To this convenient line the German artillery had withdrawn some batteries of field guns for the express purpose of shooting down the tanks as they appeared. As the sun broke clear their targets materialized as if done on paper with poster paints. Each machine came under a hurricane of fire, a hurricane shared by the infantry following along behind. Most of the thirty-seven tanks that reached the railway line were knocked out on it. Had the mist lasted for but another half hour they would have been able to deal with the enemy gunners themselves; as things fell out, it became necessary to whistle up the RAF. Machine-gun fire and small bombs soon saw the gunners off, but they had done their work.

Every post-battle report again told of how heat and fumes were far more serious enemies than anything the German Army could produce. Men, even the most hardened, passed out completely and on resurfacing found that their memories had gone; most of them recovered after a few hours but Mr Ricardo had made a bad error in believing the exhaust-covering and internal fan, admittedly makeshifts, 'served its purpose'. It did so only for the time needed to warm the engine up nicely.

Squadron 20 bore responsibility for testing and, with all their accumulated experience, they had found nothing to worry about. Which goes to show that the only worthwhile test of a weapon of war is its performance in war. Only under battle conditions was it discovered that once the exhaust pipe had reached a certain degree of heat the joints warped and neat carbon monoxide fumes continued to be pumped inside the hull. As a form of suicide this has long been popular; even the most salted tank crews could endure it for only a little while.

For all its excellent qualities the Mk V was still not good enough. Even if Squadron 20 had reported upon this joint in the armour, as it may well have done privately, it would have made no difference. The Mk Vs had got to be used; there were no others.

On 23 August 'Uncle' Harper again demonstrated his tank expertise. Late in the morning, says Williams-Ellis, 'some of the Whippets of the 6th battalion were operating with the infantry of IV Corps to the east of Courcelles. It was suddenly noticed that the artillery barrage table had been altered, and that the rate of progress of the barrage was now 100 yards in four minutes, that is to say considerably slower than had been originally intended. The Tanks were therefore obliged to manoeuvre and wheel about in order to let the barrage keep ahead. They were constantly under anti-Tank gun fire at this time.' It was in spite of, rather than owing to, 'Uncle' Harper's staff work that the Whippets got themselves out of a nasty scrape and went on to give strong help to the taking of Achiet-le-Petit, squashing a number of machine-gun positions on the way.

Still there was no rest for tanks or crews. The small numbers of both left fit for duty meant that it was the same people who went back in time after time; it says a lot for the mechanical reliability of the new machines, despite their limitations, that they were able to keep going for so long. Stern says that the endurance of a tank in battle was reckoned to be three days. Many of them, though crying out for overhaul, had been at it for twelve. By the time for the attack on the Drocourt-Queant Switch, hard by the old Arras battlefields, a hundred new machines had arrived. They were just in time; the old ones were very nearly played out.

Though the scent of victory was breast high for all the advancing armies nobody was under any illusions about what lay ahead. So far the defences they had penetrated had all been the usual kind of field work. The next would be very different. In the Spring of 1917, under the pressure of the battles of the Somme and the

Ancre, the Germans had made a decision of first importance. For probably the only time in history a communique saying that 'our troops had retired to prepared positions' meant exactly what it said. The Hindenburg Line – called that only by the British – was no scambling trench and wire system, put up by fatigue parties in the dark, usually under fire. It was an elaborate piece of civil engineering carried out under peacetime conditions by non-combatant labour, mostly Russian prisoners and impressed civilians. It had all the mystique of the Maginot and was, for its day, just as effective. Acre upon acre of blue-gleaming barbed wire of the thickest kind gave the boldest observer cause to think. On the front of the old Arras battlefield lay a substantial outwork, begun just before Allenby's battle and designed to link the Hindenburg position around Bullecourt of awful memory to the old La Bassée-Lens system. In April, 1917, in its unfinished state, it lay just beyond the furthest point reached by any part of Third Army. By August, 1918, it was complete in every detail.

Under Sir Julian Byng the Third Army stormed it in the course of a single day. The Canadians, who practically owned Vimy Ridge, 63rd (Royal Navy) Division and 52nd – lowland Scottish Territorials brought from Palestine during the German Spring offensive – moved off on the morning of 2 September covered by a barrage of a million shells. Eighty-one tanks took part, about forty of them heading for the Switch itself. What the German Army called *Tankschrecken* – 'Tank Funk' – had been spreading since 8 August almost as widely as the influenza that affected all armies. The attackers moved off at 5.30 am; by lunch time all was over bar some

Supply Tank at Bucquoy, 19 August, 1918.

Mk V Star Tank on railway truck.

clearing up. Further south the Australian Corps, with an audacity that only that irrepressible formation could have managed, chased the Germans from the almost equally impregnable Mont St Quentin.

Though the cry was now going up in France for more tanks, the prospect of their arrival in a continuous and ever growing stream was far more remote than anybody realized. During the victorious month of August James Borrowman Maclean was appointed Controller of the Mechanical Warfare Supply Department with the right of direct access to Mr Churchill. Maclean was a professional engineer from Clydebank who had already served the Ministry as Director of Shell Production and Controller of Gun Manufacture. No man knew better than he the ins and out of the entire munitions business and he took up his new post with a grim suspicion that all was not well with tank production. He found matters far worse than he had expected.

The official estimates of production of all kinds of tank gave figures of 203 for September, 1918, rising to 747 in the following April. These estimates had already been vetted by Mr (later Sir Percival) Perry who reckoned them on the high side for the first few months but pessimistic when 1919 should arrive. Maclean got down to them in detail. His conclusion was that, thanks to a falling labour force and a great deal of of muddle, the two sets of figures were wildly optimistic. His own showed that at best we could hope for only 2,320 by April as against an official estimate of 4,334. Of the 900 Mk IXs ordered in September, 1917, not a solitary one existed;

178

nor did any of the Mk VIII hulls promised to the Allied Commission. 250 Medium Bs had been bespoken at the same time; there was just one sample machine finished.

The blame was placed almost entirely upon the Ministry. Two firms, one of them Beardmores, came in for heavy criticism because they had piled up armour-plating beyond their machining capacity. Maclean calculated that 'over 5,000 tons of unmachined plate were lying about the country'. D'Eyncourt concurred with the report and Tritton had something to add to it. In his evidence to the Royal Commission he asserted that 'Many months were lost in the construction of these machines through the non-delivery of parts by the Mechanical Warfare Supply Department. This Department undertook to supply the engines and gear-boxes and they fell twelve months into arrears with gear-box deliveries.' In a letter to the MWSD dated 31 August he complains that 'The Lannoe Committee orders smoke bomb equipment for the Hornet. The Edkins Committee says they are not wanted'. What was he to do? It was not the first letter of its kind. Nor was that all. A report from the Chief Testing Officer of Squadron 20, dated 11 July, says that 'The failure of a large number of the sprockets and their replacement is by far the most serious matter the Tank Corps have now to face.' He blamed it on sheer bad workmanship.

Maclean took over in the first week of August, just as the tanks were inflicting on Ludendorff his 'Black Day of the German Army'. His first letter to Mr Churchill says that 'I believe that a continuation of the policy which came to an end in August would have resulted in a *complete cessation of deliveries before the end of this year*.' Then he took the Department by the scruff. Wilson, expressly freed from any criticism, gives some figures. By the end of the war exactly seven Mk VIIIs had been made here and 'a few in the US'. Medium Bs numbered forty-five; Medium Cs thirty-six. In all 2,696 tanks of all kinds had been completed. Maclean speaks of

German Tanks. 'Mephisto', an A7V captured by the Australians.

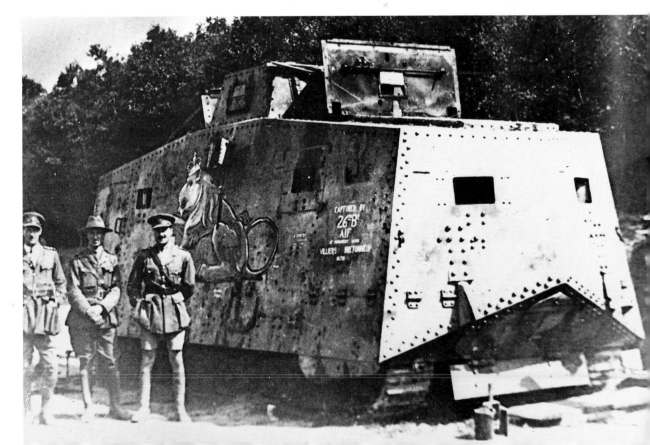

the Medium D – the gleam in Fuller's eye – in a letter to the MWSD written in January, 1919. 'Owing to a certain amount of Departmental jealousy (it) had not benefited by the experience of the main design staff.'

It all sounds so very remote from Fuller's 'Tank Programme 1919'. For what he calls 'the decisive attack' he would need 7,700 fighting tanks, plus 3,282 administrative ones ('Carriers for 80 Divisions, 1,600'). In all he required, counting reserves, 18,000 tanks with 1,500 trains to bring them near the battlefield. They were to be provided in equal thirds by Britain, France and America. Maclean's comments would have been worth hearing; the Scotch are not reckoned to have an outstanding sense of humour. Fuller, rather interestingly, talks of the need for 'thousands of tanks, both light and heavy, ranging from 2 mph to 8 mph'. No talk of the Medium D and 20 mph yet awhile. 'When can we get 20 mph Tanks?', is Item 13 at a War Office Conference that took place on 26 June. No answer appears in the record. The question was purely rhetorical.

CHAPTER 17

The Last Foothills

M R CHURCHILL, STILL MINISTER OF MUNITIONS OF WAR, visited the scene of the attack on the Drocourt-Queant Switch. Hardened though he was to the sight of battlefields, both as performer and spectator, he found something new in this one. 'It was a very fine strong, deep trench. In front of it was a belt of wire, nearly one hundred yards broad. The wire was practically uncut, and had only little passages through it, all presumably swept by machine-guns. Yet the troops walked over these terrific obstacles, without the wire being cut, with very little loss, killed many Germans, took thousands of prisoners and hundreds of machine-guns. Three or four hundred yards behind these lines was a second line, almost as strong and more deceptive. Over this also they walked with apparently no difficulty and little loss. Behind that again, perhaps a mile further on, were just a few little pits and holes into which the German machine-guns and riflemen threw themselves to stop the rout. Here our heaviest losses occurred. The troops had got beyond the support of the tanks, and the bare, open ground gave no shelter.'

He wrote a letter at once to the Prime Minister: 'Up to the present there have only been about 18,000 men in the Tank Corps and they have only had 600 or 700 tanks in action. It is universally admitted out here that they have been a definite factor in changing the fortune of the field and in giving us that tactical superiority without which the best laid schemes of strategists come to naught. It is no exaggeration to say that the lives they have saved and the prisoners they have taken have made these 18,000 men the most profit-bearing we have in the Army.... Every time new success is gained by their aid there is an immediate clamour for large numbers. The moment the impression of that success passes away the necessary men and material are grudged and stinted. I repeat that there ought to be 100,000 men in the Tank Corps.'

It was a little late in the day to say this. The work of a tank crew was the most highly skilled of any, and to train such men to concert pitch requires months of hard work.

The time had come for Sir Henry Rawlinson to take one of the most serious decisions of the war. Happily he was an imperturbable man, for two schools of thought were tugging at him in different directions. First came the 'Yanks and the

Tanks' school; their case was a good one. The American Armies were gathering strength, not merely in numbers but in battle-worthiness; the Mk VIII, with 19 mm of armour, ability to cross a 14-foot-wide trench and a range of forty-five miles on one filling of its 200-gallon petrol tank was almost in production. Or so it was believed. So was the Mk IX, capable of carrying fifty men in safety for much the same distance; the fast Medium B, C and D were not far behind. Wait until the Spring of 1919 and we shall have such a victory as the world has never seen, ran their counsel. At his other sleeve was the 'hunch' school. The Germans now are really and truly on the run; we know Charteris had been saying this for years and was talking nonsense but the cause has altered. We know the German has great and formidable defence lines but has he the men to hold them? And, if he has, will they still fight? Your army has never been in better form and another winter may harm it more than it will weaken the Germans. If we go hard for them now and win, the war will be over. If we fail, then it will be time to rely on 'Yanks and Tanks'. Sir Henry made the brave decision. The Fourth Army, including its Australian Corps and the American IInd Corps, would advance and take the Hindenburg Line at the end of September.

As matters fell out this was a fortunate decision for the Tank Corps. Excellent though the machines now in the pipeline were, the Germans had in their own pipeline something that would have been deadly. The TUF (*Tank und Flieger*) machine-gun was of 13 mm calibre and, as experiments on captured tanks had shown, it could pierce steel plates 30 mm thick. It could have riddled the Mk VIII, the Mk IX and the new Mediums as easily as 'K' ammunition had slaughtered the training tanks at Bullecourt. Six thousand of these guns were ordered from no less than sixty factories and the first deliveries were promised for December. The Minister of War set so much store by the TUF that daily progress reports were demanded and it was given priority over both submarines and aircraft. The Great

Mk Vs of the 301st (U.S.) Battalion taking a German trench. October 1918.

The Mk VIII guarded by U.S. troops.

Tank Victory of 1919 should not be regarded as a foregone conclusion even though Williams-Ellis, writing in the same year, says of the TUF that 'the modern tank fears it not at all'. He ought to have known.

Sir Henry had had one piece of luck that nobody could grudge him. When the booty brought back by Lieut Rollings and his armoured car on 8 August had been thoroughly examined it turned out to be beyond price. Every detail of the Hindenburg position was there, including some fine photographs taken from German balloons. They are still to be seen in General Montgomery's *Story of the Fourth Army*. Rollings was awarded a bar to his MC but had to wait some time for a more tangible reward. In 1931 a newspaper got hold of the story and made a meal of it. Lady Houston, benefactress to the Schneider Trophy team and to every Imperial good cause, was so taken by it that she sent Rollings a cheque for £5,000.

After 2 September the tanks were again withdrawn to reorganize themselves, patch up the holes, replace the casualties and make ready for the next and greatest battle.

The doings of the Tank Corps from 8 August onwards have tended to overshadow the early days of another armoured force. General Pershing had no intention of letting his American Expeditionary Force be outclassed by the British and French in any aspect of war so long as he had the power of influencing events. As long ago as September, 1917, he had entrusted the formation of an American Tank Corps to Colonel Rockenbach, who may fairly be called the American Swinton, and had given him a free hand as to what he did. Rockenbach set up his headquarters at Chaumont as part of Pershing's GHQ and sent selected officers off to learn the business at the French and British tank schools. During their absence he busied himself drawing up an establishment for a body of armoured troops appropriate to the great American armies that were slowly gathering.

Rockenbach thought big. The US Tank Corps should consist of five heavy battalions, equipped with the most modern British tanks, and twenty more using the Renault FT 17. The importance of this lay in the fact that as soon as the establishment was approved by Pershing, as it was very quickly, orders could go to Mr Stettinius, the War Department representative in Paris, for the full might of American industry to be put at the service of Stern's Inter-Allied Commission. Work on the Liberty (alias Mk VIII) tank began soon afterwards. Mr Henry Ford, not to be left out of anything mechanical, produced a design of his own. The Commission, fully occupied, was not interested. Mr Ford went ahead just the same and set up a production line for a midget tank weighing only $3\frac{1}{2}$ tons. It had all the virtues and all the defects of the 'Tin Lizzie' and while many were made only a few arrived in France before the Armistice. It never saw action.

The 301st Battalion spent its formative months with the British Army, using Mk Vs and being to all intents and purposes part of Elles' Corps. This state of affairs pleased both sides, for they got on famously together. Two light battalions were formed at Bourg, the Tank Training Centre of the French Army. By the time the Hundred Days battles had started the two battalions of Renaults, 124 machines strong, had been formed into a Brigade. Its commander was that George S. Patton, Jr who had so impressed his bloodthirstiness on Sir Douglas.

Patton's Brigade was shipped to the St Mihiel salient in time to begin its work on 12 September. The American Army then going into its first attacking battle had

Men of the 30th (Tennessee) Division, U.S. Army and 8th Bn Tank Corps attacking the Hindenburg Line near Bellicourt.

German troops attacking a Tank with a flame-thrower.

a touching resemblance to the British of 1916. It was enthusiastic, determined and bursting with courage; it also had everything to learn. Patton, having done the course at Wool before going on to the French school at Champlieu, was well instructed, though he thought little of either the St Chamond or the Mk V. His was not the only name familiar to a later generation. 42nd US Division was commanded by a young General named Douglas MacArthur: much of the planning for the St Mihiel offensive was the work of one of Pershing's Staff officers, Lieut-Colonel George C. Marshall. Something like half a million American troops plus 150,000 Frenchmen took part in the battle. It would have been against nature to expect a few score of light tanks to have much effect on it. Deliveries at the last moment had brought Patton's strength up to 174. Zero was 6 am; six hours later a hundred were bogged down. Most of the others ran out of petrol. It was not Patton's day. Next day, however, one of his sections had a little victory. Lieutenant McClure, caught in the open by a German battery, kept straight on in a proper 'Damn the torpedoes' style and rammed it.

The next American battle, the Meuse-Argonne, was not suited to the tank of 1918. As mud had wrecked all hopes at Ypres so did trees in the Argonne forest. Patton took a painful wound in the side from a shell splinter and was out of the war.

The rest of it, for the AEF, was old-style foot and guns slogging matches. By 1920 the US Tank Corps had ceased to exist and Patton was back with the cavalry.

Further north, on the fronts of the British First, Third and Fourth Armies, it seemed that 1759 had come again; every breakfast time produced its enquiries about what victories the previous day had brought. For the Tank Corps it had hardened into a drill. As Williams-Ellis put it, 'preparations for a battle had been so completely reduced to a routine that to attempt to chronicle the preparations for any of our set attacks would be to make a mere *cento*, whose pieces might be culled from particulars already recorded for Cambrai and Hamel and for Amiens.' Details of gallons of petrol, tons of grease and acres of maps do not make compelling reading. The critical matter was training with other arms. Wherever these were accustomed to working with tanks success invariably followed at a price that could be accepted. The two RAF Squadrons detailed for tank protection, Nos 8 and 73, were essential members of the team. Their task was to spot enemy anti-tank guns and to eliminate them by bombing or machine-gun fire. Without their help tank casualties might well have been so heavy that they could no longer be an effective force. Something like thirty per cent of the German field artillery was now reckoned to be put to work at tank-killing and when the machines were left to fight private battles in the open the odds were heavily against them.

The heat and fumes in the Mk Vs also forced the crews to shifts and expedients. So far as possible they were kept outside the machines until battle was imminent. The habit grew up of having them driven to a point just short of the start line by skeleton crews, the remainder being brought up by lorry. There were small advantages in the slowness of these machines; on one occasion a tank was attacked by German infantry throwing phosphorus bombs; when they had been chased off and the inside became uninhabitable the crew calmly got out leaving the tank in motion and walked between the horns until the fumes had cleared; then they resumed business.

On 18 September came the Battle of Epehy, a little to the south of the old Cambrai battlefield. This was an area from which the Germans had to be cleared before the main assault on the Hindenburg Line, a couple of miles in the rear on average, could be mounted. It was a strong position, not to be taken at a run, for there were old trench systems, much wire and, in a countryside that had been farmed for thousands of years, a number of sunken roads. Four Divisions of Third Army had driven the enemy from the old British trenches south of Havrincourt on the 12th but the line running from Peizières to the Quadrilateral, by Selency and only a mile and a half from St Quentin itself, would not be pushed in without a lot of hard fighting. Sir Henry Rawlinson quite deliberately entrusted the business to some very tired Divisions. He had fresh ones, but they were earmarked for the great attack on the Hindenburg Line itself.

If the infantry Divisions were worn out, so were the Tank Brigades. Only about a score of machines, all sadly in need of overhaul, could be put into the fight, all of them from Courage's Fifth Brigade. Once again it was to be an affair not of armoured fleets but of small, very vulnerable packets. Eight were to go with Butler's IIIrd

Corps on the left, four more with their old friends the Australians in the centre and the last eight were to work with IXth Corps, now commanded by Walter Braithwaite. The morning broke in rain and mist; many of the crews directed themselves into action for the first time by the naval compasses with which each fighting tank was now equipped.

In the north, Epehy itself fell without much resistance but Ronssoy proved a hard nut to crack. Anti-tank guns and machine-guns firing armour-piercing rounds seemed to be dug in everywhere. The Division charged with taking the place, the very good 18th, was under orders to press through to Lempire and The Knoll. It does not seem to have been greatly aided by its tanks. Of the seven allotted to the 53rd Brigade five were knocked out. 'So heavy had been the machine-gun fire,' said the Divisional History, 'that they had found it impossible to fight their guns.' Several veterans who had been present at almost every western front battle are on record as saying that they had never encountered such fire as this. 74th Division, the dismounted Yeomanry brought back from Palestine after the March Retreat, simply observed that 'The tanks were unable to give any assistance as they failed to reach the starting point or were knocked out before reaching the first objective.' On the Australian front things went better, as might have been expected after Hamel and the rest.

Far and away the hardest fighting was in IX Corps area, between Maissemy and Holnon. Two Regular Divisions, the 1st and 6th, moved forward. The German line had been recently strengthened by the arrival of the crack Alpine Corps. Major-General Marden, commanding the 6th had, as you may remember, had dealings with the first tanks on the Somme and did not think much of them. His 16th Brigade was on the left, with its left on Fresnoy-le-Petit and its right on the formidable defence system called the Quadrilateral. 'Six tanks were allotted to the Division,' he wrote afterwards, 'but met with various mishaps or were knocked out and were not of much use.' Another entry, three days later, says that 'the four tanks detailed to attack the Quadrilateral again had bad luck, one being turned absolutely turtle by a minefield.' This tank must have had the melancholy distinction of being the first ever to be wrecked by such means. Both sides had been laying mines since soon after Cambrai but they were not effective, usually being made out of old shell cases.

The adventures of two tanks around the Quadrilateral must not go unchronicled. First on the scene was that of 2nd Lieut Smallwood, which was caught in one of the sunken roads and brought to a halt. So heavy was the fire directed at it that any attempt to get at the unditching beam would have been suicidal. While this one was stuck a second tank loomed out of the murk with all its guns blazing. The driver was dead, the second driver grievously wounded and the commander, 2nd Lieut Hedges, was at the controls. Also aboard was the Section Commander, Captain Hamlet, doing duty as gunner. As Hedges' tank was getting to work on the defenders and seemed to be gaining the upper hand it suddenly exploded into flames. The crew, having little choice, scrambled out into the hands of the surrounding Germans. Hedges, in no mood to be taken, shot his way clear with his revolver and made for Smallwood's tank, bullets cracking all round him. When fifty yards short of it he dropped; Smallwood came out and dragged the badly wounded Hedges inside. Before long the tank was being rocked and holed to an extent that it made it impossible to stay aboard. Smallwood and the survivors unshipped the Hotchkisses, jumped down and began to open up on the Germans. They held the position for long enough to enable the infantry to cover the furlong separating them and handed over the post. Hedges was sent to the rear to find a Dressing Station. He was never seen again.

Epehy cannot be claimed as the tanks' finest hour. With a handful of machines that should have been in the workshops and a few score men who should have been enjoying well deserved leave that is hardly remarkable. But they had something to show for it. Major-General Marden, up till now one of the unenlightened, admitted on 24 September that four tanks had been of great assistance to his 16th Brigade in securing the north face of the Quadrilateral. Coming from Marden this meant much. Four tanks had saved a lot of infantry lives, and that was what they were for.

All the outer works of the Hindenburg Line had now been cleared. The tanks were withdrawn for a brief respite and for Colonel Searle to have his men work on them. As many of the crews as possible were sent on leave to the Tank Corps' almost private *station balnéaire*, Merlimont Plage. The Chinese labourers, along with others, were put to work on a new accessory. Fascines had done well enough at Cambrai; 'cribs', great oaken octagonal frames bound together with iron, would do even better when it came to crossing the Hindenburg Line. And every tank, even Baker-Carr's old Mk IVs, must be ready in time for The Day.

CHAPTER 18

To the Green Fields Beyond

IN THE SPRING of 1918 a British Army had waited grimly for an attack by forces that it knew would be overwhelming; in the autumn the pendulum had swung and it was Germany's turn. This time it was not along a single stretch of a few miles but the whole front from Dixmude to the Argonne Forest, some 250 miles in all, that was on the move. From King Albert's men in the north to Pershing's in the south blow after blow was falling upon the battered Wehrmacht and nowhere would it be more stunning than on the sector under Sir Douglas Haig.

The mighty Hindenburg Line had as a part of its protection the two canals of St Quentin and the Nord. These had in peacetime carried, as they still do, the big seagoing barges upon which so much of French commerce depends, though in September, 1918, the Canal du Nord was dry. In only two places were there no impossible tank obstacles, along the 4½-mile stretch called *Le Grand Souterrain* between the villages of Hellicourt and Vendhuille in the north and the thousand-yard-long Le Tronquoy Tunnel just north of St Quentin. The decisive battle opened on 27 September and it lasted for fifteen days. It began on the fronts of Horne's First and Byng's Third Armies, with a drive across the old Cambrai battlefield towards Bourlon Hill spearheaded by fifty-three tanks, sixteen of them old Mk IVs and the rest Mk Vs. Here it was necessary for them to get over the dried-out canal between Bourlon and Marquion as best they could. It did not look easy, for the canal was 50 feet wide at bottom, 12 feet deep and with banks of 9 feet scarped by German engineers into almost vertical faces. This was Baker-Carr's parish, with his Brigade supporting the Canadian Corps. Elles was in London, as Tank Representative at the War Office, and his replacement, Colonel Karslake (later of Quetta earthquake fame) came to Baker-Carr's HQ 'with the avowed intention of stopping me from wasting tanks on an impossible task'. He got no change from Baker-Carr. His own Reconnaissance Officer, Williams-Ellis, had made some very daring visits on his own and Oswald Birley – famous in another sphere but then First Army's aerial photograph expert – had agreed that the thing could be done. Karslake retired in a cloud of gloomy prophecies. A plan was proposed 'by some genius' that half-a-dozen time-expired tanks should be strengthened and made to serve as a bridge. Baker-Carr, unconvinced, agreed to let it be tried. Not one of them reached the canal, but this did not prevent a colourful account of how 'the wonderful feat was accomplished' from appearing in the Press. As things turned out every fighting tank, 'first one, then another, then two or three at a time, negotiated the "insuperable obstacle" and appeared going strong on the far side.' The 'swallow-dive' learned at Bovington had paid off. Bourlon Wood and Bourlon Village both fell after some hard fighting to the same battalion, 'G', which had attacked them at First Cambrai. Two days later, in a dense fog that made it necessary to navigate by compass, more tanks crossed the Canal to the south. The infantry fought their way to the outskirts of Cambrai itself.

On the Fourth Army front, further south, were concentrated most of the still serviceable tanks, about 120 in all. Numbered among them was the United States 301st Battalion whose Mk V and Mk V Stars were in support of 27th (New York) Division. There was not a rat-hole in a canal bank whose existence and location was not known to Fourth Army Intelligence but there was one particularly worrisome factor about the now imminent battle. Three very important positions from which the route of the attackers would be commanded, the Knoll, Quennemont Farm and Bellicourt, had not fallen as expected during the preliminary battles. The original intention had been that the inexperienced American Divisions should not be put in until these features had been secured. Once again Sir Henry Rawlinson was faced with a hard decision and once again he refused to shrink from it. The 27th Division, with its own willing consent, would have to attack the outpost line on 27 September and have it securely in their possession before the main attack began on the 29th. Twelve British tanks were allotted to them. Resistance was strong and the attack failed utterly. The result was that another fearsome decision had to be made. The British artillery was now a superb instrument and the orchestration of barrage plans was as demanding as the scoring of a Beethoven symphony. Small bodies of American troops were known to be somewhere in the zone upon which the barrage must fall, along with many American wounded. If the plan remained unchanged they were in mortal danger; if it were to be tinkered with the barrage would be ineffective. With great courage General Read, the US Corps Commander, accepted that the lesser evil would be to carry on as arranged and let the men lost in front take their chance. Even as it was, the fact that the Germans still held Quennemont and the Knoll meant that the Americans would have to start a thousand yards behind their barrage line and risk being cut up by machine-gun fire as they tried to catch up with it.

The veteran German machine-gunners were presented with unmissable targets and the US troops were laid in swathes, just as the British had been on the Somme. The 301st Tank Battalion moved off to bring them some help. Then came one of the war's tragedies. During the early days of the March retreat, when rumours of German tanks were running wild, a line of mines – 50 lb mortar bombs filled with ammonal – had been laid exactly in the path they were about to take and had been forgotten. Probably the men who had put the minefield there were all dead. The US tanks, following carefully laid tapes, rolled straight into it. The mines went off in a succession of roars, ten tanks were blown up and many crewmen were killed. So powerful were the explosions that the bottoms of most of the victims were completely torn out. Another milestone in tank history had been passed. The crews that had passed it safely kept going.

Worse was to follow. As the mist lifted, large parties of Germans emerged from the tunnels and began to shoot into the American ranks from behind. The Australians, following up, dealt with them as only the Australians could but so long as Quennemont was untaken the American advance would make no headway. Something had to be done, and done at once. Major Hotblack has appeared before in this story. Even among the brave men of the Tank Corps his reputation was that of d'Artagnan and this was his hour. His position as head of Tank Corps Intelligence gave him no tanks to command but the moment was critical. Hotblack commandeered the two nearest, Mk Vs of the 16th Battalion waiting their turn, and headed through the storm of steel straight for the ridge. The tanks were on their own, no infantry being anywhere near but Hotblack did not hesitate. The pair drove unscathed up the south spur of the Quennemont Ridge, generally regarded as inexpugnable, drove the Germans off it and killed those who did not run. As soon as the German artillery tumbled to what had happened every gun in the neighbourhood was switched on to the two intruders; inevitably both were quickly destroyed. That, however, was by no means the end. Hotblack, partially blinded, with another wounded officer and five or six men brought some captured German machine-guns into action and held the immediate counter-attack at arm's length. Soon they were joined by an Australian officer, then by an American, each with his orderly, who had come to find out what was happening. The newcomers took a German gun apiece and brought the strength of the garrison to about a dozen. Twice during the previous week the ridge had been held in force but German counter-attacks had pushed the trespassers off. This time a dozen heroes kept them at bay for several hours until the first of the infantry arrived and took over. By that time every man had wounds of some kind to show. With even a part of Quennemont ridge in Allied hands the battle took a turn for the better. One cannot let Major Hotblack simply disappear from the story. His latest wounds, for he had almost as many as Bernard Freyberg, took him out of the remainder of the Kaiser's War. On 17 April, 1940, the First Lord of the Admiralty, Mr Churchill, picked him to take over command of the troops in Norway. After being briefed at the Admiralty until late at night he set off through the black-out and suffered a stroke whilst on the Duke of York's Steps. He was not found until next morning and was later boarded out of the Army. A sad end to such a brilliant career.

175 tanks, including those of the unlucky 301st, attacked the Hindenburg Line on Michaelmas Day. 46th (North Midland Territorial) Division of Walter Braithwaite's IX Corps performed one of the most remarkable feats of arms ever, crossing the Canal at Bellenglise by scrambling down the steep banks, swimming or wading across and then up the other side, driving the Germans before them. This being hardly tank work, the crews had to wait until they could cross the tunnel; that done, they swung south, worked down the far bank and added greatly to the German discomfiture. The armoured cars drove impudently into Bony, on top of the *Souterrain,* but were soon hustled out again.

Strong though the Hindenburg Line was, it was out of date by September, 1918. General Gouraud, in the last German attacks in Champagne, had demonstrated what a modern defensive system should be. His strength lay in depth, a depth far exceeding that of what the Germans called the Siegfried Stellung. The front lines were lightly held by sacrificial units and easily taken. Only then did the victors realize that these trenches were packed not with men but with land-mines and mustard gas. By the time these novelties had shaken them they found themselves beyond the range of their own artillery and were shot down by companies. The position in front of the British armies was a line in the most literal sense. Once broken there was not much behind.

The breaking, however, looked to be a prodigious task. Immediately to the front lay acres of wire, not in lines but in an ingenious chequerboard system. Behind the wire were deep dug-outs, built as carefully as any housing estate, in which the infantry and machine-gunners could take their rest immune from the heaviest of barrages. To cut the wire sufficiently for infantry to have any chance at all of getting through ought to have taken the British batteries a very long time; they would probably have succeeded in the end but that would only have meant launching unarmoured men through a jungle of torn-up spikes straight on to the waiting machine-guns, whose crews could have remained under cover until the last possible moment. When the works had been constructed the designers had bargained only for such an old-style attack and the tanks captured at Bullecourt had given them no cause to think again. The Mk V, with all its faults, was their undoing. Haig's plan turned over to the Tank Corps virtually all responsibility for dealing with the wire and a good part of the business of eliminating machine-gunners.

Every tank that could be made serviceable had to take its part. Once their first duty had been carried out the infantry could take over and storm the lightly fortified areas beyond. The Corps performed nobly. Its machines took heavy punishment, but from the standpoint of the Army as a whole it was a sacrifice well worth making. Sir Archibald Montgomery put it rather mildly in *The Story of The Fourth Army*; 'September 29th was perhaps the most trying day the tanks had experienced during the hundred days, but they earned the sincere gratitude of the infantry by their never-failing gallantry and self-sacrifice whenever they were called on for assistance.' It would have been no exaggeration had he said that, lacking them, the task might have proved impossible.

The heaviest burden fell upon those leading the Australian-American Corps, the 4th and 5th Brigades. Only a part of their strength was to be used on the first day, for all experience emphasized the need for reserves to be kept for reinforcing success. It was on the front of 46 Division, however, that the ball opened. The cavalry was under a cloud; one regiment, having decided to pass the night at a place midway between Divisional HQ and an important forward position cut down something like a hundred yards of the three pairs of signal cables which formed the main Divisional route in order to use them as picket lines for their horses.

Early morning mist had been the curse of British machine-gunners in March but it was a blessing to the Tank Corps in late September. The tanks of 46 Division,

The Carden-Lloyd carrier of the 1920s.

sixteen Mk Vs and nine Whippets, got safely across south of Bellicourt before it thinned. With the disappearance of the mist tanks stood out like hedgehogs and the German anti-tank gunners knew their business. One company was, says Montgomery 'quickly put out of action'. The Divisional historian tells how all five of those attached to 139 Brigade went the same way. Nevertheless some survived. As 138 Brigade came up to the strongly fortified village of Magny-la-Fosse, 'the tanks played an important part, cutting broad swathes through the wire entanglements, which here and there had been very little damaged by our artillery fire. Wheeling after their passage through the wire, the tanks then proceeded northwards along the line of the trench, and sunken road enfilading them and giving the crews of the machine-guns such a bad time that they fell comparatively easy victims to the Infantry pouring through the gaps in the wire. The tanks, closely followed by the Infantry, then advanced towards the village, and after a little street fighting the resistance of the enemy garrison was overcome.' This, as Sir Raymond Priestley

A Crossley 6-wheeler of the 1920s.

says, 'was indeed a breakthrough'. It was, however, the last contribution the tanks were able to make on that sector on Michaelmas Day. As the 32nd Division leap-frogged the 46th their quota of tanks was 'unfortunately unable to reach their rendez-vous in time to take part in the advance and concentrated at Magny ready for the next day'.

Away to the left the most troublesome area was still around the Knoll and Quennemont whose stout defence by the Germans had come near to throwing the whole operation out of gear. The 4th Tank Brigade (including the American 301st Battalion) had been given the special task of mopping-up around these strong-points and its success was very limited. Of thirty-nine machines that crossed the start line, twelve received direct hits, seven became ditched and only one crossed the Bellicourt tunnel. Seven drove to within a hundred yards of Quennemont Farm but all of them were knocked out as the mist rose. Fortunately the Australians were not far behind. At 9 am 5th Division crossed the original American start line led by the tanks of 5th Brigade whose crews were almost honorary Australians. Two of them, closely followed by two infantry battalions expert at working with tanks, approached Belli-court as the last shreds of mist were dispersing and by skilful co-operation cleared the village. Then, in the clear air of early autumn, the German anti-tank gunners around Nauroy got to work. Ten out of the twelve went down almost at once. Some hours later all four of those working with the 8th Brigade went the same way; of four Mk Vs and eight Whippets attached to 15 Brigade all but three Whippets were put out of action. The air support does not seem to have been conspicuously successful, probably by reason of the smoke expelled by hundreds of thousands of bursting shells.

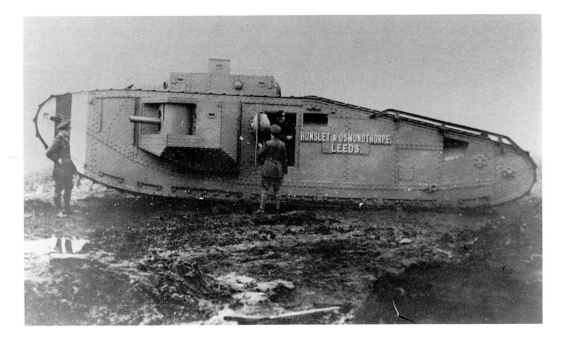

A British made Mk VIII Tank.

The Tank Corps was dwindling as observers watched. New battalions existed in various states of training but none was yet fit for battle. The same old faces were to be seen, though every day more and more dropped out for ever. It was not shortage of machines that was the critical factor now; it was shortage of the men who knew how to use them. The Germans, in spite of wide-spread '*tankschrecken*', were beginning to get the measure of the Mk V and the Whippet. With their low speed and thin armour – less than $\frac{3}{4}$ inch against about 6 inches in the later war – they were too vulnerable except in conditions of their own choosing and they relied for survival upon infantry skills that were themselves becoming rarer. Stern and his associates were working frantically and, though they now had every sort of official encouragement, the hour was very late. Neuvy-Pailloux was nowhere near finished. The International Mk VIII, was near to undergoing engine trials in America and the first Medium Bs were coming to the end of the production line in England. Everything henceforth was going to depend upon the speed with which these could be turned out, for otherwise the British Armies in France might waste away before the end came. Already Sir Douglas Haig's rifle strength had dropped to a figure about equal to that he had taken over from Sir John French nearly three years ago. Far too large a proportion of his infantry consisted of boys whose gristle had not yet set into hard muscle and middle-aged men who had no business to be there. Some Divisions retained nothing but a number to remind people of what they had been. The 50th, for example, was no longer the old Northumberland Territorials. It consisted almost entirely of malarial units brought back from Salonika. There were plenty of others in much the same case. Unless the war could be quickly won the

A Mk VIII Tank made in the United States.

baton would have to pass, as it had passed from France, to America. And the American Army, however brave and willing, was still green. The Germans, though savagely mauled, were falling back upon their own country and their own supplies. Naturally there were weak elements in it but a hard core remained determined to fight it out to the last, as Lee's men had done in the twilight of the Confederacy.

'*Tankschrecken*' was an important factor. There were occasions when, for want of real tanks, wooden dummies were employed, sometimes on the backs of mules. They brought in a gratifying number of prisoners. On the last day of September twenty tanks fought once more, back again in the old 'penny-packet' way that the Corps had hoped had gone for good. No notable success was achieved, largely because the infantry with whom they worked had no experience of the right kind and the tanks were left to fight little private battles on their own. Next day a few were engaged in the assault of Joncourt where, for the first time they put down their own smoke screens. It worked very well. 32nd Division took the village with ease. Incidentally 1 October, 1918, has a place in the history of the Army at large. It was the day on which it adopted the 24-hour clock, advocated by Haig since 1911. It took a little while getting used to saying things like 'twelve hundred hours' but it was better than having to learn about metres and litres.

There were no tanks engaged on 2 October but their presence was still felt. Major Freiherr von der Bussche, Ludendorff's emissary, made a statement to the party leaders of the Reichstag in Berlin. It was a long statement, treating of all the battle fronts in addition to the west, but only one part of it concerns us. Having announced that the High Command had decided that there was no longer any probability of the Allies suing for peace, he went on to explain why: 'The enemy has made use of tanks in unexpectedly large numbers. In cases where they have suddenly emerged in huge masses from smoke clouds, our men were completely unnerved. Tanks broke through our foremost lines, making a way for their infantry, reaching our rear and causing local panics, which entirely upset our battle-control. When we were able to locate them our anti-tank guns and our artillery speedily put an end to them. But the mischief had already been done, and solely owing to the success of the tanks we have suffered enormous losses in prisoners, and this has unexpectedly reduced our strength and caused a more speedy wastage of our reserves than we had anticipated. We are not in a position to make use of similar masses of German tanks. Our manufacturers, under the existing pressure, were absolutely unable to supply them in large numbers, without causing other more important things to be neglected. ... We can continue this kind of warfare (withdrawal from extensive sectors of the front) for a measurable space of time, we can cause the enemy heavy losses, devastating the country in our retreat, but we cannot win the war.' Perhaps Sir Douglas' 'minor factor' had not been so minor after all.

The Tank Corps, though worn to a rag, had not yet finished with the German army. On 8 October, when both Third and Fourth Armies attacked again on an eighteen-mile front between Cambrai and St Quentin eighty-two machines could still be found to act as spearhead. This battle saw the second fight of tank against tank, when four captured Mk IVs suddenly put in an appearance. Though they had the advantage of surprise they were soon out-classed. The only German male was killed almost at once by a 6-pdr shell; a female was also sunk by a captured German field gun operated by a tank section commander; the remaining two ran for home as soon as two British females hove into sight. On the following day the general chase began on a thirty-mile front. Cambrai was occupied by the French First Army and, with that, the Hindenburg system had collapsed. 50,000 prisoners were herded into the cages and 600 guns went for salvage.

The German Army was now doing what Major von der Bussche had foreseen, walking slowly home and destroying everything in its path. Once upon a time this would have been the moment to turn loose the horsemen, but it was 1918 and not 1318. They were quite useful carrying messages. A few more light squadrons, Hornets for preference but Whippets at a pinch, could have made retreat into rout; there were none, for the penny had dropped too late. Only painstaking plodding at the speed of a heavily-burdened man on foot was possible. By mid-October the British Army was nearing Le Cateau with its memories of Smith-Dorrien and an August day in 1914. On the 8th another of those milestones had been passed. Major Sasse of the 301st (US) Battalion led his unit from a wireless tank. On reaching Brancourt and seeing nothing of interest he left it and climbed a rickety ladder to the top of the church tower. From that advantageous position he could see, as nobody else could, that a German counter-attack was developing. In proper Tank Corps tradition he dismounted his light machine-gun, took the retreating infantry in hand and stopped the rot. Less traditional was his use of tank-mounted wireless to send out an SOS to the rest of his battalion. Sasse held the village with great bravery until American tanks came to relieve him. His DSO was well earned.

Baker-Carr, in the last month of the war, saw a prophecy fulfilled. His First Brigade being utterly worn out, mechanically and physically, he obtained from Sir Julian Byng a release from all duties until further orders. The same afternoon he was summoned peremptorily to Canadian Corps HQ by General Currie, familiarly known as 'Guts and Gaiters'. Sir Arthur Currie 'was a huge man with a vast expanse of pallid, clean-shaven countenance.' He was in a vile temper and pitched straight into his visitor. He was, 'to tell the truth, extremely rude to me'. The trouble was this. A Canadian Division, having been ordered to carry out an attack three days thence, had flatly refused to do so unless furnished with tanks. The Divisional General had said, fairly enough, 'Why should I lose three thousand men when, with tanks, I should only lose three hundred?' Baker-Carr explained that it was on the Army Commander's personal order that his tanks were unavailable. Telephone wires grew very hot; eventually Byng told Baker-Carr that he did not want to tell GHQ that a Division refused to fight and asked whether, as a personal favour to himself, the Tank Brigadier could not do something. Such an appeal could not be resisted. A dozen worn-out tanks manned by a dozen worn-out but volunteering crews did what was needed. The Division captured all its objectives at slight cost and published a special order of thanks. But it was just what Sir Beauvoir de L'Isle had prophecied; the day would come when infantry would not play unless the tanks played too.

It is fitting that the last battle of Baker-Carr's First Brigade should have a part for 'Uncle' Harper. Immediately in front ran the River Selle; in some places it was crossed by the help of 'cribs', but First Brigade, on its last legs, had none of these. The stream in their path was nothing much but on either bank was an impassable – for tanks – swamp and a furlong beyond was a railway embankment teeming with machine-guns. 'Uncle' demanded an immediate tank attack. Baker-Carr agreed to do it, but only on condition that a causeway was first built. 'But you can't build a causeway. The Germans are only a couple of hundred yards away.' Baker-Carr knew how to handle 'Uncle' after all these years. 'No causeway, no tanks, sir. Not one would get across.' The Corps Engineer was consulted; so was the Army Commander, who sent his Chief Engineer. The upshot of their deliberations was that a causeway could be built but a lot of men would be killed in the building of it. 'Uncle' rounded on Baker-Carr. 'What is it to be, Baker? If we build the causeway, will you guarantee that it is worth the loss of the builders?' This was reprehensible of 'Uncle'. When Baker-Carr answered that he could guarantee nothing, but that, with a causeway, he could certainly clean up the railway embankment 'Uncle' demanded a straight yes or no. It was not like him to duck out of a decision that had to be his own but by then everybody was dog-tired. The causeway was built, under continuous machine-gun fire. All the Sapper officers were killed or wounded 'and of the two hundred men who had started but few remained.... Another company of RE was summoned and the causeway finished, but not before the fresh workers also had paid a heavy toll.' The tanks crossed at dawn, climbed the embankment, turned right and left and wiped out the garrison. 'Masses of machine-guns were found, in one place seventy guns in the space of half a mile. The infantry, following the tanks at a short interval, suffered almost no loss whatever, and the gallant Sappers, splendidly upholding the traditions of their Corps, had saved hundreds upon hundreds of the lives of their comrades.' When the First Brigade was finally withdrawn a couple of days later it had exactly two tanks left.

By now the season of mist and mellow fruitfulness was well established. On 19 October thirty-seven tanks helped in an attack north of Le Cateau that began by moonlight and ended in thick mist and poisonous gas clouds. In this unmarked country the tanks proved as useful at smashing down hedges as they had done in flattening wire. The same number 'chipped in' on 4 November when an Anglo-French offensive began between Valenciennes and the River Oise. Two supply tanks, unarmed and loaded with bridging materials clanked menacingly towards a German machine-gun emplacement at Landrecies; even these hard men surrendered at the sight of something on caterpillar tracks. The last fight was of five Whippets supporting the 3rd Guards Brigade to the north of the Forest of Mormal. They were about the only ones left.

Figures are seldom animating but some are inescapable. Since 8 August the Tank Corps had fought on thirty-nine days out of the ninety-six. 1993 tanks and armoured cars had been engaged; 887 had been handed over for salvage; only fifteen were quite beyond repair while 214 had been returned to their units. Casualties in men had been grievous. Out of 1500 officers 592 were killed, wounded or prisoner; from an 'other rank' strength of 8,000, 2562 had gone the same way. The number of infantry lives they had saved is beyond computation. To put the figures into the hideous perspective of First War losses, the Tank Corps had in ninety-six days suffered less than many an infantry division in a single day on the Somme. To continue such analogies would be futile. Better to leave it there.

CHAPTER 19

End of Round One

LET US NOW CONSIDER how matters stood at the moment when Marshal Foch was laying down armistice terms to a German delegation in the railway siding at Compiègne. In accordance with custom, information about the enemy must come first. That Germany was in a bad way was beyond argument. Had it been otherwise no senior officer of that proud Army would have been present in Foch's Pullman straightly admitting that they were beaten. They had been driven out of their strongest fortifications; quite apart from their dead and wounded there were not far short of a million men missing or prisoners. The combined efforts of the Royal Navy and Admiral Sim's American ships had decisively broken the U-boats. In the air the Royal Air Force, the French and the small but growing US air service had something like complete superiority. Even more serious than these serious things was the state of affairs in the Fatherland. Four years of blockade had done its work; actual starvation had not yet come, but it was coming.

The black side was black enough, but there were lighter patches. There are, naturally, many resemblances to 1945, but one factor is missing. No great Russian armies were closing in from the East. Had the Kaiser not panicked, it was entirely possible that a stand might have been made even if it had to be on the Rhine. New weapons were on the way; the Siemens-Schuckert fighter aircraft with its 11-cylinder rotary engine should have been capable of overcoming anything that the Allies then had; German chemists could still turn out poisonous gases nastier than ever; the fate of the 301st Battalion had demonstrated that tanks were very vulnerable to mines, even to makeshifts from mortar bombs, of which there were still plenty; the TUF machine-gun, added to small guns borrowed from the fleet and to ordinary field-pieces simply converted could have seen off most tanks. And there remained the High Seas Fleet, still capable, had it only the stomach for it, of forcing a naval engagement with some chance of success.

Sir Henry Rawlinson, better informed than almost anybody, had firm views: 'It has been contended by some that the armistice was premature, that in another few weeks the German Army would have been forced to lay down their arms and surrender unconditionally. I do not hold this view. It is true that, insofar as the fighting troops of the Allies were concerned, a pronounced moral ascendency had been established in all the Allied Armies throughout the whole western front, and was

The Mk IX troop carrier.

daily increasing. Owing, however, to the thorough and systematic manner in which the Germans had destroyed all railways, roads and bridges during their retreat, it was a physical impossibility for at least the British Armies, and I think for any of the Armies, to continue their advance rapidly and in strength, and to immediately follow up their successes. Had they done so, they would have starved.' Winter would not have improved their chances; whatever else the Germans lacked it was not time. Had their Generals possessed the determination to see the business out to the end, determination shown by Jubal Early in 1865 and Christiaan de Wet in 1902, they might have compelled a stalemate followed by a peace of mutual exhaustion. America and Bolshevik Russia would then have had Europe to themselves, with results beyond imagining.

Had the Allies been able to endure yet another winter their complete military victory was possible, even probable; but it was not a foregone conclusion. On the British side whole divisions had long since been reduced to cadres and more would

A Mk VIII with British and U.S. officers.

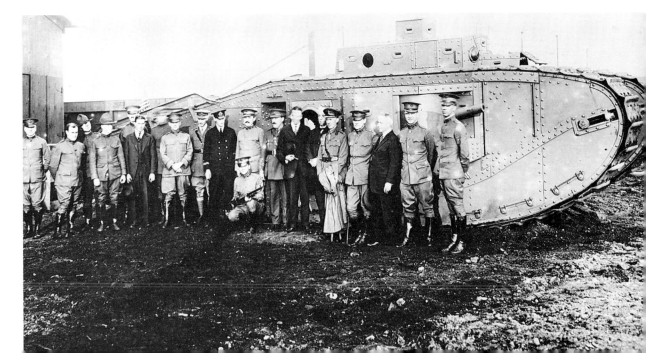

have had to go the same way. Already there were far too many soldiers whose youth or middle-age made them vulnerable to a winter in the open, and that without taking any account of the influenza epidemic that was to kill more people world-wide than the war itself had done. To press on to victory it would have been essential to cut down infantry and artillery strength in order to build up a powerful armoured force. The great, unanswered, and unanswerable question is whether this could have been done.

Had the armistice been delayed by a single week, or had some misbehaviour by Germany vitiated it, General Trenchard's Independent Air Force, based around Nancy, would have been capable of dropping 500 lb bombs on Berlin. No obvious military end would have been gained by thus punishing half-starved civilians, unless vengeance be reckoned an end in itself, but it would have brought war home to Germany as it had been to France and Britain. Here again it would be unwise to take success for granted. The new fighters in the hands of men like Hermann Goering before he got into bad company might have knocked down the Handley-Pages at their extreme range and have caused the business to be given up.

It was on 29 November that Stern, in his Paris office, received the cable from Stettinius for which he had been waiting and which told him that the International tank had passed all its tests. It was a very fine tank for its time, but it still had a top speed of only 6 mph and could travel only about fifty miles on a fill of 200 gallons. It weighed 37 tons, could cross a 14-foot wide trench and climb anything within reason. The armour was 19 mm thick. Ricardo's engine in the British model and the Liberty in the American put out 300 hp. It should have been thoroughly reliable mechanically and far less exhausting to drive than anything that had gone before. All the same, to approach a strong German position, presumably mined, at 6 mph was not a thing to be taken lightly. Great numbers would be needed, as they would be with the British Mediums B, C, and D. Nothing could be hoped of Neuvy-Pailloux for some time to come. Most of the Internationals would have to come from US factories and even that great source of production had its limits. The arrangement was for 1500 to be made in the States while Neuvy-Pailloux would turn out the same number. When the American manufacturers ran into difficulties with armour-plate and guns it was decided to move the whole enterprise to France. Accurate prediction of when this mass of machines would be handed over to their crews was hardly possible even by late November.

Then came the master-question. Given that the machines were to arrive, where were the men to be found? In his famous memorandum of 5 March, 1918, Mr Churchill had made the proposal, acted upon twenty years later, of 'putting most of the cavalry into tanks or other mechanical vehicles'. This made excellent sense, but time was against it. At a pinch men can be made into reasonable infantry soldiers in a few months. Grooms cannot be turned into mechanics and gunners in anything like so short a period. When he speaks of constructing 'armoured vehicles of various types ... to such an extent and on such a scale that 150,000 to 200,000 fighting men can be carried forward certainly and irresistibly on a broad front and to a depth of 8 or 10 miles in the course of a single day' it sounds more like Mr Wells than the

Early mine-clearers. A Mk IV fitted with rollers.

sober Minister. The war had reached a point much like that in South Africa after Lord Roberts had gone home convinced that all was over. It soon became clear that Wellington's Peninsular Division was not the kind of formation needed for war on the veldt; instead of a number of miniature groups of all arms it became necessary to raise a completely new army made up almost entirely of horsemen. This had been done after a fashion, but it took a couple of years. To do the business again, making an infantry army into a mechanically propelled one, would be a much longer affair. And until such an army existed the idea of using cavalry tanks for raiding far behind lines, disrupting communications and smashing up headquarters, was a pipe-dream. Some of the elements existed, such as the armoured aeroplane that could defy ground fire and pick off anti-tank batteries; already the Tank Corps was working on machines pushing rollers that might be able to clear ways through minefields. The idea was sound enough, as the last stages of the second war were to demonstrate; but in November, 1918, it was not yet practical.

Fuller's 'Plan 1919' is well known, with its emphasis upon using 20 mph tanks for raiding deep behind the lines and wrecking enemy headquarters rather than pushing the whole line forward as it had been pushed during the battles of the hundred days. It is difficult to regard this as more than a TEWT on the grand scale with a touch of Tennyson's *Locksley Hall* for good measure. In the first place the plan of campaign would not be devised by the War Office but by Sir Douglas Haig and his advisers. It is far from certain that Fuller, a Staff Officer of only field rank and already known by his self-chosen adjective of 'unconventional', would have been asked for an opinion.

Mr Churchill put his point of view many years later in an article called *Shall We All Commit Suicide?* 'Had the Germans retained the morale to make good their retreat to the Rhine, they would have been assaulted in the summer of 1919 with forces and by methods incomparably more prodigious than any yet employed. Thousands of aeroplanes would have shattered their cities ... Arrangements were being made to carry simultaneously a quarter of a million men, together with all their

Above and opposite: *The medium D Tank, Fuller's 'White Hope' for 1919.*
Both photographs are post-war.

requirements, continuously forward across country in mechanical vehicles moving ten or fifteen miles each day. Poison gases of incredible malignity ... would have stifled all resistance and paralysed all life on the hostile front subjected to attack. No doubt the Germans too had their plans.' They had. One of them was a delay action fuse, used to deadly effect in the last days, that could set buried mines to go off at any time from hours ahead to months. It came near to stopping all rail traffic. Mr Churchill had, on his own authority, ordered 10,000 caterpillar tractors from Henry Ford and he spoke of the Mk VIII as 'the tank we are counting on for 1919'. He acknowledged the difficulty in finding crews, with men of fifty already called up, and suggested that the Navy and the Marines should provide the men 'necessary to steer and manage the last 2,000 tanks to be completed before the battle'. Although he wished to see the Tank Corps raised to a strength of 100,000, he admitted that 'you will have large numbers of these invaluable weapons without the men to man them'. Nowhere is petrol mentioned. Cambrai alone had used up a quarter of a million gallons. Every first war tank was what the Americans call a 'gas-guzzler'.

Mr Churchill was at least planning from a known base, for the Mk VIII was nearly ready in prototype and its capabilities and its limitations were understood. Fuller worked on what must be called visions. The Medium B and C tanks were certainly improvements on the Whippet; from the crews' standpoint they were great improvements, for the 100 hp Ricardo engine was more reliable than the Tylor and, for the first time, engine room and fighting compartment were separate. All the same they were still not good enough for lightning raids; their speeds were only slightly more than that of the Medium A and their radii of action small. Neither ever reached France, though a few were sent to General Maynard at Murmansk shortly before his force was withdrawn. He does not mention ever having used them.

Fuller's plan was based on the Medium D, which did not exist. It was the brainchild of Lieut-Col Philip Johnson, a professional engineer and one of Searle's bright young men at Bermicourt. He had begun experimenting in February, 1918, searching for something that would come up to the magic speed of 20 mph, and by October his plans were sufficiently advanced for him to be given a free hand. A Mk V was sent to his old firm, Fowlers of Leeds, where it was stripped of tracks, rollers, sponsons and much else. Johnson fitted what remained of the hull with new tracks of his own design. This consisted of an ingenious suspension system based upon pulleys, bogeys and steel cables; the old Tritton-Wilson plates were scrapped and replaced with a curious arrangement shod all the way round with wooden shoes.

Model of a German 100-ton Tank. Never completed.

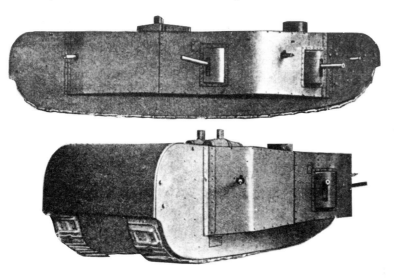

A Mk IV Tank towing a Naval airship.

Opposite, Top: *The 'store roller'. Designed for the campaign of 1919.*
Centre: *A Mk IV Salvage Tank, with the 'electro-magnetic collector'.*
Bottom: *A Mk IV Salvage Tank with crane jib.*

These were described as 'expendable', an apt enough word since, as soon as the machine gathered speed, they tended to fly off in a shower. The Medium D did not emerge in its final form until May, 1919; even then the unenlightened were sceptical about its queer appearance, saying that it looked as if it had just had a serious accident. It did indeed touch 20 mph in ideal conditions but whether it would prove battleworthy was much open to question. Only five were ever built and none went into service.

The Army is often accused, not always unjustly, of preparing for the last war over again. Fuller prepared for the next but one. Anything said about the prospects of success for Plan 1919 can only be guesswork. It seems fair, however, to suggest that any grand attack undertaken that Spring would not have been based on anything dreamed up by a middle-grade British Staff Officer. Smashing up enemy headquarters was an obvious ploy and it could have been better carried out by the heavy bombers of the RAF, for the four-engined Handley Page o/400 was in squadron service. The tank part of the business would have had to be entrusted to the Mk VIIIs, mostly American-manned and certainly not numbered in thousands. Foch would, no doubt, have retained his post but the decisions would have had to be those of General Pershing who was not a tank fanatic. He had only recently asked Haig for the loan of 25,000 horses. Fuller, one suspects, would have been ignored.

Even Mr Churchill was the Churchill of 1919, far removed in power from the great War Lord of 1940. He and Sir Douglas did not carry mutual admiration to excess. The CIGS, Henry Wilson, could claim that in him Mr Churchill detected signs of military genius but Sir Douglas loathed and despised him. Anything suggested by Mr Churchill, however inspired, would have been greeted with cries of 'Gallipoli' and rejected out of hand as a matter of course. A further imponderable was the great influenza epidemic of 1919 which killed more people worldwide than all the battles had done.

For all that, a plan did exist. Sir Philip Neame, in October, 1918, had been ordered to quit his appointment as GSO 1 of 30th Division in order to become chief operational Staff Officer to No 2 Tank Group. Three such formations were to be formed, each of three Tank Brigades of four 60-tank battalions. The armoured force of 1919 would, had it come into being, have contained as many tanks as seven armoured divisions in the next war without counting the 10,000 tractors. As none of these formations ever existed one must regard them as the army of a dream. Twenty years later it became a nightmare.

Plan 1919 came off when tried, but by then it was Plan 1940 and was written in German. Even that, against French Generals of Foch's kind, might have failed. It is a large question and there is no point in worrying it to death. One thing is certain. In the Kaiser's War the Empire lost some three-quarters of a million of its best young men, killed outright or died of wounds. Had the pioneers not had the brains, the skill and the pertinacity to make their tanks and the hardihood to fight for them against entrenched prejudice that figure would have been far higher. The descendants of those infantrymen who came safe home might give them a thought every time the Two Minutes' Silence comes round.

Thus the war terminated, and with it all remembrance of the Tank Corps' services. It reckoned itself lucky to escape disbandment.

PART TWO

'*And the King of Israel answered and said, Tell him, Let not him that girdeth on his harness boast himself as he that putteth it off*'.

I KINGS, ch. 20, v. 11

CHAPTER 20

Vickers Take Over

IT VERY NEARLY HAPPENED. In the moment of victory the tank did not lack for friends but after a pause for thought cautionary voices were raised. Sir Douglas Haig included in his Final Despatch a section quaintly headed 'The Value of Mechanical Contrivances' whose conclusions were both firm and reasoned. 'Weapons of this character are incapable of effective independent action. They do not in themselves possess the power to obtain a decision. To place in them a reliance out of proportion to their real utility . . . would be a disservice to those who have the future of these new weapons most at heart.' On 8 August, 1918, and the following days, Sir Douglas pointed out, 'A scrutiny of the ammunition returns disclosed the fact that in no action of similar dimensions had the expenditure of ammunition been so great.' Sir Henry Rawlinson made a similar point in his Foreword to *The Story of The Fourth Army* which he wrote in December, 1919. After giving tanks the praise they deserved he qualified it: 'There is always a tendency on the part of a new service like tanks, aeroplanes, or even machine-guns when first employed in a general

The Vickers Light Mk 4. A slightly later version of Mk. 2.

The A9 Tank of the 1930s.

The Vickers Light Mk 2 Tank. Another between-wars machine.

action to think that they can win the battle on their own.' The 'all-tank' idea was officially disapproved. Tanks were a useful addition to the traditional arms but they were no substitute.

There were many and various committees dealing with the future of all the armed services. This was the period when *Punch* joked about a new uniform for the RAF appearing every week and strange-sounding ranks like Reeve and Third Ardian were being seriously proposed. The Tank Corps was humbugged in much the same way. One suggestion that came quite near to being adopted was that it should be treated on a par with the African Colonial Forces and officered by people seconded for short tours of duty. Nobody knew quite what to do with an arm that was undeniably useful but with functions that could not be called merely defensive.

The war to end war had left the British Army stretched as never before. Quite apart from ordinary peacetime functions, it was faced with a campaign in Waziristan, something very much like a campaign at Archangel and Murmansk and the possibility of yet another in the near East where a new Turkey was manifestly not disarming in accordance with the Treaty, but was up to something. There were formations scattered about from Tiflis to Constantinople and smaller ones in Persia and Mesopotamia; Ireland demanded troops; an Army of Occupation stood on the Rhine; the Palestine Mandate demanded its share in addition to the forces in Egypt. All these contingents had to be found from an Army that was melting away like a snowman in the sun. Conscription did not end until the Spring of 1920 but drafts seemed to become smaller and smaller.

The old Regulars were nearly all gone, dead, maimed or time-expired. The Territorials, their numbers saved only by the return of the three Divisions sent to India and thus unscathed, reverted to the condition known as disembodied. The remainder, Kitchener men, Derby men and conscripts, were clamouring to be released before all the civilian jobs had gone. New Regulars were enlisted as quickly as possible but they were few in numbers and very young. The Tank Corps melted faster than most, for it was made up almost in its entirety from non-Regulars. Mitchell put the professional soldiers at no more than two per cent of the total; most of these were the senior officers who, fortunately, were senior enough to compel attention when they spoke.

The pioneers dispersed in much the same fashion. Crompton returned to electrical engineering and in 1926 won the coveted Faraday Medal. The Admiralty claimed back d'Eyncourt, though he remained a member of the War Office Tank Committee. Swinton, who had been on a long lecture tour in the United States, left the Army and became Controller of Information for civil flying at the Air Ministry. Stern rejoined the higher reaches of money-lending, becoming a Director of the Midland Bank as well as of various overseas finance houses. Tritton, having beaten ploughshares into swords, resigned himself to beating them back again. Wilson likewise continued with his own particular mystery and founded the company called Self Changing Gears Ltd. Ricardo also went back to his beloved petrol engines and made a considerable name for himself in the world of mechanical engineering.

Not much remained of the Tank Corps once the Victory Parades were over and a number of surplus Mk IVs had been posted in market squares as reminders to a new generation of what their crews had once achieved. Of the rest of the machines, most were dumped around Bovington to await either purchasers or the scrap-merchant. Their military value now was about equal to that of HMS *Victory*. Williams-Ellis indeed suggested that the best thing we could do would be to sell all the Mk Vs and Whippets to any potential enemy we might have. A few Whippets went to Denikin's White Russian Army and fell into Bolshevik hands for nothing. Some remaining armoured cars, the last ones made by the American Peerless Company to Austin's specification, roamed the muddy roads of Ireland to provide targets for the IRA. A few Mediums were sent to India in order to ascertain whether they would be of any use on the North-West Frontier. They were not. The Tank Corps was reduced to four battalions, one for each Home Command from which in the laughable possibility of another European War the four Divisions would presumably be raised again.

The general belief was that the tank had been created for one purpose only, to break the Hindenburg Line. Having done that, its occupation was gone. There was no case made out for persevering with the long battering-rams of 'Mother's' brood but one might exist for something lighter and faster that could be employed in open warfare. Even this was far from certain. The Army, bidden to get rid of everything not absolutely essential, obeyed. The mighty Machine Gun Corps was disbanded, such of its guns as were not sold being handed over to the Support Companies of infantry battalions. Practically everything relating to chemical warfare was hurriedly scrapped; all that was allowed to remain was the unarguably defensive respirator; to test it tear-gas chambers were permitted. These were not unpopular with recruits for they were held to be the best cure for the common cold. Thanks only to Mr Churchill the heavy guns were laid up in mineral jelly on the off chance that they might be needed some day. They were.

The greater part of the equipment of the Royal Air Force was sold off at thieves' prices. The entirety, aircraft, engines, spares and everything else, fetched £5,700,000.

Over everything hung the shadow of the American Debt. Some of Mr Churchill's writings suggest that he did not find President Coolidge's 'They hired the money, didn't they?' entirely worthy of a Power that had got off so lightly. When he had taken on the job of furnishing the AEF with all the heavy artillery it demanded there had been a simple word-of-mouth agreement. We would make no profit; they would underwrite any loss. Times had changed. Though the reasons were not the same as in Mr Asquith's day every half-penny spent on the armed services was grudgingly doled out as if it had been the last one in the Treasury.

Bovington remained, a shadow of its former self like some little Norman church huddled in a corner of an abandoned Legionary fortress. Throughout 1919 and 1920 it clung to such tanks as remained serviceable, constantly patching and mending. Sir Hugh Elles stayed on as Commandant until 1923 when he was given an infantry brigade and moved upwards along the usual lines. An uneasy feeling was growing up among tank men that he was no longer to be counted on as their champion. Like many other people he was veering towards the view that anti-tank weapons were now so strong that no armoured vehicle could stand against them. Not that this was of more than academic interest, for the Ten-Year Rule laid it down firmly that no war would happen during that time. All the peripheral tracked weapons, the gun-carrying tank, the mine-roller, the folding bridge, the wireless tank, the crane-carrying salvage tank and the rest, withered and died. Mr Churchill, in *The World Crisis*, asserts that the neglect of the torpedo-carrying seaplane was 'one of the great crimes of the war'. Language rather strong, perhaps, but neglect of the self-propelled gun was every bit as bad. When the bell sounded for Round Two all these lost arts had to be rediscovered.

Two men remained in the Service to speak up for Mechanical Warfare. Fuller and Martel alone kept alive some interest in the subject during these critical years. Even they could not have achieved much but for a stroke of good fortune. From January, 1919, until February, 1921, the Secretary of State for War and Air was Mr Churchill, probably the only Minister who had not deluded himself about the possibility of the Army having again to fight a serious war. 'Kill the Bolshie; kiss the Hun' was his admirably succinct description of the policies needed. Nor did he require any homily about tanks and the need for them. Suggestions that new ones were essential got from him a sympathetic hearing.

There were no tank manufacturers left. Once production had ceased, companies like Metropolitan, Marshalls, Fosters and Fowlers wasted no time over returning to their ordinary business. The only possible candidate for producing new machines was the firm of Vickers. Though long established in the armament business Vickers had never made a tank. They were, however, willing to add tank production to their other interests, but only upon terms. It was not seemly for Vickers merely to build to other men's designs. They would recruit their own experts; this they did, eventu-

The Vickers Medium Tank Mk 1A.

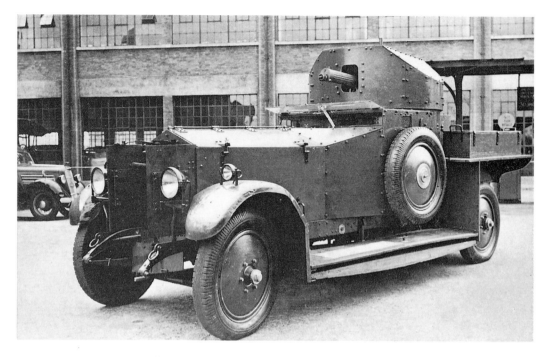

The 1920 Rolls-Royce armoured car.

ally setting up a design office in Sheffield. When the Master-General of the Ordnance asked for a new design they produced it themselves. Neither Fuller, at the War Office, nor Johnson, who had planned the Medium D, was consulted.

In 1921 the first Vickers Medium Tank made its debut. It was mechanically a good machine, built with the loving care that men had once put into the building of cathedrals. Rough wartime finish would not do for Vickers. Their tanks were built to last; which was just as well as this model and its immediate successor would have to do duty for many years to come. The armour was still very thin. More weight spelt more fuel consumption. The Mk I weighed 12 tons, much the same as a Whippet but there the comparison ends. An Armstrong Siddeley engine of 90 hp gave it a top speed of 18 mph and a cruising range of more than a hundred miles. The track had been completely redesigned, for the Tritton-Wilson, though a splendid performer on slow machines, was not up to these much greater speeds. Like the Renault FT17, it carried a revolving turret in which was mounted the same Vickers 3-pdr gun that had been rejected in 1916 as being too small. The crew numbered five and the tank could cross a trench six feet wide. This was considered quite enough since trench-crossing was no longer of first importance. Major-General Sir Louis Jackson, lately Director of Trench Warfare, had made this quite clear in the course of an RUSI lecture in November, 1919. 'The circumstances which called (the tank) into existence were exceptional and are not likely to recur. If they do, they can be dealt with by other means.'

Vickers held a monopoly in tank production for the better part of twenty years.

216

It was not of the Company's seeking. Nobody else wanted work in which chopping and changing of specifications by people who only half-understood what they were doing went on far too much. The taxpayer did not suffer. During the 1920s and early 30s Vickers, without any help – if that be the right word – from the War Office produced a notable range of light tanks as part of their ordinary commercial activities. For home consumption they built between 1923 and 1928 160 of their Mediums but these were only part of the Company's output. Foreign Governments subsidised research and development by buying the machines the War Office did not want. The 6-tonner of 1933, for example, was sold all over the world, even to customers as unlikely as Bolivia and Siam. Soviet Russia and Finland were both purchasers, the Russians basing their own light tanks upon Vickers' models. The Finns were less fortunate. The last half-dozen they ordered in 1939 had not been handed over when the Russian invasion came; they ended up as training machines for the British Army. It might have been better to have disbanded all the inexpert War Office Committees and to have turned the whole business over to the professionals. With Generals of the quality of Sir Herbert Lawrence and Sir Noel Birch on the Board they would not have lacked for competent advisers.

Armoured cars were treated differently. The solid-tyred, twin-dustbinned models looked absurdly out of place on English peacetime roads. They were soon phased out in favour of the far more chic Rolls-Royce, Lawrence's 'Blue Mist' with a turret; even with this piece of camouflage they could not help looking the aristocrats they were. The Peerlesses, being fairly new and having cost a lot of money, were handed over to the Territorial Army, itself re-born in 1921.

The fingers in the pie from which a new tank might be pulled out were many. First came the Master-General of the Ordnance himself; his department was divided up into four Directorates, the one with responsibility for tank production and many other things being the Director of Mechanization. His office was divided into three parts, the first dealing with engineer and signal stores, the second with all kinds of tracked vehicles and the third with second echelon, non-fighting, motor transport. Superimposed upon the Director was an advisory body called the Mechanization Board, mostly officers serving at the War Office but thickened up with civilian experts. To assist in their conjoint efforts was the Tank Testing Section – later known by other names – at Farnborough. Once a new machine was over all these obstacles, it was submitted to the Chief Inspector of Armaments at Woolwich where every component part was supposed to be keenly scrutinized. For the Medium tank this meant the examination of some 2,500 parts set out in the inventory contained in a thick book. It is hardly remarkable that years might elapse between design and prototype; delays were often prolonged by constant tinkering with plans which halted production and the insistence on a high standard of finish more suitable to the Motor Show. It was rare indeed for any member of any Board or Committee to be drawn from the Tank Corps. All the same, in the late 1920s the arrangement seems to have worked. British tanks were still the best in the world and there was no call for any 'Boot and Saddle' over their production.

Unfortunately the Medium was expensive. Almost at the same moment as it

The Crossley-Martel wheel-and-track machine.

appeared Herbert Austin surprised and delighted the world with his baby car and the cry inevitably went up 'Why build a tank comparable with a Daimler when, for same money, you can have half a dozen Austin Seven equivalents?' To this there was no answer. Martel, himself a qualified mechanical enginer, decided to have a try on his own. His tiny machine was trooped around the Staff College and gave everybody a lot of fun. It was not, however, anything to be taken seriously.

When Sir Edmund Ironside was appointed CIGS in September, 1939, to his own indignation as he had been expecting the fighting command, he had much to say about the then tank situation. One remark is interesting. Our tanks, he said, were unfitted for war in Europe. He may very well have been right. The League of Nations in its starry-eyed phase, along with the various pacts, had reduced the British Army to an armed colonial police force. Its enemies thenceforth would not be Hohenzollerns and Hindenburgs but the likes of the Akhound of Swat, the Fakir of Ipi and the Grand Mufti of Jerusalem. Against such as these the smallest and cheapest tank would do. If, indeed, any tank were needed at all.

Then, in 1924, came the first Labour Government and the voice of the conscientious objector was heard in the Cabinet. The word of power was 'disarmament'; strictly defensive weapons, such as the ageing guns sunk in concrete and overlooking Dover Harbour, were legitimate. The same guns taken out and mounted on carriages were offensive and unlawful. Good socialists can tolerate armies provided that they are not efficient. Everything of an offensive description must go. Disbandment of a Corps that could by no stretch of Socialist imagining be called defensive was once

An experimental airborne machine from the same stable. Only the one was made.

again on the cards. Fortunately the Administration did not live long enough to attend to it.

The Locarno Pact of 1925 declared war to be illegal. The War Office, with all its faults, did not subscribe to the view that its duties were now limited to calling an international policeman when something blazed up. Orders were placed with Vickers for a new tank, not merely an improved Medium – though the Medium Mk II did appear in the following year – but something that would make possible the mechanized war of Fuller's dreams. It was to be big enough and powerful enough to take on fortified positions with a decent chance of success, but it was to be more than an up-dated Mk VIII. The proposed machine would also have to be fast enough and of sufficient endurance to work in large bodies of its own, no longer tied to the pace of heavily burdened foot soldiers. It must be capable both of fighting Cambrais and of improving upon Rolling's armoured car raids on enemy headquarters.

Sir George Buckham, head of the design team, had been with Vickers since 1895 and by now had a seat on the Board. Under his guidance the designers and engineers came up with a very fine tank indeed. Officially it was styled the AI, first of a long line of 'A's, but the name used for it by everybody was the Independent. AI weighed in at 32 tons, a monster for its day, and could carry its 47 mm gun and four machine guns in their separate turrets at a steady 20 mph. Its armour was no better than that of a Mk V but in every other respect Independent was years ahead of its time. Buckham's men showed it off at the Imperial Conference and received polite applause. Here was the machine constructed as its name implied for warfare of a new kind. Squadrons of Independents would be able to do in reality all that the free range Medium Ds had accomplished in Fuller's dream and more besides. A few hundred of them with their eight-man crews would be of more value than an old-style Army Corps. Neither the Army Council nor the Treasury saw it that way. Only the one specimen was made. You may see it sitting forlornly in the yard of the Tank Museum, a monument to the barnacled minds of elderly gentlemen. No price would have been too high for an updated Independent in the hot summer of 1940. It was fortunate that Soviet Russia, of all countries, discerned its merits and copied many of them into their highly successful KVI. Sir George's work was not entirely wasted: Nazi Germany came to know all about the KVI.

Though Fuller went on and on about the tank versus tank battles that must abound in any future war – another of those blinding glimpses of the obvious that some military minds refuse to see – the policy reverted to the old one. As the best tank in the world had been wantonly thrown away the obvious next step was to settle for the worst. Not that there was anything wrong with the Vickers Light Tank; except, of course, that with no more than a machine-gun and with armour proof only against small arms fire any tank that carried a gun could kill it quickly. No tank in the later 1920s was even contemplated as the means of bringing down fire from anything heavier than rifle-calibre weapons, the only exception being the elderly 3-pdr. One cannot but suspect some members of the Royal Regiment of Artillery of bringing this about. Guns are sacred things, the equivalent of Colours. They must not be degraded by being put into the hands of non-gunners, not even very small guns.

There were many Gunner officers in positions of power and few of them trusted 'Boney' Fuller. He was indeed a strange figure, in some ways reminiscent of Robert Craufurd in the Peninsula. Both were capable of brilliant planning; Craufurd's operations on the Coa and Fuller's at Cambrai are examples. Against that, both were capable of what the Duke called 'mad freaks'. Fuller, as he grew older, seemed to withdraw from reality into a Jules Verne world. His 1919 essay on 'The Application Of Recent Developments In Mechanics And Other Scientific Knowledge To Preparation And Training For Future War On Land' won him a medal; but it frightened many staid men off the tank idea. The devil they knew was at least a familiar devil. Had they known Fuller to be on corresponding terms with Aleister Crowley, alias The Beast 666, they would have been more frightened still.

The plans he had long ago matured for the perfect destruction of a hostile army had become common knowledge. To Fuller the number 3 possessed a mystic significance and all his calculations were based on that digit. The Rule of Three had worked at Cambrai and it would work even better at the Cambrais yet to come. Three semi-independent forces would be needed. First to go in would be the Disorganizing Force, Medium Ds or something better, whose charge it would be to pierce a hole, pour through it, and beat up all headquarters from Corps down to Divisions. It would not, if it could help it, smash up communications; these would be better left to wail out demoralizing messages to the troops in front of them about what was happening in rear. Then it would be the turn of the Breaking Force of heavier tanks and self-propelled guns to smash through a line that, with any luck, would have become disorganized. Lastly, behind the Breakers, would flood in the third wave of fast light tanks and their attendant mounted infantry in lorries to cut down the fleeing rabble. It sounded excellent sense, provided only that the enemy played fair and sprang no surprises of his own. When the German Panzer divisions put it into operation it proved needlessly complicated. The French Army disorganized itself.

In a perfect military world where men of high intelligence were available in great numbers and money was no object Fuller might have achieved great things. In a very imperfect one, where infantry depots were glad to scrape up any recruits they could find and Adjutants went prematurely grey in having their drafts ready for the Indian trooping season, his imaginings were rich in academic interest but barren of much practical importance. Fuller's influence upon the Army as a whole was not profound, at any rate after 1927.

The cavalry for some years to come went on its elegant way, unburdened by worse things than the Aldershot Tattoo and the King's Birthday Parades. They had nothing further to learn, for the whole business of horse-soldiering had been mastered centuries ago and it was only a matter of passing it on. Infantry battalions still took a proper pride in their standard of march discipline.

The tanks, though little seen by the public, worked away at their trade. Baker-Carr's old friend Colonel George Lindsay assumed command at Bovington; no man was better equipped for the task. Fuller's days with tanks were drawing in by the mid-twenties but another star was rising in the East. Percy Cleghorn Stanley Hobart came from the Indian Sappers and Miners, with whom he had experienced some of the pre-tank battles on the western front in 1915. When the Indian Corps had been withdrawn Hobart found himself in Mesopotamia where he had as rough a war as most men. If Fuller bore some resemblance to Craufurd, Hobart is reminiscent of Mangin, for he was a fierce man and suffered no fool near him. Fool, in Hobart's vocabulary, meant any man who disagreed with his ideas. He himself wrote his views, tersely enough, on military matters in a confidential report. 'This officer plays cricket. Need I say more?' Though he had seen nothing of tanks in battle Hobart was determined to learn, for he had a clear grasp of what future war would be like. In 1924 he transferred to the newly christened Royal Tank Corps, but for serious business he had a long wait ahead of him. His first three years were passed still in India where only a few armoured car companies represented the Corps, but he entered at once into a spirited correspondence with Lindsay at Bovington. Each struck sparks off the other. By the time he arrived at the same place in 1927 Hobart was well marinated in tank doctrine.

The other protagonist of the future, Colonel Martel, was still busy inventing things. In 1925 he had met Sir John Carden, 33 years old and a 7th Baronet, who was joint proprietor with a Mr Loyd of a small London garage. Carden possessed something like a genius for design and the two men worked happily together. Out of the garage came some very small machines of the two- and even one-man kind. The most successful was a simple tracked affair which without many changes was to become the Bren carrier which every Second War soldier knew. Some of the other

The A1 'Independent' Tank of 1926.

designs were less successful. Mitchell tells of Martel's plan for a four-tracked tank, 'long and low and looking like a dachshund'. It never got further than the drawing-board. He also wrote of a tank equipped with a hinged pole by means of which it could jump ditches. Again, it was never more than an idea. The French stuck to Louis Renault's little machine which seemed good for a long time to come. The main thrust of Martel's thinking was towards the very small and cheap, to be turned out in great numbers. His 'tankette' – a name mercifully forgotten – was made from ordinary commercial parts and cost, at £500, about the same as the Rover saloon car. The idea was that swarms of these machines should move ahead of the Army, as Napoleon's Tirailleurs had done, until they struck opposition. If it was not too heavy they would press on and prepare the way for the bigger machines following behind; if it proved too much for them they would halt and convert themselves into minuscule pill-boxes. In all this there was an air of strident unreality. In practice the 'tankettes' served a small purpose by bringing instruction in driving and main-tenance to men who otherwise would have had none. Stern, who had always had a fancy for the heavy tank, was scornful. These toys were not for fighting. Martel might have privately agreed with him, but he was in much the same case as Elles before Third Ypres. Better to have something, however feeble, that boasted an engine and a pair of tracks than nothing at all. And nothing at all seemed the alternative.

Money was not the only limiting factor. Since 1919 the Army had gone back to proper soldiering as understood before the Kaiser's War. Sir Philip Neame tells of how 'I served at Aldershot in 1924 under a Major-General who took me to task for introducing tanks into a military exercise, as he said that he was not going to have his infantry frightened by the idea of any ... tanks!' Exactly what had once been said of machine-guns.

Fuller had one last blow to strike for his Corps. In 1926 Sir George Milne had been appointed CIGS with Fuller as his Military Assistant. Milne, who had won in Macedonia the rare distinction of being known to his troops as 'Uncle George', was a Gunner but prepared to listen to a man from the younger arm. The upshot of it was that before the summer of 1926 was out Milne, against much opposition within the Army Council, had persuaded Sir Laming Worthington-Evans, Secretary for War, to allow him to form an experimental armoured force and try it out on Salisbury Plain. It was not only Fuller who had worked on the CIGS. Captain Liddell Hart had dined with him at the Norfolk Arms, Arundel, and had reinforced the argument.

It was left to Fuller to work out the details and he came up with a plan. It had fairly modest beginnings: a tank battalion, a company of armoured cars, a lorry-borne infantry battalion and machine-gun battalion along with a battery of self-propelled guns and another drawn by the tracked machines known as 'dragons'. The self-propelled gun would be the 'Birch', of which more later. There was much tinkering with the Experimental Force but for the time being it came to nothing. The Treasury refused to find the money. In the year of the General Strike it is hard to blame them. The cash was found in the year following.

The summer of 1927 was distinguished for almost incessant rain. It was remarkable also for the first appearance since 1918 of an armoured, mechanized force at work. Fuller, through his own fault, did not command it. Instead he forced a silly quarrel upon the CIGS because he was not allowed to escape the humdrum duty of commanding an infantry brigade as well as having the fun of directing the great exercise. The quarrel ended with Fuller being translated to work where he had nothing further to do with tanks. Command of the Experimental Brigade passed to Colonel Collins who neither had nor claimed to have experience of the necessary kind.

Before the exercise began the Army, to show how modern it was becoming, put on an exhibition of its new machines for the benefit of a party of Colonial Governors. All the latest cross-country vehicles were put through their paces. Some, like Morris' 6-wheeler 30 cwt truck, were excellent. Others were downright freakish, such as the car with a detachable undercarriage which could suit itself to either wheels or tracks as the situation demanded. A half-tracked Morris Cowley, capable of perhaps 60 mph, pulled a hickory-wheeled 18-pdr gun capable of about 5. The Governor of Nigeria, Sir Graeme Thompson, said politely that it would have a great effect upon the future of our Colonies. This was not borne out by subsequent events.

CHAPTER 21

Years of Futility

THE GREAT EXERCISE OF 1927 ought to have had more effect upon the future of mechanized warfare than it did, for it was pretty much of a success. The correspondent of the *Illustrated London News* wrote enthusiastically about it. The object of it all, he said, was to find out whether it was more advantageous to advance with machine-gunners carried in tanks or to send the tanks off first and let the guns follow in the old style. Every Vickers Medium and every tankette available was used, along with every horsed unit and every horse-drawn gun. In the battle of 24 August the 'Blue' force of tanks drove the 'Red' infantry off a hill. On the following day a cavalry brigade mixed it with the Experimental Force, with surprising results. The *Times* man reported that 'I was in time to see an interesting fight between the Lancers and armoured cars in a large field. The mix-up between horsemen and machines was indescribable. Owing to the good placing of the anti-tank machine-guns of the cavalry the umpires gave the decision in their favour.' The 'anti-tank machine guns' were, of course, still the pre-1914 Hotchkisses, which might as well have been red flags. The *Illustrated London News* carried a picture of horsemen scrambling up a bank, apparently to avoid being run over, with the caption 'Cavalry crossing a road on which are seen two captured tanks.' How the cavalry captured them is unclear, but umpires can work miracles. Another picture shows clusters of horses slowly dragging artillery pieces across a skyline. 'A picturesque view of a battery advancing during a battle.' Nevertheless, on the same authority, 'it was ruled that tanks are the decisive arm and infantry are in support'. The RAF amused itself by flying low over the performance in order, perhaps, to frighten the horses, and a gesture was made towards the use of smoke. Tank Corps officers marked the transitional nature of it all by wearing berets and spurs.

On the serious side, the exercise gave both the 'all tank' men and the 'co-operation between arms' men a lot to think about. It was, none the less, a mere beating of the air until some high authority should pluck up its courage and remove horses from the battlefield where they no longer belonged.

Fuller, you will remember, had spoken of self-propelled guns being part of the Experimental Force. No such weapon had existed since Wilson's tank carrying a 60-pdr had been degraded to coolie labour. General Sir Noel Birch - 'Curly' to his peers - had been Sir Douglas Haig's chief artillery adviser; with the possible exception of his German opposite number, Bruchmuller, he knew more about the business of gunnery than any other man. The 'Birch' gun – an 18-pdr mounted on a cut-down Vickers Medium chassis – had been constructed to his design; no fault could be found with it nor did any officer of stature speak other than in terms of praise. General Birch could never have been called an enemy of the horse, for in his spare time he had written books on equitation and he was a well-known coaching whip. In spite of all these things he was unable to persuade the Royal Artillery to take up his new weapon. There was no reasoned argument against it; merely that if such a thing were taken on Gunners would have to dress themselves in dungarees, cover them-selves in grease and develop new smells. Not only would the 'hairies' who pulled the guns have to go but in all probability their hunters and polo ponies also. A cavalry regiment, they knew, was listed to become rude mechanicals but not the artillery. 'Curly' was due to leave the Army before long, and authority forgets a dying king. The Birch gun made its last appearance in 1928. It would have been beyond price in 1940.

The anti-mechanicals movement was not confined to comparatively junior officers. Sir Douglas Haig had won great battles with tanks and had given them enthusiastic praise. Retirement seemed to have switched him to General Jackson's opinion: tanks had been created for a specific purpose that no longer existed. In his counter-blast to Liddell Hart's *Paris, or The Future of War* he set out his thoughts on paper; 'I believe that the value of the horse and the opportunity for the horse in the future are likely to be as great as ever ... I am all for using aeroplanes and tanks, but they are only accessories to the man and the horse, and I feel sure that as time goes on you will find just as much use for the horse – the well-bred horse – as you have ever done in the past.' The year was 1925. General Birch's reputation stood very high but none equalled that of the old C-in-C. The Horse Artillery could thus appeal to Caesar with confidence. A mere five months after the 1928 exercise Sir Douglas died. Like Caesar, the small piece of evil that he had done by this lived after him; the good was interred in Dryburgh Abbey.

Horse-magic lived on far too long. With the Birch gun sunk without trace the artillery moved a step backwards. Their pieces were, undoubtedly, now pulled by mechanical vehicles but they still pointed in the wrong direction, as guns had done from the very beginning, and needed to be unshipped and hauled round before they could perform their office. One regiment, however, succumbed. In 1927 the 11th Hussars, the famous Cherry Pickers, acquired a new name. On being deprived of horses they became known as the Sparrow Starvers. As a douceur they were put not into tanks but into 1920 vintage Rolls-Royce armoured cars. The 11th still retained a high degree of tone. The 4th Hussars, personified by the Chancellor of the Ex-chequer, were not jealous.

Another Salisbury Plain exercise took place in 1928. An armoured car battalion, a battalion of Mediums, a field brigade of artillery and a motorised infantry battalion took on the 3rd Division. With leaders like Martel, Pile and Hobart to do the planning and execution, it comes as no surprise to learn that the Experimental Brigade cut rings round their opponents, who moved at the pace of Marlborough.

The Division, apart from the presence of many new faces, was still the Division of 1918. It possessed no weapon that it had not had then and was helpless when attacked suddenly from an unexpected quarter. The prophets of the future war naturally gained much kudos. The oddest thing about it all is that none of them seemed in the least interested in anti-tank weapons. When these eventually came, many years later, they were no more than slightly improved versions of the German equipment of 1918, rifles or small guns that threw a solid slug of metal at great velocity. A modest prize put up in 1928 would surely have produced something that could have changed the entire state of affairs. When matters became desperate the Sticky Bomb, the PIAT, the Blacker Bombard and the Bazooka seemed to spring up overnight. At a time when the RAF High Speed Flight was winning the Schneider Trophy with regularity it can hardly have been beyond the skill of scientists to have produced some weapon of this kind, however crude, by whose agency a couple of infantrymen might stand a chance of knocking out the thin-skinned armoured vehicles of the day. Instead, infantry battalions on training exercises were kitted out with a series of coloured flags that could represent anything from a Soyer stove to a battleship.

In a way the unsurprising success of tanks over marching infantry was as much to be regretted as the 'Dash To Kimberley'. The parts of the army moved by petrol and by animal-power began to draw away from each other. Tanks pursued their own interests while the remainder – and by far the greater part – of the Army continued in the old way. Drafts were made up for India, Egypt and Palestine and training was as unrealistic as ever. In January, 1927, a Division had been hurried to Shanghai where a little-known Chinese war lord named Chiang Kai-shek was on the rampage. No tanks went with it but SS *Karmala* carried a dozen of the Rolls-Royces belonging to No 5 Coy, RTC in her hold. Armoured cars had been useful during the regular Hindu-Muslim 'cow-rows' and would no doubt come in handy here. There was no knowing where the next brush fire would break out but wherever it was it would be a job for the under-strength, under-trained second battalions from Catterick or Tidworth. Tanks and their accomplices were, to the War Office, an eccentricity far removed from the mainstream of proper soldiering.

In 1929 France took a decision which was to alter much of the thinking about mechanized warfare. It was the year in which Foch died, and his assertion that there was no more than a twenty-year armistice, half of it gone, had not been forgotten. Stories had been current for a long time about how von Seeckt was quietly building up a new and more formidable German Army. A deal had been done with Stalin, so the rumour ran, and Germany was making and training with tanks somewhere in Russia. No tank, however, could overcome the combined effects of great ditches, mines and anti-tank guns. The French Army had no intention of being caught as it had been caught in August, 1914; no more bands playing 'La Marseillaise' and columns of men marching up to the expectant guns. Next time the Germans could try it. France had suffered enough for one century, as a visit to Verdun will still testify. Every village had its long bronze scroll naming its dead, scrolls still unweathered by rain or time. Ex-Sergeant André Maginot was one of 'Ceux de Verdun' where he had lost a leg. With him at the War Ministry the digging began.

It is now considered a mark of sophistication to sneer at the Maginot Line. Nobody sneered when excavators started work on the elaborate tunnel system. The Line was regarded with awe, even though it was imperfectly understood in this country. On the outbreak of war in 1939 one of the most popular maps on sale was the 'All In One' No 5, put out by the Geographer's Map Company of London. It showed a comfortably thick black line running from a point in front of Metz to the sea by Dunkirk. Few people queried it; possibly because the Chamber of Deputies had resolved in 1937 to make the needed extension. The fact that no sod had been turned was not advertised.

It was not only the beginnings of the Line that marked out 1929 from other years. America had been growing fat. Strube's *Daily Express* cartoon for 19 March, 1927, pictured two tramps on a park bench looking across water at Uncle Sam counting masses of notes in a skyscraper office labelled 'US Treasury; £120,000,000 Budget Surplus'. One tramp, Strube's Little Man, remarks to the other, the Chancellor of the Exchequer, 'I say, Winston, aren't you glad you haven't got to sit up all night counting money like that poor fellow over there?' The money was all borrowed and Nemesis duly caught up with Hubris. When New York caught its cold the droplets took some time to cross the Atlantic but the warning was there. In the eye of the storm that was about to hit London there was a moment of peace. The first Vickers Light tanks of just over four tons and carrying two-men crews put in an appearance in 1931 and for the next few years they were to be the mainstay of the Corps. The tank addicts thought themselves lucky to have even that, for current thinking was on other lines. With M Maginot's works nearly complete what possible need could we have of an Armoured Division? Those in positions of authority seemed to have lost sight of one plain fact. The British Army throughout the nineteenth century had won its big battles from Bussaco to Omdurman by way of Waterloo by adhering to the Duke's philosophy. Organize yourself with as much fire-power as possible, encourage your enemy to attack and after you have decimated him march out and finish off the business. The Maginot Line ought to do the first part but only a force of powerful tanks could do the second. This axiom was not understood by many politicians nor, as time would show, by all Generals. When suggestions were put about that the troops in the Line might be starved of supplies by aircraft cutting off the railways on which they depended, or that the glacis might be fogged by smoke under whose cover obstacles might be circumvented, they were brushed off. Men who said such things were 'croakers'. Few, if any, said it twice.

The cold drove the Army into a kind of permafrost. When Lord Gort took over 4th Division its strongest battalion could parade 350 men; the weakest mustered 185 all ranks. Drill movements were carried out by two men with a rope extended between them, pretending rather pathetically to be a rifle company. Depots gladly took in anything that was recognisably human, male and over five feet two. False teeth were no bar. It speaks volumes for the quality of the between-wars NCOs and those under-appreciated men the Army Schoolmasters that the soldier who emerged at the end of six months was a different being. There were just enough of them to keep the units in India, Egypt and Palestine up to Peace Establishment. The Army at home was not even the Second Fifteen; it was the Colts, supported by the veterans. In 1931 even the miserable pay allowed by the Warrant was cut by 10%. This was bad enough from the point of view of recruiters; it was far worse for officers. No subaltern could be seriously expected to live like a gentleman on a ploughboy's wages. It was generally reckoned that even the cheapest foot regiment demanded a private income of £200 from its aspirants; most required more like £400. The Tank Corps suffered along with the rest.

In spite of everything that had happened during the Kaiser's War the Army was still class-conscious. Sir Douglas had told in his Final Despatch of how 'A Mess Sergeant, a railway signalman, a coal miner, a market gardener, a Quartermaster Serjeant and many private soldiers have risen to command battalions'. They would never do so again. The Army Classes of the Public Schools were almost the only source of supply and competition from the RAF College at Cranwell was very stiff. As late as 1945 General Martel (late of Wellington) was writing that 'the secondary school boy is handicapped. He has led a sheltered life. He usually lives at home and runs to his mother if he is in difficulties. The stern test of fending for himself which the public school boy has had to face is denied him.' Even when the 'Y' Cadetship scheme came in there was little chance of a Grammar School boy joining the commissioned ranks. The intake of new Second Lieutenants began to show signs of drying up.

In the senior ranks, however, the Royal Tank Corps was fortunate. Apart from Martel, the founder-member, new names were coming forward. Lindsay, Broad, Pile and Hobart, all Lieutenant-Colonels, stood ahead of the world in armoured warfare lore. None had spent any part of his war service with tanks but by 1931 they had, with all a convert's zeal, thoroughly mastered the subject. Charles Broad, an 'all-armoured' man, wrote the first training manual, commonly called the 'Purple Primer'. He did his best to interest the RAF in the work of army – particularly mechanized army – co-operation but was given no encouragement. He therefore addressed himself to working out drills for armour alone. The general belief in 1931 was that wireless communication between vehicles on the move was not possible. By hard work and experiment Broad proved the experts wrong. It was imperfect, but it could be done. Once the technique was mastered tank commanders would not be left without orders, wandering aimlessly around in search of something useful to do. Under wireless control groups of machines could act together and show the power of the new machines. As Murat's great voice had once rung from wing to wing of his charging squadrons so could Broad's quieter tones direct his ironclads to move as one at speeds greater than any cavalry gallop.

Before the Wall Street crash, orders had gone to Vickers for a new Medium tank to replace the ageing machines still in service. The Company came up with something rather good. The Vickers 16-tonner was designed on much the same lines as the Mk II Medium but it was bigger and faster. It was also, at £16,000, much dearer. As soon as three pilot models (the last with a new Wilson gear box) had been sent out for testing the order was cancelled and only three went into service. A

Italian CV 3/35 and German Pz.1B. Both derived from British machines.

request went out from the MGO's office for something just as good but much cheaper. There was considerable argument about what it ought to be; so much that it disappeared altogether. The 16-tonners were the star turns of the 1931 exercise but never went into general issue. Vickers, who had bought out Carden's patents in 1928, went to work on small carriers and light tanks instead. For the 1931 exercises there were about 230 machines in all. Fifty new light tanks, about eighty machine-gun carriers of various kinds and about 130 elderly Mediums. Of necessity they were mixed together even down to Company level. The exercise this time lasted a fortnight. German observers watched it with interest.

Twenty years earlier 'Jacky' Fisher had written in praise of Admiral Sir Arthur Wilson. 'Three big fleets that had never seen each other came from three different

Vickers Light Mk6B. The last of the Vickers light tanks. Used by the BEF in 1940.

quarters to meet him off Cape St Vincent. When each was many hundred miles away he ordered them by "wireless" exactly what to do, and that huge phalanx met together at the prescribed second of time ... and dropped their anchors with one splash. Are we going to look at his like again?' We were. The First Tank Brigade of 1931, though no great phalanx by later standards, might have given an answer to Fisher's rhetorical question. It began its exercises in a thick Salisbury Plain fog and as the sun began to disperse it the watchers saw battalions of tanks, one of them Hobart's, drilling like Guardsmen to Broad's orders given by the same medium.

Another aspect would have won Fisher's approval, for he had long since laid it down that 'speed is armour'. The special idea was to demonstrate that speed had now come to the battlefield. Medium tanks pinned down the enemy to their front,

Lieut.-General Sir Giffard Martel, KCB, KBE, DSO, MC.

while the fast, light machines peppered him from all manner of unexpected quarters. Broad, with his R/T and his corps of liaison officers, kept a complete grip on the attack. In the following year, under Brigadier Laird, the exercise was developed to show how an infantry column on the march could be surprised and cut up five miles away from the tanks' assembly position. That done, Laird was warned by R/T of an imminent counter-attack by enemy armour. His change of dispositions to meet it took exactly ten minutes. The sheer expertise of the Corps won loud praise from all observers but the War Office was not won over. In 1933 the First Tank Brigade was disbanded and no exercise took place. The reasoning was simple enough. In a time of great financial stringency we should never have enough tanks to perform this sort of evolution in a real war. Since there could be no question of cutting down the meagre force of infantry we still possessed the only possible course was to limit tank activity to providing them with support in the old way. That war had become a possibility again, however remote, was proclaimed by the abandonment of the Ten Year Rule.

For this there were sound reasons. For some time past the newspapers had been recording the doings and saying of a Herr Hitler, as the name was then usually spelt. When, in January, 1933, he became Chancellor of Germany minds were concentrated

The Vickers 16-tonner.

wonderfully. Mussolini had always been regarded as a figure of fun and never taken seriously as a potential enemy. Four Divisions had gone to Italy after Caporetto and their fund of stories about the Italian Army were still good for a laugh. Hitler looked equally comical but the idea of a resurgent German Army was not funny at all. In 1934 the First Tank Brigade was put together again and command was given to the now Brigadier Hobart. He worked his crews mercilessly and the summer exercise of 1934 was reckoned to be the best and most imaginative yet staged. For the last time Britain demonstrated that in this new kind of warfare she had complete superiority over all possible competitors.

This could only remain true for so long as those competitors had no tanks of their own superior to the small Vickers and its much older brother. The limitations of the small tank were obvious and the Mediums were wearing out. Something better was needed to replace them and both Martel and Hobart rallied all the support they could find. There was little enough. Carden, now working for Vickers, drew out the plans for a cruiser tank – bigger than the light machines but not sufficiently protected for infantry work – and put it before them. Martel soon saw that the suspension was quite inadequate and bade him take it away and try again. This design was officially called the A9. There had been an A8, designed by Lord Nuffield, but it never got beyond the stage of drawings. Vickers' design team went to work on the A9 and a heavier version to be called the A10 but progress was pitifully slow.

There had been changes at the top during the last couple of years. 'Uncle George' Milne finished his time as CIGS in 1932, saying wistfully as he departed that he was sure that tanks still had a future. His successor, General Sir Archibald Montgomery-Massingberd, had been Chief of General Staff to Fourth Army and had written its history. The new Master-General of the Ordnance was Sir Hugh Elles. From these two, reasonably enough, the RTC expected great things. They did not get them. Elles, long away from the tanks, had veered round to General Jackson's opinion that they had been a 'one-off' thing, as gliders were to be in the war that lay ahead. The antidotes appeared now to be too strong for the kind of armour to which everybody was accustomed. Rumours were coming out of Germany of something called the Halger-Ultra bullet which was so powerful that it would make a colander out of any tank that might dare to show its face. It seems quite probable that there never was a Halger-Ultra bullet and that the story was deliberately put about with the purpose of discouraging those pressing for better tanks. After a time Elles changed course again but not to anything like full circle. He conceded that there might be a place for the very heavily-armoured infantry support tank – the 'I' tank for short – and he personally attended to the design of a machine to meet his own specifications. It was called the A11.

The French did better. Not all their Generals were hypnotized by the Line and France has never lacked for skilled mechanical engineers. While some of them were designing thoroughly bad aircraft, others were working on very good tanks. Three new models came out of the factories in 1935, the Hotchkiss 12-tonner, the medium Somua of 19 tons and the great Char B of 31. There was no split mind amongst their designers. These machines were designed for European war and for nothing else. The Somua could travel at 25 mph, was well armoured, and mounted a powerful 47 mm gun; the Char B was a giant, by the standards of 1935, and carried a giant's punch in the shape of a genuine soixante-quinze. The later model, the Char B bis, could cruise at the respectable speed of about 18 mph, though its range was limited to about 90 miles. During the early Hitler years France led the world handsomely in tank design and construction. Unfortunately the French Army had no Broads or Hobarts to teach them how big formations should be handled. Radio equipment for them was not even ordered until November, 1939.

Everybody knew that Germany was surreptitiously building tanks in defiance of her Treaty obligations, for everybody had heard of the friend of a friend who, on a motoring holiday, had rammed one and found it to be made of cardboard. The German Army, in sober truth, was experimenting with small machines much like the light Vickers and only just working towards the heavier kind. Mention 'German

Tanks' and the mind leaps to huge affairs like the Panther and the King Tiger. In 1935 these were still a long way into the future. The Panzer Divisionen began to form on the sly in 1934 with machines less effective than those in Hobart's command. Their speed towards improvement, however, vastly exceeded anything in this country.

Here tanks were once again pushed to the bottom of the queue. The first task of the Army was the defence of these islands, and that meant in very large degree defence against the bomber. Much of the manpower that might have been available for an Expeditionary Force was switched into anti-aircraft guns and searchlights, though progress in these things also was lamentably slow. The second task was the defence of Egypt, which included keeping the peace between Arab and Jew in Palestine, the result of conflicting promises left over from the war. A new tank battalion, the 6th RTC, was raised in Egypt but it got nothing beyond some of the old tanks. The Army in India had to be kept up to strength and garrisons found for Hong Kong and Singapore; these began to look like something more than peacetime stations with the Japanese cutting loose on mainland China. Anything left over from these might be used for a Field Force on the Continent, but it was the lowest of priorities; and lowest of priorities for the Field Force was its tank element. The Army Estimates for 1934 were cut from forty millions to twenty millions. The estimates for 1914, computed in peacetime, had been just under twenty-eight millions.

CHAPTER 22

'Eavy-sterned amateur old men

(*Stellenbosch*), RUDYARD KIPLING

HAVING HALVED THE ARMY ESTIMATES, the Government became afflicted by the condition known to soldiers as 'wind up'. This was due more to the antics of Mussolini than to the really serious threat from Hitler. What was called 'a limited degree of rearmament' was suddenly ordained. There was little enough support from the electorate. In a by-election at Fulham they had put in a pacifist; a body of undergraduates announced loudly that on no account would it fight for King and country; even in the Public Schools the OTC was despised. It was a bad period for Government and governed alike, and no leader comes out of it with credit.

Hobart became Inspector of the Tank Corps and laboured mightily for improvements. The best he could achieve was the raising of one more battalion at home. With the tools available to him he strove to make an effective armoured force, but it was uphill work. The First Brigade was again exercised as an entity and pitted against an unarmoured force under Brigadier Lindsay. More lessons of a tactical kind were learned but as soon as it was over about a hundred of the best tanks were sent to Egypt, leaving only a few dozen veterans at home. Talk continued, as it had been doing for a long time, about sending the Cavalry finally to the knacker's yard and turning troopers into tankers which would put some flesh on to the proposed Mobile Division. It achieved nothing. Mussolini's smash and grab raid on Abyssinia gave evidence that tanks could perform well in the least likely places but the consequences were little more than articles in the service journals.

The War Office had other things to think about, the biggest single one being how to attract more recruits. It is not remarkable that promotion for officers was painfully slow. The retiring age for a General was 67 and for a Major-General 62; there was no shortage of either. Far down the ladder good middle-aged Captains waited glumly for somebody to die or go in order to create a Major's vacancy. The barrack squares everywhere were thinly populated, even though some establishments were set up merely for the purpose of bringing under-nourished youths up to the not very exacting standards demanded for infantry recruits. Most of the new money

went, very properly, to the Navy and the RAF. Democracies do not like opening their wallets for soldiers.

In November, 1935, the Secretary for War, Lord Halifax, bowed out. His place was taken by Alfred Duff Cooper, yet another of those from whom much was expected. He had risen in the social scale by his marriage to the famous Lady Diana. He had been an Ensign in the Grenadiers during the last months of the war and had won himself a DSO, something very rare for a subaltern. Though only 45, he was to the elderly Generals 'one of us'. Unfortunately he was also lazy. Under his management little enough happened. There was, of course, one man among the King's subjects who could have brought something formidable out of even a limited degree of rearmament. Mr Churchill, a giant amongst pygmies, was never seriously considered. Had He been appointed, the whine of 'Gallipoli' from some political quarters would have drowned the noise of machine-tools working day and night at Essen.

There is something about the atmosphere of that fine Edwardian building in Whitehall that seems to induce coma in most of those sent to the highest War Office positions. The office of the CIGS, though not exactly the place where elephants go

Major-General Sir Percy Hobart, KBE, CB, DSO, MC.

Opposite: *The A10 Tank.*

to die, seemed only one remove from it. Sir George Milne had commanded great armies and won great victories; Sir Archibald Montgomery-Massingberd had been Rawlinson's Berthier. They left, neither having much to show for his having been there. Now, in 1936, came Sir Cyril Deverell, once commander of 3rd Division and commonly reckoned amongst the best officers of his rank in France. Each in turn fell victim to the inertia.

To sneer at these elderly, distinguished officers would be monstrously unjust. Each of them, and many others also, looked upon the Army as a landed gentleman might look out upon a noble landscape, known and loved not merely since boyhood but since the boyhoods of ancestors long dead. There must be changes, to be sure, but changes of a natural kind as trees die and others replace them. What cannot be suffered is vulgar commercial intrusion, the building of a factory or power station where the Folly used to be. The business of the tenant was to preserve all that was best on the estate, to keep up its good traditions and to hand them down to following generations. To contemplate pulling down the stables and replacing them by a garage was no part of the duty.

For all that, 1936 saw the beginnings of change. It began with Martel's visit to the Red Army manoeuvres in the suite of the Russian-speaking General Wavell. This was terra incognita for everybody and it caused eyes to open wide. Over a thousand battle-worthy tanks – five times as many as the British Army's entire stock – took part and they were certainly not made of cardboard. Ever since the Five Year Plan of 1928 the Soviet engineers had been working away and they had much to show for their pains. The backbone of the force was a big machine looking uncommonly like the Independent and carrying a 76 mm gun along with several machine-guns in its four turrets. Even more impressive was the performance of a lighter machine called a cruiser; it had faults, but Martel reckoned the suspension to have been designed by a genius. It had been the poor design of suspension that had damned the A 9. On his return home Martel, just appointed to the War Office for duties of this kind, took the matter up.

The name of the genius, he had been told, was Mr Christie, and he was an American. Martel sought out Lord Nuffield, with whom he had worked on the aborted A 8, and arranged for his people to get hold of a Christie tank by whatever means he could find. Nuffields ran it to earth. It seemed that, suspension apart, the Christie tank was so bad the the US Ordnance Department had refused it. Nuffield bought the only surviving specimen by means of a telephone call to New York. Then the trouble began. Christie was hard up and somebody had a lien on his machine. Nuffield paid off the mortgagee but his difficulties were not over. As a result of the Spanish Civil War the US Government was sensitive about the export of war material and a tank was indisputably that. Christie rather ingeniously converted the thing into a tractor and as such it was shipped to Nuffield's works with patent rights included in the bargain. It had all been uncommonly quick work. Martel arrived home on 26 September: by 17 November the soi-disant tractor was at Cowley. This was the last demonstration of how things could be done quickly, for much slow work lay ahead. Christie's suspension system became familiar to all newspaper readers from 1940 onwards. The pairs of big wheels around which the track ran – early models had been made to work without any track at all – were unmistakeable. The idea promised speeds previously thought unattainable, but suspension was the tank's only virtue. Steering and transmission were not of the same engineering brilliance. For a power unit Nuffields acquired a number of 1919 Liberty engines and worked them over. They served surprisingly well.

Martel looked around for somebody capable of putting these things to rights and the task fell to Dr H. E. Merrit of Woolwich Arsenal. As some sort of guide he was given a design, made by Wilson some years previously but never developed, of a double differential system. It was something to work on but Merrit made it very clear that a mass of detailed work was going to be needed before results could be expected. It took him three years and was considered rather quick. One man who could have been of great use was missing. In December, 1935, Sir John Carden was killed in an air crash. His death was a serious loss to everybody concerned with mechanized warfare in Britain.

Early in 1936 the Army once more handed back to the Navy its interests in tank design. Engineer Vice-Admiral Sir Harold Brown, lately Engineer-in-Chief to the Fleet, had been snapped up on retirement and appointed Director-General of Munitions Production. Like Admiral Moore before him, he was no landship expert, but he was a ready learner. Martel was given charge of the department dealing with tanks under the Director of Mechanization, General Davidson. All this promised well, but the Treasury still remained as senior partner.

Before 1936 was out Germany had re-occupied the Rhineland and most of the tanks in England had been sent to Egypt. The Army's total stock consisted of 209 light and 166 medium machines, nearly all of them obsolete. Things were, however, beginning to move at last. In February, 1937, Mr Baldwin screwed up his courage and announced a rearmament programme that would cost the enormous sum of £1,500,000,000. In May Duff Cooper vacated Kitchener's chair at the War Office and Leslie Hore Belisha, of beacon fame, moved into it. Hore Belisha is the rebuttal of the common assertion that personalities matter less than policies. It is difficult to do justice to him for he was his own worst enemy. To the elderly Generals he was emphatically not 'one of us'. Sir Henry Pownall, Director of Military Operations and Intelligence, called him 'an obscure, shallow-brained, charlatan, political Jew-boy'. This was a superficial, if widely shared, judgment. Hore Belisha was certainly not obscure; his talent for self-advertisement had seen to that. That he was a Jew proclaimed itself; that, at least, he had in common with General Sir John Monash. All Ministers were, of necessity, politicians. 'Shallow-brained' is hardly the description of a graduate of both Oxford and Heidelberg, let alone of a man who, like Haig, had been at Clifton. There might be a stronger case for 'charlatan', for Hore Belisha delighted in playing to the gallery. He was accused of knowing nothing at all about the Army and he made no effort to deny this. In fact he had known a good deal, joining up in August, 1914, serving two years in France and another two in Salonika, rising to the rank of Major at 25 and earning himself a mention in despatches. His service had, admittedly, been in the unexciting Army Service Corps but it was entirely creditable to him.

Less creditable was his demeanour. Duff Cooper had been rude, but more stylishly so than Hore Belisha. Comparison between the two men is interesting. It was Duff Cooper who had come late to the war, had performed a rather showy act of bravery and been decorated for it; one cannot somehow picture him sweating out dreary years in the ASC, but it is easy to imagine Hore Belisha having done what Duff Cooper did. Both had excellent brains. Cooper's idleness prevented him from any display of intellectual superiority when among slower-thinking elderly Generals; Hore Belisha made no allowances. His demeanour and habits were not of the kind to which they were accustomed and they liked neither. Sir Edmund Ironside was fascinated by his cloth-topped boots with zip fasteners and reminded himself that 'French had never been able to work with a man who wore Jemimas'.

On policies he did better. Time promotion for officers - eight years to Captain and seventeen to Major - came as a blessing to many. In other respects he was, as everybody knew, the mouthpiece of Captain Liddell Hart, late of the Army Education Corps and a mighty writer about all things military. For a time this did no harm, for there were senior men quite willing to listen to new ideas. The novelty wore off quite soon. General Deverell, CIGS and a very experienced commander, came to loathe the name of Liddell Hart. Pownall eventually confided to his diary that 'He needs to be shot dead, a sinister influence who has done the Army much harm'. This was a little hard. Many foreign Generals have proclaimed their debt to Liddell Hart's teachings. No such acknowledgment was to come from Field-Marshals Alexander, Slim or Montgomery. Possibly not all of them had heard of him. Ideas that might have worked wonders with the huge Red Army – now busily engaged in purging itself white – were of little value to the War Office of the late 1930s. The combination of Hore Belisha and Liddell Hart was too much for General Deverell; putting him into the same room as the Secretary of State was tantamount to mixing the two halves of a Seidlitz Powder. One of them had to go. Sir Cyril Deverell bowed out and was succeeded, as much to his own surprise as anybody else's, by the Military Secretary, Viscount Gort, VC. A mere boy of 51, grumbled Sir Philip Chetwode from his Club.

From the tank standpoint it was a change for the better, as Deverell was known to be seriously considering disbandment. In fact the saviour of the Corps was probably not Gort but Mussolini. After Waterloo the Duke had preserved the Army by hiding it in the Colonies. The greater part of the Royal Tank Corps was already in Egypt with practically every serviceable tank to its name. Obviously these could not be withdrawn and to keep them in being some sort of establishment at home was essential.

The Corps could, in fact, look forward to better days; the final row that had driven Deverell from office concerned it intimately. On paper there was a Mobile Division. It had at last been agreed that the time had arrived for it to become a reality. Other regiments had joined the Sparrow Starvers and were learning to drive armoured cars; the remainder of the Cavalry of the Line would soon have to go the same way. After all, the Germans already had four demonstrable Panzer Divisions. A commander had to be chosen for this new formation; Deverell thought it only fitting that he should be a horse-soldier; the Secretary of State saw no such necessity. They quarrelled, and the CIGS lost. The command went to a Gunner, Major-General Alan Brooke.

It was in October of 1937 that the great decision was taken. The 12th Lancers were already mechanized; in 1935 the 3rd Hussars had suffered the indignity of becoming 'mechanized mounted infantry' because there were not enough tanks or armoured cars to go round. The 11th were now well acquainted with the Rolls Royces they had been driving for the past ten years. The Royals and the Greys were to be exempted on grounds of seniority; all other cavalry regiments would be mechanized as soon as opportunity offered. There were mixed feelings at all levels but the inevitability of it was generally accepted. The tone of war was lowered for ever.

CHAPTER 23

As We Sowed

IN 1934 THE ROYAL TANK CORPS had possessed the best machines in the world and the men who knew how they should be handled in battle. By 1938 all that had gone, save for the quality of the tank crews. The Army was 20,000 men short even of its Peace Establishment. Sir Edmund Ironside, about to leave for Gibraltar, wrote in his Diary that we had 'obsolete medium tanks, no cruiser or infantry tanks, obsolete armoured cars and no light tanks apart from one unit in Egypt.' There were a few light machines and armoured cars in India but they hardly counted. 'This,' he concluded, 'is the state of our Army after two years warning. No foreign nation would believe it if they were told it.'

The warnings were clear enough. Fuller, long retired, had become a Fascist of high degree and as such had been invited to inspect both the Spanish Civil War and the new German formations. At the request of the General Staff he wrote of what he had seen. His letters made gloomy reading. The light tank was 'a wretched little object', while the Germans were producing powerful machines in great quantity. This was confirmed by Hotblack, now Military Attaché in Berlin. Mr Baldwin's extra money was all being spent by Mr Chamberlain - 'J'aime Berlin', the French pronounced it - on anti-aircraft guns and the like. Even these, in 1938, were only noticeable by their absence.

Things were, however, on the move in the tank business. Dr Merrit was well on the way to overcoming the difficulties with the Christie. The solution seemed to lie with a form of modified version of the controlled differential, using light brakes which absorbed little power but retarded the track upon the side to which the driver sought to turn and transferred its energy into the other. It was to prove entirely successful, but not in 1938. Martel pressed on with a resurrected A9. Carden had left plans for a form of suspension, known in the trade as 'the Bright Idea' which was not as good as the Christie but still better than anything that had gone before. The first three marks were, in Martel's words, 'not successful', but by the summer the prototype of a Mk IV came off the line and looked promising. Its top speed was only 23 mph and its armour no better than the 1918 Mk V but at least it carried a gun. The 2-pdr anti-tank gun, with a semi-automatic breech, was regarded as formidable. One was on exhibition at the Netheravon Wing of the Small Arms School and was hidden away in the Museum when the Japanese Military Attaché paid a call.

The A11 Infantry Tank, commonly called Matilda 1.

An old horse artillery 13-pdr was put in its place and the Attaché's chauffeur was observed making copious notes about it. The A9, originally conceived as a cheap version of the Vickers 16-tonner, behaved as cheap things do. It was not mechanically reliable.

Something in the nature of a close-support tank was also demanded and dust was blown off the plans for A10. As Vickers had no more capacity, contracts for building the A10, designed to carry a 3″ howitzer, were placed with several commercial companies. Inevitably very few were made by September, 1939, although the establishment provided for six of them to a battalion.

Last of the new breed was the A11, Elles' 'I' tank and his legacy to the Corps. 'I' tanks, by their nature, need armour heavy enough to keep out more than rifle bullets and experiments were put in hand to find something thicker. It was soon found that protection from a 2-pdr shot demanded a thickness of 60 to 70 mm. Nobody had ever made a tank with armour anything like as thick, but it had to be done. A contract had been placed with Vickers as long ago as October, 1936, but progress had been slow. In March, 1938, the machine emerged. Such was the weight of the armour that it could only lurch along at 8 mph, the pace of a 'Stop Me And Buy One' ice-cream tricycle. A glance suggested at once that either the machine had

242

been involved in a serious accident or that many vital parts were missing from the outside. It had a turret, but so small that it could only accommodate a single heavy machine-gun. The waddling gait called to mind Matilda, the name of a duck in a contemporary comic strip. It could as well have been Donald. Matilda it was, however, and it was the only infantry tank we had. It could absorb endless punishment but was so feebly armed that it could deal out none in return. The cruiser, on the other hand, could hit hard but any gun would kill it immediately. Matilda turned the scale at 11 tons, most of it armour. The Russians were near to completing their 47-ton, 20 mph KV1: the Germans already had, in large numbers, the PZKw III and the French their Char B bis. To comment on this state of affairs demands intemperate language. Only about fifty Matildas existed in September, 1939. A further fifty were promised by June, 1940.

There was no pattern to the business. Germany, by contrast, went to work systematically, The first tanks were small affairs, no better than the light Vickers. Each, however, was given a rigorous testing in every particular. That done, and every weak point discovered and corrected, the makers moved upwards to a bigger, faster, better-armoured and better-gunned machine. The British way was more eclectic; if a tank was unsatisfactory, then bring another even if it is worse. This state of affairs was to continue for a long time. Nobody suggested that we might buy superior tanks from France or build them here under licence. When Anthony Eden, who had done an attachment to the tanks as a TA officer, canvassed the idea he found no supporter.

French Tanks of 1939. The Somua S35.

Then came the humiliation of Munich. Time was certainly bought at the cost of honour; the fact remains that had we gone to war in 1938 we should have been soundly beaten and the Swastika would have been flying over London by Christmas. Possibly, before too long, over Washington and Moscow as well. Mr Wells, still active, coloured up the picture with his film *The Shape Of Things To Come* where the tower of St Martin's-in-the-Fields crashes down upon the crowd in Trafalgar Square. Stories abounded about gases of unbelievable nastiness. The anti-aircraft element of the Army was increased first to four Divisions and finally to seven. Vickers concentrated their efforts on new and better guns for them. Tanks remained in their familiar place, at the end of the queue.

From 1936 onwards there had been White Papers and other papers about our continental commitment with much said about four Divisions and an Armoured Division. What actually existed was explained by Major-General Hawes in a letter to the *Daily Telegraph* published on 6 October, 1981. A fortnight before Mr Chamberlain went to Munich Colonel, as he then was, Hawes of the War Office G Staff took a party of officers to France to make arrangements for the reception of the British Field Force. It would have amounted to three infantry battalions, ten bomber squadrons from the RAF and nothing more. In such a state of affairs there was not a lot of value in talk of expanding torrents and great tank raids. The blame must go to successive Governments but His Majesty's Loyal Opposition ought not to escape scot-free. The Leader of that Opposition was a former Tank Corps officer, Major Clement Attlee. His attitude is hard to understand, for he had a fine war record and his patriotism was never in question. Neither of these could, however, be said of some of his colleagues.

If war had come at Munich time the French Army would have had to fight alone. There was only one spot on the map which remained a British responsibility. Egypt was still reckoned in as much danger as in Lord Kitchener's day and something had to be done to strengthen the defences. The 1936 Treaty limited the number of troops that might be kept there. The task was to make them more effective, for the Italians had, in the M13/40, a better tank than anything that could be put against it. Lord Gort sent for Hobart, then in the Staff Duties Directorate at the War Office, and sent him off to form an Armoured Division in Egypt while there was still time.

Hobart arrived a couple of days before Mr Chamberlain's last call on Hitler. He was greeted by the Commander British Troops in Egypt with 'I don't know what you've come here for, and I don't want you anyway'. This did not endear General Gordon-Finlayson to the tank expert; nor did it inhibit him from getting down to work. Hobart inspected his troops. There were two RTC battalions equipped with a few worn-out Vickers Mediums as the only thing more formidable than various Marks of the light tank. There was in addition a Mechanized Cavalry Brigade. On closer scrutiny this turned out to be the 11th Hussars, still clinging to their 1920 Rolls Royces, the 7th Hussars with an early model of the light tank of strident unreliability issued on their mechanization a year before and the 8th Hussars in Ford trucks. There was a mechanized Horse Artillery battery of 3·7 howitzers and a single battalion of lorried infantry.

From this mechanized scrap-heap Hobart began to build the formation that was to become the famous 7th Armoured Division. For something over a year he brought to bear his unequalled skill in matters of tank warfare and, as equipment trickled in, he began to see something like a genuine Division taking shape. His reward was to be sent home with an Adverse Confidential Report. The officers reporting on him were Sir Robert Gordon-Finlayson, about to go home himself in order to become Adjutant-General, and General Sir Henry Maitland Wilson. Of the former Pownall wrote in his Diary that 'It's time he left Egypt where he has done much but has not succeeded in keeping up morale too well'. Sir Edward Spears dealt more suavely with the latter: 'Military historians may discover in his decisions a sagacity which my own shortcomings no doubt prevented me from detecting.' Few, if any, have accused 'Jumbo' Wilson of being amongst the Great Captains. Between the two of them they threw away the best commander of armoured troops in the British, perhaps in any, Army. Seventh Armoured had to manage without 'Hobo'.

The dreadful year of 1938 passed into history. Early in the next one the War Office received a new Permanent Under Secretary who was something out of the ordinary run of Civil Servants. P. J. Grigg – never called other than 'P.J.' – had been a Gambardier, an officer in the Royal Garrison Artillery, during the Kaiser's War and although much of his service had been of a financial kind, part of it in India, he enjoyed the advantage of having been Private Secretary to Mr Churchill with whom he remained in close touch. P.J. was reckoned the rudest man in the Civil Service and he feared nobody, Minister, General, Admiral or anything else. The impression he gained on arrival was one of confusion.

Official policy seemed to be that when war came the Army would not be expected to do more than defend these islands, mainly against air attack, and find garrisons for the usual places. In spite of the fact, explained by General Hawes, that we had no troops, it was decided early in 1939 that we should have to accept a land commitment in Europe and that much of the burden would have to fall upon the Territorials, starved of everything though they were. It began with a promise of two Divisions and later it was increased to four. There was no longer any mention of the Mobile, or Armoured, Division. This was hardly surprising, for it did not exist.

Mr Hore Belisha had ideas of his own. In March the ancient office of Master-General was abolished and its duties transferred to a civilian Ministry of Supply under the colourless Dr Leslie Burgin, assisted by Admiral Brown. They were not to be envied and Martel said, mildly enough, that 'it took the Ministry a long time to find its feet'. This was undeniable in the matter of tanks. Nothing was on offer better than the A9, the A10 and the A 11. Production even of these was held up by friction between the soldiers and the engineers which resulted also in mechanical defects being allowed to go unrectified.

Vickers showed once more how the business could be done. When their 16-tonner had been turned down as too expensive, they had been asked to come up with something else. The plans produced in 1935 were once more rejected as showing something both too slow and insufficiently armoured. They redesigned it yet again with thicker armour and a new kind of track. The Valentine, not quite ready for

*French Tanks of 1939. The Char B. Usually called by the Press 'the French
50-ton (occasionally 70-ton) Tank'. Its actual weight was 33 tons.*

production by September, was neither as well-protected as Matilda nor as fast as
the Cruiser, but it was utterly reliable; probably the only British tank of the day
about which this could be said. Before the war was over it had gone through nine
marks. If the Ministry of Supply had adopted methods of quality control equal to
those of Vickers much grief might have been saved.

In April, 1939, the month that saw the re-introduction of conscription, the
cavalry rode sadly away. All line regiments, save only the Royals and the Greys,
were mechanized; the old names were retained by Cavalry of the Line, along with
eighteen Yeomanries, though all now became part of the Royal Armoured Corps.
The RTC also changed into the Royal Tank Regiment, though this made no difference in practice, except that its precedence in the Army List was now ahead of the
Royal Artillery. It was inevitable but it could not be expected to achieve universal
popularity. The cavalry, on the whole, did not take unkindly to the change for war

The Universal Carrier. One of the few success stories.

The A13, ancestor of the Cruiser Tanks.

The Infantry Tank Matilda II. Briefly queen of the battlefield.

was in the offing and it had no place for horses. They set themselves to learn all about the Vickers Light Tank. All but the 12th Lancers, who were given a new armoured car. Bovington did not greatly care for the change, for it was a very professionally organized establishment and had no means of expanding to take over training masses of new and possibly reluctant entrants.

On organization a kind of convention grew up. Divisional cavalry regiments were nothing new. The mechanized variety could at short notice be converted into Armoured Reconnaissance Brigades, though they would need a lot of training. What did not exist was the equivalent of the old Bermicourt Central Workshops. It was not until yet another new Corps, the Royal Electrical and Mechanical Engineers, came into existence that repair and maintenance ceased to be matters of great difficulty. Under the convention ex-cavalry regiments would be the light troops, doing what cavalry had always done, and the RTR would be the heavyweights.

At long last the old Vickers-Lewis-Hotchkiss-Madsen controversy was settled. When the infantry adopted the Czech ZGB light machine-gun and called it the Bren it was re-made to take the old rimmed ·303 cartridge. The Armoured Corps also adopted it but in the original form, including the rimless ·276 round. This was wise, for the old cartridge was far freer from stoppages than the new. Later a heavy, 15-mm model was taken over under the name of Besa. It proved a valuable weapon.

The tanks, under whatever name, remained a race apart, having little or no training in conjunction with other arms. Neither artillery nor RAF had time to spare for training in joint operations. The Germans made excellent practice in Spain with their JU87 dive bomber and made no secret of it. Vickers' chief test pilot, Summers, was allowed to fly one and on his return home was rebuked by the Air Ministry for presumption. To criticize the RAF would be absurd; its plate was full with far more important matters.

Lack of interest in Army affairs did, however, inhibit the tanks' effectiveness. The events of 1918 had shown how much need armour had for air support. The JU87 was highly effective as close-support artillery and further earned its keep by beating-up unarmoured units. Its effectiveness was mainly gained by spreading a kind of 'Stukaschrecken'; steady troops soon came to rumble it for what it was – a machine that made fearsome noises but did little damage and had no taste for controlled rifle fire from the ground.

With war creeping nearer and tank production reckoned at no more than three or four a month, the Armoured Division was, says Martel, 'dreadfully short of equipment'. The first A13s, the Christie Cruisers, began to dribble in from Nuffields but much work was needed on them before they could be called battle-worthy. The 2-pdr was a good enough weapon for the immediate future but armour was becoming thicker. Martel prudently arranged for drawings to be made of a 6-pdr which could be put into production as soon as the need arose.

Defence against tanks had been neglected even more than tanks themselves. The new infantry weapon was the Boys ·55″ rifle. It was a slight, very slight, improvement on the German monster rifle of 1918. Given a tank a few paces away and unaware of the rifle's presence it might, with luck, break a track-pin before the crew were seen off. In practice its main use was as a form of field punishment; it was heavy, awkward and entirely suitable to be given to the Company drunk to be carried as a penance. Then there were the mines. At the Hythe Wing of the Small Arms School instruction was given in these. They came in three sizes, the Mk I, the Mk II and the French mine. The first two resembled grey slab cakes, the last a good-sized wedding cake. The lectures began with a caution; the Mk I and Mk II were unreliable and the French one not much better. It was given out that the Army was buying a number of small French 25 mm anti-tank guns on handcarts. Few people appear to have come across one and the loss does not seem to have been great.

In 1938 and early 1939 there were numerous wild-eyed men about the place who claimed much knowledge of anti-tank makeshifts picked up during their service with the Communist International Brigade in Spain. Several of them published pamphlets about heroic miners from Galicia or the Asturias who had knocked out German tanks by means of bottles filled with petrol and other things or by flinging sticks of dynamite under their tracks. The trouble with the Tom Wintringhams was much the same as that with Mr Hore Belisha. Their demeanour did not inspire enthusiasm. The Bolshieness could have been overlooked; it was their cocksureness that people found rebarbative. Which was a pity, for they might have had something useful to sell.

Hore Belisha, with all his faults, did an honest best to make the Army better. Pay was increased and recruiting picked up. His efforts at re-clothing soldiers was less successful. Several specimens of a uniform proclaiming modernity were put on display; the most eye-catching was a kind of D. H. Lawrence gamekeeper suit complete with deerstalker hat, the whole carried out in mustard yellow. The idea was sensible enough, for far too much time was wasted with button-stick and blanco. The final choice was not pleasing. 'Battle dress', the top half of a golfer and the bottom of a skier along with the most ridiculous headdress imaginable, smacked more of Dartmoor than of Caterham. There was no escape and the Army went to France dressed as convicts.

In the busy month of April the first conscripts, all 20-year-olds, arrived. There were no weapons for them. Passers-by at Sir John Moore's Shorncliffe Camp watched parties of young men practising Cuts 1, 2, 3 and 4 with cavalry sabres. It probably built muscle.

Nothing more came the way of the RAC. In April, on Ironside's figures, tanks present with units numbered less than 45% of establishment. By 3 September there were exactly fifty 'I' tanks, all Matilda Is, out of the 450 on paper. The Territorial Army was doubled, a circumstance that the CIGS learnt for the first time from his morning paper. In August, 1914, Lord Kitchener had demanded to know whether the then Government knew what it was doing by going to war without an Army. This time it was far worse.

On 3 September, 1939, the long-expected blow fell and Foch's Twenty Year Armistice was over. The Field Force went to France exactly as it had done in 1914 but neither as well-equipped nor so well trained. Its numbers were less than half those of Sir John French's Army. The modern part of it, coming along by degrees, amounted to some Divisional cavalry regiments in useless light tanks or armoured cars. The Army Tank Brigade was made up of two battalions of Matilda Is, inexpugnable but powerless. The German General von Manstein later described its contribution as 'quite insignificant' and it is impossible to gainsay him.

His own Army mustered 3,200, mostly light machines but with about 300 of the formidable Mks III and IV and a number of the excellent Skoda T21s, the booty of Munich. France could call upon 2677, nearly 500 of them carrying a cannon of 47 mm or bigger. Even Japan was reckoned to own about 2,000. The Red Army had more than the rest of the world put together, something in the order of 20,000, but most of them were out-dated. The feebleness of Britain's contribution passes belief. To be an 'Old Contemptible' is one thing: 'Old Insignificant' is quite another. The campaign of 1940 is outside the scope of this book. Suffice it to say that it did the Army some service. Along with masses of equipment, much of it obsolete, Hitler collected a good many middle-aged Lieutenant-Colonels and Majors who had out-lived their usefulness.

In the course of a meeting on 16 May, 1940, Mr Lloyd George expressed his view of the matter to the CIGS, General Ironside: 'Baldwin ought to be hanged'. Ironside made his own note that 'Milne and Montgomery-Massingberd ought to be shot'. There was more to it than that.

Appendix I

In 1919 the Royal Commission On Awards to Inventors assembled at Lincoln's Inn under the Chairmanship of Mr Justice Sargant to consider claims for payment. Their findings began with a tribute to one of the men who claimed nothing: 'In the first place the Commission desire to record their view that it was primarily due to the receptivity, courage and drive force of the Rt Hon Winston Spencer Churchill that the general idea of the user of such an instrument of warfare as the Tank was converted into a practical shape.' This could not be gainsaid.

Of the serious claimants Wilson and Tritton, who put in a joint claim, were given £15,000 between them. D'Eyncourt, because he had been a Government official on full pay, had to be content with £1,000. Colonel Swinton, who merely said that 'I claim a very large share of the credit and, so far as the Army is concerned, the sole credit for the introduction of the Tank as a weapon of war' received the same. Stern claimed nothing. Crompton put in a claim but was turned down. Mr de Mole was awarded sympathy for 'a very brilliant invention' but got no money. Not all the armourers throve. Murray Sueter demanded £100,000 but his claim was dismissed. He wrote a book to complain about the unfairness of it all.

There were many claims not far from the frivolous. A Naval officer who asserted that he had invented a detachable running-board for armoured cars got short shrift. Best of all was a lady, a Mrs Capron of Louth. Tritton wrote to Wilson warning him of her probable descent upon him. Mrs Capron, 'a young woman who wishes to be very fascinating', was in the habit of going into trances of several hours' duration. In the course of one of these she had invented the tank. It does not appear that her claim was pressed very hard.

Stern, in his book, praises Sir Eustace Tennyson d'Eyncourt, 'who was the real father of the Tanks and nursed the development from the beginning to the end'. He also speaks generously of both Wilson and Tritton, along with Mr Dudley Docker and Mr Squires whose Metropolitan Carriage Wagon and Finance Company turned out something like three-quarters of all the tanks produced in the UK. It is pleasant to be able to record how their fierce quarrels came to an end. In 1939 Mr Churchill, once more First Lord of the Admiralty, sent for Sir Eustace, Sir Albert, Major Wilson and Mr Ricardo, charging them to do once more what they had so well done earlier. Each was now in his sixties and in the front rank of his chosen profession but the years dropped away and they worked once more as in the happy days at the White Hart, Lincoln. The tank they designed was christened by Stern. 'TOG', he called it; 'The Old Gang'.

TOG would have been a splendid tank for about 1920. You may see it in the yard of the Tank Museum. It turned the scale at 80 tons, carried armour as thick as a brick wall and mounted a 17-pdr. From the outside it looks big enough to accommodate a small private dance. Sad to say its maximum speed was only 8½ mph. It was bigger by far than even the German Royal Tiger; but the Royal Tiger carried an 88 and could travel at four times the speed. TOG, like the great Tortoise that followed it, was never more than a curiosity. But it brought old friends together again. If they had indeed participated in 'the absurd scramble for credit' it was forgotten now. The last monument is the gear-box of the 'Chieftain'. Wilson designed it.

Appendix 2

In the last weeks of 1916, whilst the battles on the Somme and the Ancre were fading away, Mr Lloyd George was preparing his bid for taking over the Premiership. Being far-sighted in such matters he well knew that in order to justify his actions he would need some striking proof of the superiority of his administration, and that soon. The Western Front had nothing to offer. In Mesopotamia General Maude had already taken Baghdad. One possibility remained. If only the Turk could be driven from Jerusalem the newspaper headlines would be heart-warming. Mr Lloyd George needed the fall of Jerusalem more than any man had done since Godfrey de Bouillon.

Before Jerusalem could be approached, however, one obstacle had to be overcome. Gaza, now a fortress by Middle Eastern standards, barred the way. Neither Sir Archibald Murray nor his subordinate Sir Charles Dobell was a Wellington, but they must be given every means of cracking this particular nut. The Egyptian Expeditionary Force, though of fine quality, was an old-style army. It needed bringing up to date so far as resources permitted. During the last month of the year eight tanks, all contemporaries of 'Mother', arrived to help along with 22 officers and 226 other ranks. Nobody was awestruck at the sight of them. Cyril Falls, writing many years afterwards, called them 'a handful of ancient tanks'. This was unkind, for they were still the last word in armoured fighting vehicles. Colonel (as he then was) Wavell, in *The Palestine Campaign*, merely observes that the eight were 'not in the best condition'. By common consent they were regarded as curiosities rather than as serious weapons of war.

The Second Battle of Gaza, in mid-April, 1917, took place at about the same time as Arras and Bullecourt. The eight machines in Palestine were luckier. They were given impossible tasks – tasks that Stern claims would have demanded a couple of battalions in France – and in spite of valiant efforts they achieved very little. In this place the adversary was not mud but sand; sand so loose that not only did it engulf lorries to axle depth but that infantrymen at times found themselves knee-deep in it. The various histories hardly mention armoured vehicles. Stern, who had access to men who had been there, made the best of it: 'What the Tanks could do they did.' One was knocked out by a shell, another had a track broken and fell into Turkish hands. The entire battle was muddled and the actions of the tanks were hardly worth a mention. Very few accounts give them one.

Wavell makes two excellent, though hardly consistent points. The battles fought later by Allenby were, in the main, cavalry battles and were highly successful. This, however, was not a vindication of those devoted to the horse or camel. The winning factor was mobility, and in 1917 and 1918 only animal transport could provide this. Wavell mentions that the most dangerous enemy to horsemen was the aeroplane. Luckily for the British Army they were not all that numerous and the RAF had them well under control. At a later stage in the campaign MacAndrew's 5th Cavalry Division demonstrated the superiority of the armoured car.

When the time came at the beginning of November, 1917, for the third and final attack on Gaza three Mk IVs had arrived and once again eight tanks went into action, this time to help 54th Division. Allenby does not even mention them in his Despatch of 31 October, 1918. Even Stern could say no more than that they did useful work but not all that was asked of them. This was hardly surprising. Six tanks were assigned twenty-nine different objectives. All the same they earned their rations. Five reached the first objective, four the second, third and fourth, and one the fifth. The two reserve machines were used to bring up sandbags; both caught fire. One man was killed and two wounded. Thus ended the first public appearance of tanks in the desert. Much needed to be learnt before they could cope with it.

Bibliographical Note

At the end of his book *Napoleon and his Marshals* the late A. G. Macdonell wrote these words. 'I am profoundly suspicious of almost all bibliographies. Nothing is easier than to hire someone to visit the British Museum and make a most impressive list of authorities, which will persuade the non-suspecting that the author is a monument of erudition and laboriousness.' This I hold to be great truth.

In the half-century or more that I have interested myself in the subject I have read, or at least dipped into, more books than I can begin to remember. The loci classici are so well known that it would verge on insult to any possible reader of this to affect that he might be unaware of them. To continue my borrowing, 'I propose, therefore, to confine myself to the simple statement that every single detail of this book has been taken from one or other work of history, reference, reminiscence, or biography.' Where unpublished papers have been ravaged I have set out details in the Source Notes.

A Note on Sources

There is a lawyer's maxim to the effect that he who asserts must prove. Up to a point this is good counsel, but it has limits. I am not captivated by pages of print pock-marked by tiny numbers which eventually guide the persistent reader to a numbered box in some distant seat of learning. In doctoral theses such things are all very well: in books I hold them to be deprecated.

The information upon which this one is based comes from published books, official papers, unofficial papers, the experiences of my seniors of which they have told me and, towards the end, in a very small way, upon experiences of my own. The books are not all that numerous. In 1919, when memories were fresh, there appeared Stern's *Tanks: the Log-Book of a Pioneer*, William-Ellis' *The Tank Corps* and Fuller's *Tanks: 1914-18*. All bear signs of having been written in haste but they are essential reading and have been laid under contribution. Equally, the Divisional Histories tell what men thought at the time. Admiral Murray Sueter did not publish his *The Evolution of the Tank* until 1937; it contains much that is informative about the earliest days. Sir Harry Ricardo's *Memories and Machines*, (Constable, 1968) is of the greatest interest, and about many things other than tanks. Everything about Sir John Charteris comes from his *At GHQ* (Cassell 1931) and all the Churchilliana, save where the context suggests otherwise, from *The World Crisis*. Brigadier-General Baker-Carr's autobiography, *From Chauffeur to Brigadier* (Benn, 1930) is not merely essential but a joy to read. Lieut. Mitchell tells his story in *Tank Warfare* (Nelson 1933).

Amongst official papers, all in the Public Record Office, I have used a very small part of Lord Kitchener's monumental 'The War: August 1914 to 31st May 1915'. There is no substitute for this to understanding what happened during the period. Its reference is CAB 37 5929. The CID Report and Recommendations upon 'The Question of Caterpillar Machine-Gun Destroyers' of 24 December, 1915, is now called CAB 42/7 XP4919. The Cabinet paper on the Madsen gun is CAB/4215 XP 4919. Under the same reference comes Sir Douglas Haig on 'Cavalry in France', of November, 1916.

Two sets of private papers are of first importance. Those of Sir Albert Stern are lodged with the Liddell Hart Centre for Military Archives at King's College, London. The Tank Museum at Bovington Camp has those of Major Wilson. His copy of Stern's book with his notes on the contents is with the archives of the County of Clwyd. The Stern Papers add a little to the matters of which he treats in the book but consist mainly of routine notes and correspondence. The great value of those at Bovington is that they contain transcripts of all the proofs of evidence prepared by the claimants to the Royal Commission on Awards to Inventors, and copies of Wilson's letters to various highly-placed people, mostly about his quarrel with Stern. The letters passing between him and Sir William Tritton contain nothing surprising but they demonstrate the cordiality between them.

For the between-wars period there is much to be learned from th diary of Lieut-General Sir Henry Pownall, published in edited form by Leo Cooper in 1972. Sir Basil Liddell Har's *The Tanks*, published in 1959, is the locus classicus on the entire subject. Sir Giffard Martel's *Our Armoured Forces* (Faber, 1945) and his 1934 book *In The Wake Of The Tank* are, as one would expect, important, and authoritative.

General Index

Index of Tanks

Back end-paper: *Machine Gun Corps men with a tailless Mk I.*